Global Newsrooms, Local Audiences
A Study of the Eurovision News Exchange

Akiba A Cohen

Mark R Levy

Itzhak Roeh

Michael Gurevitch

John Libbey
JL
LONDON · PARIS · ROME

British Library Cataloguing in Publication Data

Cohen, Akiba A.
Global Newsrooms, Local Audiences: A Study
of the Eurovision News Exchange
I. Title
070.195

ISBN: 0 86196 463 2 (Paperback)
       0 86196 451 9 (Hardback)
ISSN: 0956-9057

Series Editor: Manuel Alvarado

Published by

John Libbey & Company Ltd, 13 Smiths Yard, Summerley Street,
London SW18 4HR, England.
Telephone: +44 (0)81-947 2777; Fax: +44 (0)81-947 2664
John Libbey Eurotext Ltd, 127 rue de la République, 92120 Montrouge, France.
John Libbey - C.I.C. s.r.l., via Lazzaro Spallanzani 11, 00161 Rome, Italy

Contents

About the Authors

Akiba A. Cohen is the Danny Arnold Professor of Communication in the Department of Communication and Journalism at the Hebrew University of Jerusalem.

Mark R. Levy is Professor of Journalism and Director, Center for Research in Public Communication at the University of Maryland.

Itzhak Roeh is Senior Lecturer in Communication and Journalism at the Hebrew University of Jerusalem.

Michael Gurevitch is Professor of Journalism in the College of Journalism at the University of Maryland.

Preface

Every day, 22,000 miles above the earth, the images that become the substance of television news are fed across time zones, continents and cultures by supranational wholesalers of television news stories. 'The sky is full of stuff', says one broadcast news executive. 'We just take it down ...' .

In an ever more interconnected world, that 'stuff' – television news – becomes the subject of controversy, study and concern. Is, as some have charged, the world's supply of television news pictures controlled by a small clique of London, New York, or Atlanta-based broadcasters? Do television news viewers around the world indeed get the same stories on their evening news programmes and how does that affect what they know and believe? Has McLuhan's 'global village' truly arrived, courtesy of the Eurovision News Exchange, Reuters Television, Ted Turner or Rupert Murdoch?

Claims concerning the power of the media to create the global village are not new, of course. The printing press crossed national and cultural boundaries long before television. The international news agencies have been in the business of disseminating print news around the world for almost a century and a half. Radio and films have been oblivious to national boundaries almost since their inception. Yet the advent of satellite technology and the growth of institutional arrangements using that technology to deliver television news around the world may well have ushered in a qualitatively new age in human experience. For the first time in history, it is routinely possible for almost the entire population of the globe (give or take a few millions) to be exposed to a common set of events. This potential for universally shared experience cannot be assumed to be trivial. Even if individuals – and societies – decode or interpret these mediated experiences in different ways, globalised television news has increasingly become a fact of our global lives, and has thus acquired immense power as an actor in human affairs around the world.

Awareness of the significance of these changes has led us, over the past few years, to examine and to analyse some of the processes and impacts of globalised television news. We call our research project 'The Global Newsroom'. The metaphor of the global newsroom is meant to suggest the 'gatekeeping' function performed by a relatively small number of journalists – men and women who day in and day out co-ordinate the dissemination of a large volume of television news, exchanged among the world's broadcast organizations by satellite.

In this monograph, we present a detailed examination of one key player in the global newsroom – the Eurovision News Exchange (EVN), the journalistic arm of the far better known European Broadcasting Union (EBU). Started in May 1961 with a once-a-day exchange of news items by satellite, the Geneva-based Eurovision has grown to become an important clearing house for TV news. With its own 24-hour-a-day satellite links; with its own news bureaus in Washington, New York, and Moscow; and with a cadre of field producers able to co-ordinate coverage from the hot-spots of the world, the Eurovision News Exchange is a video 'wire service' for the electronic age.

We have been studying the Eurovision News Exchange for more than seven years. When we began, Akiba Cohen and Itzhak Roeh visited the headquarters of the EBU in Geneva and discovered to their surprise that virtually no academic researchers had ever stepped inside the home office of the 'global newsroom'. There were a few older studies (Pollock & Woods, 1959; Sherman & Ruby, 1974; Kressley, 1978a and 1978b; Fisher, 1980; Melnick, 1981) and a few more recent ones (Wallis & Baran, 1990; Hjrvard, 1991, Parker, 1994); but few, if any scholars had spent much time recently investigating either the EBU or its news service. Indeed, as of this writing (Spring, 1995), it seems that the EVN remains a well-kept secret, at least among students of broadcast journalism.

We believe that the Eurovision News Exchange is very much worthy of study and we hope that the findings presented here will convince readers of that. In its broadest and most theoretical sense, this monograph can be seen as exemplifying a research strategy first put forth by Cohen and Bantz (1989). They wrote: 'We believe that one useful, even necessary, and not altogether impossible strategy for television news research in the future is what may be termed research from start to finish. By this we mean research projects that examine the various aspects and phases of the news, at its various levels ... This commences with production of the news, including the various internal and external factors that constrain the process (e.g., journalistic norms and political pressures); it continues through the news content itself; and it ends with the way audience members consume and make sense of the news. Many previous studies of news focus on one of these three phases, sometimes on two, but rarely have researchers engaged in comprehensive projects that have dealt with these three elements. . . . Nevertheless, such an approach could add much coherence to the research on news, providing closure to what is probably one of the more complex subjects of mass communication' (pp. 142–143).

Our study of the Eurovision News Exchange should therefore be seen as an example of 'start-to-finish' research, an attempt to bring together questions – and some answers too – about the production, the content, and the consumption of globalised television news.

We could not have carried out our inquiry without the help and patience of many talented and interested journalists and staff members. We begin with special thanks to three individuals at the Israel Broadcasting Authority who were instrumental in helping us create our initial contacts with the EBU: Nathan Cohen, the now retired legal advisor and liaison with the EBU; Yair Stern, former head of television news and currently head of television; and David Witztum, head of the foreign news desk.

We continue with special thanks to Mr. Tony Naets, the current head of the EBU News Division, and his predecessor Michael Doherty, both gentlemen and scholars, whose support was invaluable for our efforts. If fact, Tony Naets was kind enough to read and comment upon the accuracy of parts of the manuscript. We take responsibility, however, for the remaining errors.

We also wish to thank the following present and past journalists and staff members of Eurovision and the global newsroom for sharing their time and insights with us: Catherine Bergon, Katherine Brown, Robert Burke, Clive Clisshold, Roger Creyf, Jeff Dubin, Ahmad Fawzi, Antonio Fernandez, Kevin Hamilton, Susan Henderson, Horst Jancik, Peter Knowles, Gernot Lindmuller, W. Lowndes Lipscomb, John Mahoney, Lorraine Mottola, Isabel Raventos, Paul Reid, Angela Thomae, Jacques van der Sichel, Marine Vegliante, and Miro Wilcek.

Sincere thanks too to our academic colleagues and students Gabrielle Bock, John Cordes, Anandam Kavoori, Archana Kumar, Timothy Leggatt, Hagit Ringel, and Jocelyne Tinestit who conducted focus groups for us with television news viewers in the England, France, Germany, Israel and the United States.

Funding for this study was provided by the Israel-US Binational Science Foundation; the Smart Family Foundation Communication Institute of the Hebrew University of Jerusalem, and the L. John Martin Fund of the College of Journalism, University of Maryland. We are grateful for their support.

Akiba A Cohen
Mark R Levy
Itzhak Roeh
Michael Gurevitch

Foreword

Somewhere among the heavyweights of international broadcast journalism – somewhere between the three US networks and CNN and the three television news video agencies and the BBC World Service and Deutsche Welle and TV5 – the interested professional (and he or she is more likely than anything else to be a television editor working a foreign desk) will find the Eurovision news exchange system. Started by the European Broadcasting Union in 1958, the Eurovision News Exchange (EVN) now provides its participating broadcasters with an astonishing, daily flow of news video.

Its first experimental attempts to exchange television news pictures coincided with the death of Pope Pius XII - which led to the memorable phrase from the then chief editor of Dutch television, Carel Enkelaar: 'I want the dead Pope live'. The News Exchange has developed considerably since then. It has built ambiguous ties to the television video news agencies, with which it cooperates, but at times also competes; and it is considered a model of international comity, improving the free flow of information. The Eurovision news exchange is in fact the only internationally recognized organization in which countries at war with each other continue to cooperate. This was very much in evidence throughout 1995 when coverage from Serbian television found its way into exchanges, which were received in both Zagreb and Sarajevo.

Despite this obvious success and Eurovision's very tangible presence in Europe, where it is a prime source of news pictures for broadcasters and where it does set the editorial agenda, the workings of the exchange system are surprisingly unfamiliar even to editors who use it daily.

Fortunately, Professors Cohen, Levy, Roeh, and Gurevitch have had the patience and insight to explain it thoroughly in this well-researched book. To produce their insights, Cohen et al. had to know as much and perhaps more about the exchanges, their arcane rules and traditions than those of us who deal with them on a daily basis. The curious reader will find tantalizing traces of their learning process in this book as it explores the decision-making process in an industry, whose products are the instantly outdated information of the television news bulletin.

Most importantly however, the authors of this monograph have time on their side. The broadcasters involved in the exchanges are too close to their daily grind to see the patterns that academic researchers detect and describe. It therefore also takes skilled observers to see that the news exchanges are indeed the product of what Cohen and Company have come to call global newsrooms, dealing with each other on a daily basis through a continent-wide communication system.

Reading the book also gives me time to pause. The Eurovision News Exchanges has occupied a dominant position in the newsgathering process for decades. They came about after all, because the emerging international television news agencies did not want to commit to an electronic newsgathering and distribution system. Deregulation in the European broadcasting industry (and to a lesser extent in satellite communications) has created a new environment. The European Broadcasting Union has been forced to reconsider its own role: from being the representative organization of all European national broadcaster, it has become the representative of one interest group, the public broadcasters. This has made the Eurovision news exchange system an exclusive network of news backhaul for public service broadcasters. Although there are still many areas where these broadcasters and the television news agencies share the same interest and the same editorial policies and practices, there is a tension in the relationship now that was not there in the 1970s or 1980s. While the television news agencies and the EBU still cooperate in many places, and the EBU provides them with transmission facilities in places like Sarajevo or Grozny, agencies and the exchange system compete with each other to bring correctly tailored coverage to smaller groups of subscribers. Commercial broadcasters in Europe too are looking at cooperation, whether it is within the framework of one major media holding company such as the Luxembourg-based CLT group, or through a loose affiliation, such as the one that operated for some time with the Belgian Flemish commercial broadcaster VTM.

It may prove encouraging for the public broadcasters and confirm that they found the right way to cooperate and to provide themselves with a balanced coverage of European affairs. Or it may give them cause to think about the need for the exchange system, to think about which items to exchange for which audience. This book comes therefore at the right time and the work of its authors is highly appreciated by those of us in the global newsrooms. Finally, I hope that *Global Newsrooms, Local Audiences* also conveys to the reader the pride we all take in the work we do and the coverage we bring to Europe's television news audiences.

Tony Naets
Head, TV News Division
European Broadcasting Union
Geneva, Switzerland

1 Studying Global Newsrooms

A sk the average European television viewer what 'Eurovision' means to him or her, and you are likely to get a response about the 'Eurovision Song Contest' or some international sporting event. Ask the average TV-watching American what Eurovision means, and you are likely to get a blank stare. But if you query almost any broadcast journalist on any foreign news desk, you probably won't be told about euro-pop or soccer matches. For broadcast journalists, Eurovision means the Eurovision News Exchange (EVN), the oldest and most successful of the news exchanges, a 'regional' exchange with the capacity to cover news worldwide and to share its news footage with a global cooperative of national broadcasters.

In this chapter, we trace the growth and development of the Eurovision News Exchange, examine its current structure, and contextuate the Eurovision exchange in an ever more competitive context of global news-gathering and broadcasting. A final section outlines our research methodology. Thus, this chapter provides the background for the detailed analyses of news creation, content, and reception which follow.

From EBU to EVN

In the beginning, there was the European Broadcasting Union. It was founded in 1950 with 23 members and a meagre by-broadcast-standards budget of 447,000 Swiss francs (then about US$103,000). The EBU was the world's first professional association of national *television* broadcasters. It was started because Europe's broadcasters had common interests and concerns about the growth and regulation of radio and television, primarily in Europe. The EBU replaced the dormant International Broadcasting Union, which had collapsed following World War II. Its successor, the EBU, was designed to be a non-commercial, non-governmental, international organization. Its watchword was and still is *cooperation* in broadcasting between nations (Fisher, 1980).

For its first thirty-some years, the EBU was almost the only non-commercial source of television programmes and news film for broadcasters in Western Europe. However, Intervision, an Eastern European consortium of 19 Soviet-bloc broadcasters, was started contemporaneously with the founding of the EBU. Intervision exchanged television programmes using the Intersputnik network of the former-USSR and daily exchanges of news footage between the EBU and Intervision took place as early as 1965 (Kressley,

1978). In 1984, a group of Asian countries, including India, China, Japan, and others established the Asiavision News Exchange or AVN (Lansipuro, 1987). An EBU-AVN link was quickly established and in 1984, for example, news footage of the Bhophal, India chemical disaster was sent by Asiavision to the EBU and received widespread distribution. In 1985, 22 Arab countries, under the auspices of the Arab States Broadcasting Union, launched a regional news exchange and in 1988, the Caribvision news exchange was established to serve Barbados, Curaçao, Jamaica, and Trinidad (Flournoy, 1990).

Although the EBU was quick to form ties with each of these regional exchanges, the flow of programming and most especially news was much greater from the EBU *to* the regional services than the reverse (Kressley, 1978; Varis, 1989). This pattern of news and information flow continues more or less unchanged to this day.[1] In 1994, for example, when the EBU's news exchange transmitted a total of 22, 383 news item (see Table 1 below), it received and thus transmitted no stories from SIN, five from Caribvision, 110 from Arabvision, and only 455 (or about two per cent of the total) from the Asiavision news exchange.

In January 1993, the EBU merged with Intervision, making the enlarged EBU, the world's largest professional association of national broadcasters. The EBU then had 62 'active' members, 44 of which are in Western Europe and the Mediterranean Basin and 18 in Central and Eastern Europe. In addition, the *European* Broadcasting Union currently has 54 loosely affiliated 'associate' members (see Appendix A for a complete list of members of the European Broadcasting Union). To become a member of the EBU, a broadcaster must provide a *national* broadcast service, producing a significant proportion of programming themselves, aimed at all sectors of the population.

The general operating budget of the EBU was approximately 70 million Swiss francs in 1995, although for accounting reasons the figure is not precisely comparable with the 1950 budget mentioned earlier.[2] EBU costs are shared among members according to their ability to pay. Budget decisions and general EBU policies are set by a General Assembly, composed of all EBU members. Day-to-day management of EBU affairs rests with a Secretary General and Permanent Services staff of some 230 people, drawn from more than a dozen different nations. The principle work of the EBU centres in three areas: (1) creating and exchanging radio and television programmes; (2) operating the EBU's six analogue and four digital satellite channels on the Eutelsat satellite and its 13,800 kilometres of permanent terrestrial broadcast circuits; and (3) research into new broadcast technologies and into the legal aspects of national and trans-national broadcasting.

The need for news

Almost from the outset, members of the European Broadcasting Union were interested in using the new organization to facilitate their coverage of 'foreign' news. National

---

1. For similar findings, largely about print-oriented news exchanges, see Boyd-Barrett & Thussu, 1992.

2. In 1995, the EBU's budget for television news coverage *alone* was approximately 31 *million* Swiss Francs.

broadcasters, of course, could cover the 'domestic' news of their own country. But newsworthy events often happened in other nations; and this meant that to get coverage of 'foreign' news, a national news organization either had to send its own, expensive-to-maintain correspondents and camera crews to the scene or it could rely on the for-profit news film (later videotape) agencies such as Visnews or World Television News (WTN). Either way, getting non-domestic news footage was often expensive and fraught with delays. But the EBU had a technological solution to the growing demand for foreign news. Then housed in the dome of the Palais de Justice in Brussels, EBU technicians commanded a complex of permanent telecommunication circuits, linking member services. These terrestrial circuits were already being used to exchange entertainment programmes and cultural events among EBU members.

In October 1958, the first trials of a daily news exchange were carried out. Five EBU member services participated. A year later, a second round of experimental exchanges took place with seven national news services participating. On 29 May 1961, the Eurovision News Exchange began regularly scheduled transmissions with a daily feed, called, in Eurovision News shorthand, EVN-1. At 17.00 Central European Time, in the late afternoon, the earliest EVN-1's transmitted a dozen or so news and sports items by landline to member services. Before each EVN-1, a Eurovision News Co-ordinator conducted an editorial conference by radio circuit with the Eurovision News Contacts and newsfilm agencies. Led by the News co-ordinator, the 'conference', as it came to be called, became the forum for discussing the day's news and the availability of TV news pictures. Whenever possible, the film and later the video tape provided to the exchange was supposed to be 'raw' footage, that is pictures only, without voice-overs or on-camera appearances by the reporters/anchors of the offering service.

EVN items were also supposed to provide more footage than a station might ultimately use, which meant that items for the EVN often ran several minutes in length. A brief description of the item, a shot-list, and identification of speakers were provided, initially by telex and more recently by fax and/or an internal EVN computer network. These procedures, as well as a host of other norms and rules, were established in the earliest days of the news exchange. They continue relatively unchanged to this day. And thus was born the global newsroom.

With EVN-1, the members of the European Broadcasting Union had a means for making their news coverage available on a reciprocal basis to each other. The materials were available free of copyright restrictions and could be used in the news bulletins of the receiving country in whatever fashion the local news editors wished. Member broadcasters committed themselves to covering news events on their home turf and offering that footage without restrictions to the news exchange. News materials provided by one national service would, however, not be able to be used by a competing news organization in the same country. The television news agencies (CBS International, Reuters Television, Worldwide Television News, Associated Press Television) could also offer news footage. However, if a given agency story were accepted by the EVN News co-ordinator, it could only be used by an EBU member service, provided that the national broadcaster already had a separate, bilateral contract with the agency.

By 1966, a morning editorial conference had been added to the routine of the global newsroom; and on New Year's Day, 1968, a second transmission (EVN-2) came on line with daily transmissions, now of colour videotape, at 18.30 Central European Time. In 1974, a third regular exchange (EVN-0) was added at midday. By 1995, there were nine regularly scheduled news exchanges, each allocated twenty to thirty minutes transmission time. In addition to EVN-0, EVN-1, and EVN-2, exchanges currently include:

* EVN-E, the Eurovision morning news exchange (05.30 Central European Time), which is limited to European originations only and which is designed, along with EVN-M (see below) to meet the needs of so-called 'breakfast' television programmes.

* EVN-M, which immediately follows EVN-E and which is based solely on news footage relayed from the Eurovision News Exchange bureau in New York City.

* EVN-Y, a mid-morning exchange with a 10.30 Central European Time start time.

* EVN-W, which has a mid-afternoon transmission, commencing at 15.15 Central European Time.

* ERN-E, which is an exchange between the Eastern European members of the EBU and which is managed by its participants. It is transmitted immediately after EVN-W.

* ERN-N, which starts at 16.00 Central European Time, is an exchange run by and for Nordic EBU members.

Despite the increased number of EVN feeds each day, the morning conference before EVN-0, is still the traditional rendezvous for most member services. It is what one EVN journalist called, 'the meeting place next to the coffee machine'. However, since there are so many transmissions throughout the day, many News Contacts continually monitor the

Table 1. Growth of the Eurovision News Exchange

	1964	1974	1984	1994
Number of active EBU members participating in EVN's	21	33	38	62
Total number of news items transmitted	1,134	5,085	8,555	22,383
Percentage of total news items from agencies	10.0[1]	50.3	45.7	48.3[2]

[1] In 1963, only one per cent of all news items came from newsfilm agencies; while in 1965, the number had risen to ten per cent. Thus, this estimate may somewhat overstate the 1964 contribution of agency materials.

[2] Includes 4,836 items supplied by Reuters Television; 4,062 from World Television News (WTN); 663 from CBS International; and 327 from Associated Press Television.

Sources: For 1964–1984, annual *EBU Review: Programmes, Administration, Law.* For 1994, Mr. Tony Naets, Head, TV News Division, European Broadcasting Union (personal communication).

EVN audio circuit 'with half an ear', just to be certain that no important items have suddenly come up.

This phenomenal growth of the Eurovision News Exchange is further demonstrated in Table 1. Between 1964, which is to say three years after EVN's inception, and 1994, the most recent year for which we have complete data, the total number of news items carried on EVN's increased by a factor of almost twenty. Thus, in 1964, the news exchange transmitted just over 1100 news stories for the year; while in 1994, the number had soared to more than 22,000 items or roughly 61 news stories each and everyday. Although EVN initially did not rely heavily on the newsfilm agencies for items (and its relatively meagre output showed it), by the 1970s roughly half of all the material in the daily transmissions was coming from agencies. That ratio of service-to-agency materials has held essentially constant for more than two decades.

Not only has the total number of EVN items sky-rocketed, but the number of national services participating in the exchange has increased substantially, almost tripling from 21 in 1964 to 62 in 1994.[3] Increases in the 1970s were largely the result of decisions by EBU to allow broadcasters outside of Europe (e.g. Israel, Jordan) to become active members of the organization. Increased participation in the 1980s came when new non-commercial or commercial broadcasters were created in old-line European countries such France and Italy and were, after some fretting by some EBU traditionalists, admitted to the EBU 'club'. Additional, new EBU-affiliated services joined up following the dissolution of the Soviet Union, as broadcasters from the former Soviet republics sought ties with the West.

By the mid-1990s, the Eurovision News Exchange found itself caught up in an institutional environment of ever-growing competition between news organizations offering to supply various forms of television news to broadcasters and audiences worldwide. From the international video agencies, to scores of new international broadcasters, cable systems, and other satellite-delivered news, the EVN is getting a run for its money. How well the EVN is doing and what are its prospects for the future will be two key points to which we return in the final chapter of this monograph.

Co-ordinators and contacts

Day in and day out, the work of the Eurovision News Exchange falls to the News Co-ordinator and the News Contacts. (Recently the title of News co-ordinator has been changed to News Editor. However, since the term is relatively new and since many EVN journalists still refer to the News Editor as the co-ordinator, we will use the older terminology.) The News Co-ordinator is a journalist, 'on loan' for a week to the Eurovision News Exchange, but still working out of his or her national broadcast house. The News

---

3. The price of any given EVN item is based on a formula that includes certain pro forma costs and the number of potential viewers in a given EBU-member nation. The number of services which actually download any given EVN feed varies, since a service may 'withdraw' from any particular day's exchange, if it believes that none of the items about to be transmitted will be useful to it. By withdrawing, the service is not charged for the cost of the items in that particular feed.

co-ordinators take one-week shifts on a rotating basis and during that week are responsible for the content of the news exchanges. News Contacts are also journalists from EBU members and they act as the liaison between their home service and the Exchange.

Table 2. National television services providing News Co-ordinators (editors)

Station		1987	1994
ORF (Austria)	Osterreichischer Rundfunk	x	x
BRT (Belgium)	Belgian Radio and Television	x	x
CyBC (Cyprus)	Cyprus Broadcasting Corporation		x
DR (Denmark)	Danmarks Radio		x
YLE (Finland)	Finnish Broadcasting Company		x
TF1 (France)	Television Français 1	x	x
FT2 (France)	France 2	x	x
FT3 (France)	France 3		x
CPF (France)	Canal Plus		x
ARD (Germany)	Arbeitsgemeinschaft der offentlich-rechtlichien Rundfunkanstalten	x	x
ZDF (Germany)	Zweites Deutsches Fernsehen	x	x
NOS (Netherlands)	Dutch Broadcasting Foundation	x	x
NRK (Norway)	Norsk rikskrinkasting	x	x
SVT (Sweden)	Sveriges Television	x	x
SRG (Switzerland)	Schweizerische Rundspruch Gesellschaft	x	
BBC (UK)	British Broadcasting Corporation	x	x
ITN (UK)	Independent Television	x	x
	Total	12	16

News Co-ordinators are drawn from a pool which has been agreed to by the News Working Party, the inner-circle of EVN veterans who meet twice-yearly to discuss policies and problems which have arisen in the news exchange. In principle, a duty News co-ordinator is appointed *ad personam*, based on his or her talents and experience. There is no requirement that there be a broad geographical, cultural or linguistic distribution of News co-ordinators, and they serve no fixed term. As Table 2 makes clear, the pool of News co-ordinators has not expanded at the same rate as overall EBU membership. In 1987, one dozen different national broadcasters provided News co-ordinators. While many of these editors came from the largest and wealthiest news organizations (e.g. the BBC, ZDF, TF1), a number of News co-ordinators were from smaller nations such Belgium or even non-continental countries (Norway, for example).

By 1994, the number of national services represented in the News co-ordinator pool had grown to twenty. All but one of the services which had News co-ordinator responsibilities in 1987 continued in that role. New editors were added, however, from two non-continental services (the Finnish Broadcasting Company and the Cyprus Broadcasting Corporation) and one relatively new French broadcaster (Canal Plus). The slightly more diverse membership in the News co-ordinator pool represents an attempt by EVN to democratise its decision-making by introducing some additional variety into the geographic location of News co-ordinators.

Whether geographic diversity produces significantly different patterns of news decision-making or whether there is a common core of news values which all EVN journalists share is a question that we will examine later in this monograph. At the very least, the geographic diversity of the News co-ordinators reinforces the metaphor of the global newsroom. Given enough computer networks and satellite links, broadcast journalists can co-ordinate global reporting from anywhere, share what they have with each other, and never meet face-to-face in a central newsroom.

If the News co-ordinators and News Contacts are the avatars of an emerging virtual journalism, then it might be important to know more about their personal characteristics, professional experience and journalistic values. To that end, we conducted a mail survey of News co-ordinators and News Contacts. (Methodological details may be found in the methods section of this chapter.) Here, we will present findings about personal and professional background of the News co-ordinators and News Contacts. Findings about the journalistic norms and values of this group of EVN broadcasters are found in Chapters 2 and 5.

In general, News co-ordinators and News Contacts appear to share similar social characteristics. Roughly half of each group, for example, is female, although a slightly larger proportion of News co-ordinators were men. News Contacts are a somewhat younger group, with two of the twenty News Contacts surveyed being thirty years old or less and an additional four, being thirty-five or less. The modal age-range for News co-ordinators was 36 to 45; while roughly half of both groups were forty-six or older. All forty EVN journalists who replied to our survey were college graduates. Among News co-ordinators, slightly more than half had been language or literature majors at university; while News Contacts were divided approximately in equal numbers among three courses of study (Journalism/Broadcasting, Languages/Literature, and Social Sciences) (see Table 3).

News Contacts and News co-ordinators alike are comparatively seasoned broadcast journalists. Three-fifths of the News Contacts and three-quarters of the News co-ordinators reported eleven or more years of television news experience. Only five of the forty respondents had worked in TV news for less than five years. News co-ordinators seemed to have slightly more time with their home service. Almost every News co-ordinator and News Contact responding said that, in addition to working with the Eurovision News Exchange, she or he also held another job with his or her home service. In fact, one quarter of all respondents said they were the foreign news editor for their national service and slightly more said they held other 'news administrator' positions. As Mr. Tony Naets, head of the EBU television news division, told us in an interview (11 January 1994), the News co-ordinator 'has to be somebody who can react as a journalist and where in his own organization he's holed up I really don't care'.

Whether the News co-ordinators and News Contacts are 'holed up' in their own organizations or not, when it comes to Eurovision, they seem to be a gregarious group. Almost

7

Table 3. Characteristics of EVN news co-ordinators and news contacts[1]

		Co-ordinators	Contacts
Gender:	Male	12	9
	Female	8	11
Age:	21–35 years old	1	6
	36–45 years old	10	4
	46–55 years old	6	7
	56–60 years old	3	3
College major:	Journalism/broadcasting	2	6
	Languages/literature	11	7
	Social sciences	7	7
TV news experience:	1–2 years	2	1
	3–4 years	1	1
	5–10 years	2	6
	11 or more years	15	12
Concurrent jobs:	News administrator	5	7
	Foreign news editor	6	4
	Producer	5	1
	Translator	0	4
	Other	2	2
	No other position	2	2

[1] Data reported in this table represent actual counts and not percentages. Respondents classified as News Editors either have been or are currently serving in that role.

all we surveyed had attended at least one of the annual Eurovision meetings for News Contacts. Twelve of the 20 News Contacts and 15 of the 20 News co-ordinators had been to at least three or four of the annual get-togethers. Both groups almost unanimously found the annual sessions 'very useful' or 'quite useful' in their EVN work. Indeed, the opportunity to interact with news colleagues from other countries, both on a daily basis during the conferences and at the annual meetings, seemed to be an important gratification for these journalists.

Methods for understanding the global newsroom

The research reported in this monograph is the outcome of a multi-method study. The multiplicity of methods we used reflects the multi-faceted nature of our subject matter, international broadcast journalism. In beginning our study, our first concern was to obtain access to the key journalists at Eurovision and in selected services. Happily, this proved not to be difficult, as cooperation for the overall project came early and easily both from the EBU headquarters in Geneva and the national services and agencies.

For this study, we also wanted videotapes of EVN feeds and national newscasts; and documents, describing the work of the Exchange. We obtained most of what we needed simply by asking. Sometimes, however, we had to rely on jerry-built or improvised data collection procedures. This improvised approach added to the complexity (and frustration) of our task and meant that we were not always able to get what optimally we might have planned. Indeed, not all the data sets we created are complete, a fact of research-life which, as we shall see later, somewhat hindered our analyses.

The data-gathering for this study went through three distinct phases. In the first (February 1987 to June 1987), we focused on decision making process in the Eurovision News Exchange, the news agencies (Visnews and WTN) and in several European news services. Data gathering spanned many months for two main reasons: first, because of the scope of the project itself, we had many research sites to visit; and second, because we wished to build some greater generalizability into the study by expanding our data collection, observations, and interviews beyond a single, limited period of time.

In the second phase, in late 1990, we focused on the news-viewing audience and attempted to learn about how the global newsroom's output was received by the global 'villager'. Then, for a variety of reasons all-too common in academic life, we put this project on hold. We picked up the thread of the research again in 1993 and have been at it ever since. We saw this third phase of data-gathering as an opportunity to revisit some sites and journalists whom we had seen earlier and to add a longitudinal dimension to the study, examining how, if at all, EVN and the global newsroom had changed.

Certainly, we expected changes. As we mentioned earlier in this chapter, the political and media landscape of Europe, and indeed the world, had undergone profound alterations. So we visited newsrooms, watched what was happening, and conducted another round of interviews with participants. And we concluded that despite the sea-changes which had occurred, the work of the Eurovision News Exchange seemed strikingly familiar. In short, while some of the data we present here are based on materials gathered several years ago, some is as recent as the schedule of monograph production will allow. Moreover, we are confident that the theoretical insights and implications of our findings add substantially to our understanding of globalised news and are as fresh and as powerful as today's nightly newscast.

Given the nature of our study and our interest in the globalization of television news, we sought to frame the study in the broadest possible way. This meant including as many services as we could handle, logistically, physically and financially. We sought to avoid potential questions of validity which might have arisen had we based our conclusions on too few countries, services and or news items. We were able to work in one way or another in or with material from the following eight EBU-member countries: the United Kingdom, France, (West) Germany, Luxembourg, Belgium, Spain, Israel and Jordan.[4] This included some large countries as well as some small ones; some with several television channels (in addition to the public service stations which are the members of Eurovision) and others with only one service. Some of our work was also done in the United States where we

4. While we did some data collection in Switzerland and Austria and received some materials from Italy, these data sets were incomplete and could not be used in the final analyses.

examined the role of the New York and Washington Eurovision bureaus. Each phase of the study was marked by different methods and produced different kinds of evidence.

Editorial decision-making

The bulk of the work of the news exchange is designed to provide video material to the member services for use in their respective news bulletins. Thus in order to learn about how the exchange operates, and particularly how the editorial decision-making is accomplished, we chose to conduct field observations and interviews in 12 locations. One pair of researchers (Cohen and Roeh) spent two weeks in February 1987 visiting the following locations: the EBU Headquarters in Geneva; the French-Swiss service (SSR) also based in Geneva; German-Swiss television (SRG) in Zurich; the second French channel (A2F) in Paris; the Flemish-speaking Belgian station (BRT) and its counterpart, the French-speaking station (RTBF), both in Brussels; the bilingual service (French for France and Belgium and German for Germany) originating in Luxembourg (RTL); and the second German service (ZDF) in Mainz. Later that year, in June, Levy and Gurevitch spent a fortnight observing and interviewing at Austrian television (ORF) in Vienna; A2F in Paris; the British Broadcasting Corporation, Independent Television News, World Television News and Visnews in London; and Spanish Television (TVE) in Madrid. In July, all four of us carried out observations and interviews at the Israel Television (IBA) in Jerusalem. In the autumn of 1987, Cohen, Levy and Gurevitch visited the EBU Bureau in New York and in the Fall and Winter of 1994–1995, Cohen and Levy re-visited the Geneva Headquarters as well as the Eurovision bureau in Washington, DC.

At each of these locations, one or two-day long observations were made of the way the system operated. Further, we interviewed one or more of the key players (e.g. EVN contacts, foreign editors, heads of news departments) in each service or agency visited. At two sites (SRG in Zurich and A2F in Paris), our field work coincided with a week in which the local EVN journalist was also the News co-ordinator, responsible for the journalistic output of the entire exchange. We also obtained operations manuals and internal Eurovision documents and memoranda describing previous EVN policies and revisions made by the News Working Party and by the head of the News Exchange. We also gathered copies of the daily telex messages sent from the services and agencies to EBU Headquarters and to and from the News co-ordinators. (Recently, telex has given way to an internal computer network using the BASYS newsroom computer system.)

Ten days (16–20 February and 15–19 June 1987) which coincided with part of our field work were designated as the sampling period for our attempt to fully document the work of the exchange. Thus, for example, during this period we arranged to audio-tape the mid-morning voice-circuit conferences, presided over by the duty News co-ordinators in preparation for the EVN-0 and EVN-1 satellite transmissions. This conference, always held at 11.00 Central European Time, is the main conference of the day and generally has the largest number of member services participating or at least listening in.

Additional information about editorial decision-making, and particularly about how the News Co-ordinators and News Contacts felt about their work, were obtained in two ways.

First, we analysed reports filed by the News co-ordinators when their week-long tour of duty was over. Second, we mailed (and occasionally faxed) a questionnaire to 54 News Contacts, some of whom also serve as News co-ordinators, asking for information about themselves, about their work in the news exchange process, and about some of their professional norms and values. The questionnaire was accompanied by a cover letter from the director of the News Exchange, vouching for the scientific legitimacy of the inquiry (see Appendix A). We received completed questionnaires from 40 respondents, which, given the difficulty often associated in surveying far-flung elites, meant that we had a remarkably good response rate of 73 per cent.

The news content

To investigate the content of materials transmitted on the EVN's and to learn how EVN items were used by member services, we also mounted a multi-national effort to gather news videotapes for the ten-day sampling period to go along with documents and observations from the site visits. First, in order to study what footage was being made available each day for the services we arranged to have the EVN-0 and EVN-1 transmissions recorded on videotape. This was done for us at various locations. Occasionally, there were minor technical or labour problems and we did not always capture parts of an EVN feed or a day's newscast.

We also arranged for the videotaping of the main evening news bulletins of 11 national services which are regular EBU members (BBC, ITN, TF1, A2F, ARD, ZDF, RTBF, TVE, IBA, JTV and RTL-Plus[5]) and three US networks (ABC, CBS, NBC) which are associate members of the exchange. This made it possible for us to examine if and how Eurovision materials were actually used by EVN-affiliated services and to compare the stories aired with the raw EVN materials which arrived via satellite. The recordings were made in some locations by the services themselves and in other locations by our academic colleagues.[6]

The audience

In four active-member Eurovision countries – the United Kingdom, France, Germany and Israel – and in the United States, whose broadcasters are associate members of EBU – we introduced an audience component to the project. Our rationale for including US viewers was that, since one of our goals was to learn how European television presents foreign news (including US stories), it also made sense to examine how Americans relate to non-American news stories. In each of the five countries, we assembled 6 focus groups,

---

5. While RTL-Plus, the German language service of RTL originating from Luxembourg is not a formal member of the EBU, it does have a sub-licensing agreement with the News Exchange Service.

6. During the course of the entire Global Newsroom study, a total of 1,142 news stories were coded by trained graduate students associated with the Hebrew University of Jerusalem and the University of Maryland. We will not however report inter-coder reliability figures on content analyses presented in this monograph, first because all but a handful of the variables measured were sufficiently obvious that exceptionally high levels of reliability can be assumed; and second, because so many different coders, speaking so many different languages, living in so many different locations were involved, that it was logistically impossible to arrange for the usual tests of inter-coder agreement.

generally consisting of 10 men and women per group. Five groups in each country were selected to be relatively homogeneous based on the occupation of its members: blue collar workers, sales people, bank tellers, school teachers, and professionals. A sixth group in each country was composed of retired people who had a variety of previous occupations.

Group participants performed three tasks. First, each was given a modified Q-sort task in which he or she was asked to imagine being the foreign news editor for his or her home country's television newscast. Participants were all given the same set of eighteen *foreign* news stories and asked to select six from the eighteen. Participants were then asked to rank-order these potential foreign stories by newsworthiness. Group participants next completed a questionnaire dealing with their attitudes towards and perception of news in general, and foreign news in particular. Finally, participants were shown three news stories which had aired many months earlier on their nation's main evening bulletin and a moderator conducted a focused discussion with the participants regarding various aspects of the news stories.

Additional details about methods will be included in the chapters which follow and which present our complete findings. That presentation will be guided by the following three, large groups of research questions:

1 How does the Eurovision News Exchange work and can its processes and policies be profitably studied using the metaphor of 'the global newsroom'? Do journalists who participate in the news exchange and related organizations share a common culture of professional norms and procedures? What are some of the current controversies regarding the functioning of the Eurovision News Exchange and how well does EVN compete in the global news marketplace?

2 What is the content of the news material transmitted on the EVN's and how is that 'raw' material transformed by national news services? To what extent does the news exchange set the 'foreign' news agenda for the national newscasts of EBU members? How similar is the 'foreign' news coverage presented by each of the national services linked to the Eurovision News Exchange?

3 How does the audience decode news stories based on EVN items and how is the audience's view of the world affected because of materials supplied by the Eurovision News Exchange? What do audience members want in the way of 'foreign' news coverage and how does that compare to what is offered by the EVN and the national broadcasters? How, if at all, does the existence of the Eurovision News Exchange affect the balance between information-rich and information-poor nations and viewers?

2 The Marketplace of News

This chapter discusses the daily Eurovision conferences during which the EVN News co-ordinator and the Eurovision Contacts of the various national services establish the agenda for subsequent satellite transmissions. Although the News co-ordinator and News Contacts are not physically present in the same room, they are connected via telecommunication technology and operate much like they were part of one large editorial meeting. Thus, in many respects the conference is the operational incarnation of the 'global' newsroom metaphor.

As noted earlier, our study of the conferences is based on five sets of materials:

1 A sample of ten conferences recorded during our site visits.

2 A set of internal Eurovision documents and memos which describe the formal procedures as they have been established by the News Working Party and the head of the News Exchange, and which are revised from time to time.

3 Notes and transcribed interviews derived from our visits to various sites.

4 The responses to a questionnaire we sent to News Co-ordinators and Contacts at EVN member services.

5 A compilation of reports by News Co-ordinators about their week's work, filed with EVN in Geneva, after the News Co-ordinator has completed his or her tour of duty.

This chapter is divided into five main parts: the first describes the formal procedures and logistics of the conferences based mainly on the official EBU documents; the second offers a completely transcribed and annotated conference from our recorded sample; the third analyses the conferences as reflected in two lists of news items – offers made (to other services and agencies) by various services and television news agencies, and requests made by services and the News Co-ordinator from other services and agencies; the fourth section briefly comments on the limits of consensus in the global newsroom based on the transcripts and our participant observations; and the chapter concludes with the EVN journalists' own reflections about their work in the global newsroom.

Procedures and logistics

Before we take a close look at the conferences it is necessary to spell out the organizational parameters and premises on which they are based. These will be useful in reading the text of a sample conference which follows.

When are they held?

The conferences are the daily rendezvous of the Eurovision contacts. In fact, each day two conferences are held. The first conference, the so-called morning conference, is clearly the more important one, and hence better attended by the various Eurovision contacts. It is conducted at 10.00 hours GMT which is actually 11.00 in most of Europe, 12.00 in the eastern parts of the continent and in the Middle East, but only 03.00 in New York. This conference usually runs between 10 and 25 minutes but has known to go even longer. The second conference takes place at 15.00 hours GMT (16.00 in Western Europe) and is less well attended.

Where are they conducted?

The conferences are simultaneously organised and administered in two locations: one permanent and one that changes on a rotating basis. The Eurovision Control Center (EVC) in Geneva serves as the fixed main co-ordinating point for all activities of the Exchange. The Geneva office, for example, sets the rotating work schedule for the News Co-ordinators. Geneva also provides general and technical oversight of the conferences. (In 1989, technical control over the switching circuits, satellite transmissions, and conference radio circuit was relocated from Brussels to Geneva.)

While EVN headquarters in Geneva is responsible for the technical aspects of the conferences, the News Co-ordinator takes charge of the substantive news process from her or his national service's broadcast house. Each week, for seven consecutive days (Monday to Sunday) a different service provides the person who serves as the News co-ordinator.[1]

What are the roles?

Many people across the continent of Europe and in other parts of the world are involved in the conferences. We shall first enumerate the three most important roles.

The Eurovision co-ordinator is a staff member of the Permanent Services of the EBU, assigned to the Television News Division in Geneva. The Eurovision co-ordinator is responsible for the administration of the exchanges and the distribution of editorial information.

The Eurovision News Co-ordinator (NCORD)[2] is responsible for the contents of the

---

1. Several years ago a decision was made to change from a 10-day to a 7-day cycle because of the extremely heavy burden of the co-ordination task which begins each day early in the morning and continues until the late evening hours.

exchanges. The News Co-ordinator sets the editorial agenda based on the members' requirements and his or her own news selection. She or he defines the major stories for the upcoming EVN feeds and chairs the editorial conferences on the News Conference Circuit.

The Service Contacts are the service representatives who participate in the conferences. They have the prerogative to offer news items, to request news items, to ask for information, and to arrange bilateral exchanges with other members services or agencies. News Contacts are expected to conform to the Exchange rules and thereby help the complex conferences to operate as smoothly as possible.

In addition to the member services, representatives of the major television news services (Reuters Television, World-wide Television News, CBS International and Associated Press Television) 'attend' the daily EVN conferences.[3] Finally, also 'present' are Eurovision News Exchange journalists in the United States (both in New York and Washington, D.C.) as well as in Moscow.[4]

Pre-conference activities

Several important activities precede the morning conference, most of which are performed by the News Co-ordinator.

Offers from news agencies

During the early morning hours, prior to the conference, and in close co-ordination with the Geneva headquarters, the News Co-ordinator reviews the various offers that have been made by the news agencies.

Two categories of news agency items are created: A-items and B-items. A-items are items which the News Co-ordinator decides to accept for EVN-0 or EVN-1 based on her or his own judgement without the need to consult anyone and without bringing them up for discussion at the conference. B-items, on the other hand, are offers made by the news agencies which the News Co-ordinator decides to bring up for discussion at the conference. Both categories of items are usually offered accompanied by a relatively detailed description of the nature of the item including what will be visually depicted.

---

2. As noted in Chapter 1, it was recently decided to change the title of the duty News *Co-ordinators* to News *Editors*, which might reflect a change in the perceived role. However, throughout this book we use the better known term of duty News Co-ordinator or simply the News Co-ordinator.

3. It should be noted that each of these news agencies is inherently tied to one of the three major US networks (Reuters with NBC, WTN with ABC, and of course CBS with its mother network).

4. The Washington, DC and Moscow bureaus did not exist in 1987 when we did our field work. As to the difference between the New York and Washington EVN operations, New York was originally intended as a co-ordination point with the US television networks and the news agencies that worked with them. The EVN Washington Bureau was seen primarily as a support point for journalists from member services who did not have their own Washington facilities. However, the work performed in the New York and Washington bureaus has grown increasingly similar. As one EVN veteran told us, 'In a satellite age, it does not matter that much where you collect or interface'.

When two news agencies offer what is essentially the same material, a rotation scheme (referred to as the *Rota*) is used whereby an attempt is made to utilise each of the agency's materials in the most equitable fashion. However, the News Co-ordinator has the prerogative of circumventing the *Rota*, if she or he believes that the footage offered by one agency is of better quality.

Information on A-items is transmitted to all the services via the Eurovision Newswire – a dedicated communication network that uses permanently leased data circuits (in 1987 telex lines were used) – so that the contacts can receive some advanced information on what will become part of the satellite transmissions during the day.[5]

Consultation with EBU bureaus and other exchanges

Before the conference the News Co-ordinator also has preliminary discussions about potential items with the Eurovision bureaus in New York and Moscow and with his or her counterpart in the *Asiavision* exchange based in Kuala-Lumpur. Each News Co-ordinator has her or his own habits in this regard, but it is standard practice for the co-ordinator to check in with the Eurovision bureaus, the agencies, and with any of the two or three temporary EVN 'inject points', which are non-permanent EVN field production centres for major, breaking news stories.

These discussions, sometimes by telephone, sometimes by fax, update the EVN co-ordinator on what might be available from North America, Eastern Europe, Asia or a current news 'hot-spot', such as Haiti, Jericho, or Grozny.

(At the time we were doing our field work the News Co-ordinator also had a daily conversation with his or her counterpart at the now defunct East European news exchange, *Intervision*, then based in Prague.)

The conference scenario

While the format for the conference does not have an exact, predetermined script, it nevertheless does follow a fairly consistent pattern.

Checking attendance

Several minutes before the actual conference begins, a technical supervisor in Geneva pages each service to check the attendance. Each service contact is asked to acknowledge her or his presence on the network, to which the supervisor replies, often greeting each representative in his or her language in a personal manner[6] The supervisor records the presence of the Contacts as he goes along. When done, the supervisor repeats a call to those services which did not reply in the first round. Sometimes certain technical

---

5. All information available to permanent services can also be accessed from the BASYS database, a proprietary datalink via satellite.

6. The roll call is done just for the record as no sanctions are applied to a service representative who is not present. In fact, participation in the conference is non-obligatory, as is the entire voluntary nature of the News Exchange.

difficulties make it difficult to hear certain services or even the News Co-ordinator. Technical adjustments are usually made to the voice circuit and the engineering supervisor turns over the direction of the conference to the Eurovision co-ordinator in Geneva.

Review of 'final' line-up

When the conference begins, Geneva informs the services about the status of the anticipated line-up for EVN-0, based on the 'Final' list which was sent out to all services some time earlier. This list includes all A-items already selected and whatever other footage the News Co-ordinator chooses to include from New York and/or *Asiavision*. The News Co-ordinator has the authority to decide which items he or she wishes to include in this list, without any input from the Eurovision member services. There is no fixed number of items that may be selected; it is only expected that the sum total will not exceed the planned transmission time for EVN-0 which is usually 30 minutes. Thus some News Co-ordinators select more items than others from what is available. In addition, some potential items may be cancelled since the event may not yet have taken place or the expected footage may have become otherwise unavailable.[7] Whether 'cancelled' footage will be transmitted in a subsequent EVN depends largely on news developments during the course of the day.

Sometimes the 'Final' for EVN-0, which the Contacts already have, is left unaltered while on other days changes are announced at the outset of the morning conference. Changes to the announced 'Final' can also include the addition of last-minute items, frequently footage of highly newsworthy, breaking news. When available, information on each item (e.g. where and when shot, who speaks, what appears in each shot of the footage) is circulated by the EVN's proprietary, satellite-based datalink. (EVN journalists sometimes call this rudimentary information the 'dope sheet', a term which has nothing to do with narcotics, but is an old term-of-art from the days of movie newsreel photography.) If the basic information about an item is not available or inadequate at the time of EVN transmission, then the originating source provides further information on the EVN permanent voice-circuit.

New York and Moscow on-line

At this point the News Co-ordinator brings the New York Eurovision contact, and sometimes the EVN producer in Moscow, into the conference. Each of these Eurovision journalists may make offers on events taking place either in the United States, Eastern Europe, or which have been obtained from various sources, including the American networks. Also, at this time services can make requests for material originating from the United States.

It is interesting in passing how much the cost of obtaining news footage from the United States has declined during the past twenty years. In the late 1970s, the average rate to send news stories by Intelsat from the US to Geneva was approximately nineteen hundred US

---

7. For example, on 19 February 1987 an item about the situation in Beirut was cancelled because the material was confiscated by Syrian border guards when it was en route from Lebanon to the satellite transmitting station across the border in Syria.

dollars for ten minutes. Now, as we noted in Chapter 1, the Eurovision News Exchange operates two satellite channels of its own and the cost, which is now billed internally within the EBU, is only US$ 25 per minute (T. Naets, personal correspondence, 23 March 1995).

Offers and requests from services to services

The next part of the conference is devoted to deciding on whether or not to include in the transmission offers that are made from the different services and bi-national requests made from one service to another regarding an event in the latter contact's country. This is the most interesting aspect of the cooperative conference. It is the point where member services can inform their colleagues about events taking place in their respective countries and which they believe might be of interest in other countries as well. Accordingly they make offers which they are willing to provide their colleagues.

In addition to offers from national broadcasters to the news exchange, national services sometimes use the EVN mechanism to make requests for footage from another service. These requests usually come when the requesting service has some information regarding a possibly newsworthy event that has taken place, or is scheduled, in an EBU member nation.

According to the general principles of the conference, offers and requests are presented as options which the News Co-ordinator is expected to consider, following consultation with the other contacts participating in the conference. Accordingly, if an offer is made for which there is no expressed interest, the item would normally not be accepted. Similarly, if a request can be satisfied by the service being approached but there seems to be no interest in it from additional services, the item would not be accepted as part of the regular transmission. In this case, the requested item can still be made available to the service requesting it as a 'unilateral' transmission, the cost of which is borne directly and in full by the service making the request.

The News Co-ordinator is expected to follow the so called 'Rule of 3' (recently changed to the 'Rule of 5') which is that since many offers can be made for which there might be only very little, if any, interest, accordingly at least 3 (or 5) services should have explicitly expressed a desire to receive the item for it to be accepted. Thus the procedure calls for the News Co-ordinator to ask whether there is interest in the item at which point the services signify their interest by indicating their service call-letters (e.g. BBC, ZDF, RTL). As will be seen below, this rule is not consistently followed.

Offers from news agencies

The for-profit video news agencies try to provide the Exchange with as many items as they can. The News Co-ordinator, based on information which he or she already has, or the agencies themselves in real time, can offer the participants additional items. According to the conference procedures the same rules are applied to B-items (items previously submitted by the agencies) as with other items brought before the participants. However, since the agencies already know what is contained in the B-items, the Eurovision co-ordinator in Geneva reads the description of the items, thus providing the News Contacts with an opportunity to assess their interest in them.

Intervision offers

At this point in the conference the News Co-ordinator would report on *Intervision* items which in her or his view would be of potential interest to the services. Our observation of the conferences during our two-week site visits clearly suggested that *Intervision* was a only a minor source of information for the Eurovision member services, and as noted, no longer exists.

Summation of the conference

Once the News Co-ordinator is satisfied that all items have been dealt with, including offers, requests and B-items, the conference shifts back to Geneva where the Eurovision co-ordinator has been monitoring the deliberations (and consulted from time to time on a variety of technical or administrative points). The monitoring of the conference by Geneva is very important, since the pace and tension of the conference makes it difficult for the News Co-ordinator to keep track of all the items that have been accepted. Thus, the Geneva official is in a better position to provide a 'rundown', the listing of the sequence in which stories will be fed in the forthcoming EVN-1 transmission. With this action, the conference comes to its end.

A sample EVN conference

The daily morning conference begins each day of the year at 11.00 Central European Time (CET) on the Network Conference Circuit (NCC). Following is a detailed illustration using the complete transcript of one of the conferences. For the sake of brevity, however, we decided to present the shortest of the 10 conferences in our recorded sample. It took place on 20 February 1987 and the News Co-ordinator (NCORD) on duty that week was from *Antenne 2* in Paris.

The EVN conference text which follows includes a running time as well as our explanatory comments and observations. We have provided a verbatim text. In order to preserve the flavour of this moment in the global newsroom, we did not correct any grammatical or syntactical errors in what was said by the participants. Some minor, but necessary clarifications, appear in brackets within the text itself.

What was said during the EVN conference appears on the left side of the page, while our interpretive comments appear on the right.

Time		Text	Commentary
10.59	Brussels	Missing in the conference are Lisbon, Tripoli is missing and Zagreb is missing. Over to you Klaus.	A few minutes before the beginning of the conference the technical co-ordinator for the Eurovision Control Center (EVC) in Brussels [this function is now also performed in Geneva] checks the attendance of the various service contacts on the News Conference Circuit (NCC). He then reports which services did not respond to the Eurovision co-ordinator who then takes over the running of the conference from Geneva.
11.00	Geneva	OK, thank you very much. Good morning to all, *bonjour a tous*. Since the final went out, one cancellation: the RAI [Italian] handball is cancelled. Unfortunately, no material available until tomorrow. Everything else is on the Final.	The Geneva co-ordinator greets all the participants in the customary English and French and then reports that since the final list of items for the EVN-0 transmission, scheduled for 12.00 noon one item was cancelled. Cancellation of an item is common for a variety of reasons. In this case, some material that was promised was not available.
		Are there any questions, any remarks? [4 second pause] If not, over to Marine [the NCORD in Paris], Kevin in NY [at EBU-NY], and Charles [at EVC].	At this point the running of the conference is given over to the duty News Co-ordinator in Paris who greets the participants and goes on to report on what she has already decided and arranged with EVC prior to the conference regarding two items: one about the situation in West Beirut and the other about a Jewish dissident in Moscow who had been promised to be allowed to leave the USSR. She then switches to the EBU bureau in New York to continue a discussion which she began prior to the conference with the New York bureau.

Time		Text	Commentary
11.00:20	NCORD	*Merci*, Klaus. *Bonjour a tous*, good morning to all. Today we will have ex ORTAS [the Syrian satellite uplink station], on the ROTA [rotation scheme among the news services] there will be agency material two items: the Syrian troops deployment in West Beirut, and all the damage after the recent clashes. Charles will give us the full contents during the conference. And concerning Begun's liberation: Begun's family does not expect him in Moscow this evening and they are trying today, so for the moment the situation is still – we don't know what we are going to have this afternoon. OK, calling Kevin in NY?	
11.01:15	EBU-NY	Good morning Marine and good morning all. Not much for you today. Reagan is expected to make one appearance before the Conservative Political Action Convention, but he is not scheduled to speak until 18.30 GMT, so that's a bit late for you. Other than that, the Tower commission investigating the Iran arms affair will make themselves available for a photo opportunity this morning at 14.30 GMT. They will not be taking any questions; it's a strict photo opportunity of them allegedly at work. That could conceivably be offered for EVN-1 if you are interested.	
	NCORD	OK, thank you very much, Kevin. Are there any questions for NY? [5 second pause] OK, I'm afraid nothing for you. Thank you, Kevin. Bye-bye.	

Time		Text	Commentary
	EBU-NY	Thank you. Bye-bye.	This seems like a dull day in terms of offers from New York. The two items being offered that morning were events that had not yet taken place and already there were foreseen problems with material being made available. Since no contact seemed interested, the NCORD thanks her New York colleague and goes on to the next item of business.
11.02:25	VISNEWS	VISNEWS for Marine.	
	NCORD	Yes.	
	VISNEWS	When you were talking about the ORTAS satellite, were you talking about EVN-1 or EVN-0?	
	NCORD	I was talking about EVN-1.	
	VISNEWS	Thank you.	At this point the Visnews person asks to clarify a point concerning the previous discussion regarding the satellite feed to be coming from Syria.
11.02:40	NCORD	OK, coming back to Europe, are there any offers from services?	At this point the NCORD gets to the main business of the conference, namely, dealing with offers and requests from services. She begins by asking if anyone wishes to make an offer about an event taking place in his/her country.
	TVE	TVE [Spain] coming in.	
	NCORD	Yes.	

Time		Text	Commentary
	TVE	Good morning. I got couple offers for EVN-1. The first one is shot today in Valencia, where farmers will demonstrate cutting the roads with the trucks and tractors, protesting against the gas prices, asking for 14 pesos and protesting also against the government policy in agricultural matters. And the second item we will show today –	
	NCORD	TVE for Newscoord?	
	TVE	Yes?	
	NCORD	Maybe we can check immediately the interest in your first offer. Is there any interest in this demo [demonstration] today in Spain?	
	RAI	RAI would be interested.	
	TRT	[expresses interest]	
	ARD	[expresses interest]	
	SRG	[expresses interest]	
	NCORD	OK, so we will accept your offer, TVE.	According to the formal rules of the Exchange, the NCORD is supposed to ask whether the service representatives are interested in the item being offered. She does so in this case and 4 services indicate their interest by identifying themselves with their service call letters. The NCORD accepts the item and so informs the participants.
	TVE	OK. It will be in Valencia. The second offer is shot today, where we saw the beginning of the carnival in Tenerife in the Canary Islands.	
	NCORD	Any interest in this carnival in Tenerife?	
	RAI	[expresses interest]	

Time	Text	Commentary
NCORD	[after 4 second pause] I'm afraid, Albert, you're alone.	
RAI	OK.	Whereas the first offer from TVE Spain was accepted, the second only had the support of the Italian contact. Thus the NCORD decided not to accept the carnival item.
NCORD	Any other offers from services?	
BRT	BRT [Belgium]	
NCORD	Was it BRT?	
BRT	It was BRT, yes. Archbishop Glemp is coming to Brussels this afternoon. We could offer his arrival at the airport for EVN-1.	
NCORD	OK, thank you. We will accept it for EVN-1.	Another offer is made, by BRT. This time, however, the NCORD departs from the formal rule and accepts the item without even trying to determine if there is any interest in it from member services. This phenomenon occurs from time to time in the conference.
ITN	ITN [London] coming in.	
NCORD	Yes.	
ITN	ITN could offer for EVN-1 protesters from Norway holding a press conference and handing out petitions at Number 10 Downing street over plans to build a reprocessing plant at Donray.	
NCORD	OK, thank you. Any interest in this offer? [4 second pause] I'm afraid, ITN, nobody. Any other offers from services?	The third offer came from ITN in London. There was no interest in it, however, and it was accordingly rejected.
BBC	BBC [London] coming in, Marine.	
NCORD	Yes, Julie.	

Time		Text	Commentary
	BBC	I have a question for you, really. I gather that there's a Channel tunnel presser [press conference] in Paris at 15.30 GMT?	
	NCORD	Can you repeat?	
	BBC	There's a Channel tunnel presser in Paris at 15.30 GMT. They are looking at the logistical problems, I think.	
	NCORD	I thought it was in London.	
	BBC	I think there's one at your end as well.	
	NCORD	Yes, I have to check. I think we are not going to cover, but I'll check it again for you.	
	BBC	OK, thanks.	At this point the BBC contact brings up what she believes is an expected press conference on the English Channel tunnel project. A discussion ensues indicating some lack of clarity are the forthcoming event. Even more noteworthy, however is the fact that the implied 'question' from BBC to the NCORD was in fact a request for material from her own service in Paris, even though the NCORD is not supposed to act as her service's contact while she is NCORD. In any event the NCORD agreed to check but assumed that no material would be available.
	NCORD	Any requests? [3 second pause]	
	SRG	SRG [German Swiss TV] has a request.	
	NCORD	*Oui*, Catherine.	
	SRG	*Oui*, Marine, good morning. It's a request for TVE Madrid. I wonder if they could offer today the first session of the Basque parliament?	

Time		Text	Commentary
	TVE	Yes, for sure. I think that will be OK for EVN-1.	
	NCORD	OK, thank you. So we will take this for EVN-1.	
	SRG	*Merci*, Marine.	Here we witness another request. Note that the TVE contact in Madrid was paying close attention so the NCORD did not even need to contact him. Also note the item was also accepted by the NCORD without polling the participants of the conference.
	NCORD	Any other questions, requests, or offers?	
	NOS	NOS [Netherlands] has also a question also for TVE. If they have coverage from the latest let's say, apparently, ETA attack on the Renault showroom ...	
	TVE	Yes, the material comes in EVN-0.	
	NOS	Thank you.	The question by NOS regarding the ETA attack was also dealt with quickly by the TVE contact. Since the material was going to be fed for EVN-0 there was no need for the NCORD to take any action.
	NCORD	OK, any general questions?	
	ARD	Marine, good morning. Just a general advise: tonight is the opening of the 37th International Film Festival in West Berlin. We are not expecting any coverage, maybe for our later bulletin, but it could be offered for EVN-0 in case there is interest. It would help me if I'll know already today.	
	SRG	SRG [Switzerland] will be interested.	
	NOS	[expresses interest]	

Time		Text	Commentary
	ORF	[expresses interest]	
	RTL	[expresses interest]	
	NCORD	So it will be very good offer for tomorrow. Thank you.	ARD [German] informs the NCORD about the Berlin Film Festival and without the need for the NCORD to ask the participants several services interject their interest.
		OK, we have several, no one B item, Charles?	
11.07:00	CHARLES	Yes. Good morning to everyone	The NCORD then wishes to deal with the B item [the news agency offer which she had received prior to the conference] but TVE interrupts her with some information on the Basque parliament item discussed earlier. It seems that TVE was too quick to make the offer for EVN-1 since the parliamentary session will not take place at all.
	TVE	Moment, Charles, TVE coming in. The first session of the Basque parliament will not take place today. It has been postponed, and so as soon when I get any confirmation from Vittorio we will let you know when it takes place.	
	CHARLES	In principle, there is no session today anymore?	
	TVE	That's right.	
	SRG	Thank you very much, Cesar.	
	TVE	Welcome, Maria.	Finally Charles in Geneva can get to the B item which was labeled 'Shelter' in the list of B items. He provides the detailed description of what the item contains. As it turns out, however, there was no interest in that item.

Time	Text	Commentary
CHARLES	All right. Coming then to the B item: from WTN 'SHELTER' material shot the 17th in Teheran. Iran has now international campaign to teach civilians how to build air raid shelters. It aims to counter the war of the cities being waged by Iraqi air forces in a bid to demoralise the people of Iran and end the war. Many civilians have been killed in the air raids and Iraq has warned residents of Teheran to vacate the city. The Iranian government is running training classes to encourage civilians to build their own shelters, and in Teheran a number of shelters have gone on display in a park. Signs showing the way to an air raid shelter have also been erected through the city. Material shows: display of air raid shelter in Teheran park, newspaper headline urging people to build their own air raid shelter, training class in progress constructing air raid shelter, Red Cross group setting up in area, signs with directions to shelter, students and others building shelters in their neighbourhood. All that for 2 minutes in colour, natural sound.	
NCORD	Any interest? [2 second pause] No. OK, OK, so that's all for B items. Is there any questions for agencies? [7 second pause]	
11.09:15	OK, I have received the *Intervision* list. Maybe, Charles, I will check the press conference on the question of the Soviet Jews; it's from TSS [Soviet TV].	

Time		Text	Commentary
	CHARLES	OK.	Since there were no other offers or requests, the NCORD may take one item from *Intervision* [the East European News Exchange]. She then ends her role in the conference and turns it back to Geneva.
	NCORD	Are there any questions for *Intervision*? [5 second pause] OK, so that's all from me. Back to you, Charles and Paul.	Charles wants to summarise the conference but there are two questions: one to the Sports co-ordinator and one from RTL.
11.09:50	CHARLES	All right. Any questions before we go to summary?	
	WTN	Sportscoord and Geneva for WTN.	
	CHARLES	Yes.	
	WTN	Yes, Paul, can I draw your attention to our soccer item from Brazil offer in our London 8 and 9 for EVN-1?	
	CHARLES	Yes, I think the story has already been discussed.	
	RTL	RTL has a question.	
	CHARLES	Yes, RTL.	
	RTL	I wonder if the German services can offer pictures about the house of Rudy Karel protected by police, the story between Germany and Iran.	

Time		Text	Commentary
	ARD	Sorry, ARD has no coverage.	Several days earlier a programme on Germany's ARD network presented Rudy Karel, a well-known satirist doing a comic item in which he ridiculed Iran's Khumeini. This event caused a major political crisis between Iran and Germany. The satirist was subsequently provided with police protection which was the subject of RTL's current request. ARD was unable to provide footage. It should be noted that in each of several previous days there was footage of Iranian protests of the incident but none of the satirical piece itself since it was copyrighted material and not considered to be news. Finally, Geneva can summarise the conference and indicate which items will be available for the satellite feed.
11.10:40	CHARLES	Any more questions? [2 second pause] So, summary of accepted items. We will have the satellite from ORTAS [the satellite uplink in Syria] with two items which will show the display of the Syrians and the aftermath of the bomb of the different fighting from yesterday, and the day before. Then we'll have from TVE farmers' demonstration in Valencia, Andalusia. From BRT, we'll have the arrival of Archbishop Glemp in Brussels. And from TSS we'll have the presser concerning the immigration of Soviet Jews. And if I'm right, that should be all.	
11.11:30	BBC	Charlie for BBC.	
	CHARLES	Yes.	
	BBC	Do we know who is making the presser from TSS?	

Time		Text	Commentary
	CHARLES	No.	
	BBC	Thank you.	
	CHARLES	Just a press conference, that's it.	
	NCORD	Yes, we know, Charles. No, I'm sorry.	Just when Geneva is about to end the conference BBC comes in with a question about the press conference in Moscow. Note that there is some degree of confusion about the nature of the *Intervision* item as well as what seems to be impatience on the part of Charles in Geneva. Just before signing off WTN informs Geneva about two new items on Lebanon which will become available and of which, it seems, Charles is already aware.
	CHARLES	So, any more questions or remarks?	
	WTN	Geneva for WTN.	
	CHARLES	Yes.	
	WTN	Just to let you know, Charles, I have a couple of offers on Lebanon going right now.	
	CHARLES	Yes, I received the copy. [3 second pause] Any more questions or remarks? [4 second pause] So, many thanks for attention. 'Til EVN-0 in a good half hour, bye-bye. Over to EVC.	The conference ended at 11.12:10. The next major item of business at Eurovision was the EVN-0 feed at 12.00 noon.

Offers and requests

Our detailed analysis of the 10 conferences which we recorded paid special attention to the offers and requests that were made by the various contacts. We did so because we believe that the offers and requests are the heart of the negotiating process in the conference. This is because the services have little or nothing to say regarding the pre-selection of items from the news agencies and Eurovision bureau in New York, but they have substantial input to decisions about offers and requests. Accordingly, the offers indicate items which member services themselves believe their colleagues in other countries might find newsworthy. Hence, they often attempt to 'sell' these items during the news conference.

Similarly, requests for footage might shed light on the kind of stories that members might be interested in, based on what they know is happening around the world. This interest is manifest when a service takes the initiative to 'purchase' EVN items.

Tables 1 and 2, present the complete lists of all the offers and requests that were made during the 10 days we spent monitoring the conferences. The list of offers (Table 1) includes those made by services as well as the news agencies (which were designated by the News Co-ordinator as B-items) and items suggested by the Eurovision bureau in New York (but not including any preselected items from either source). The list of requests (Table 2) consists of those made by the services (including a notation of the service or agency to whom the request was made) as well as requests made by the News Co-ordinator. The tables indicate that a total of 148 items were brought up for discussion – 84 offers and 64 requests – which represent an average of 8.4 offers and 6.4 requests per day.

We decided to exclude from further analyses the offers made by the New York bureau as well as requests made by the News Co-ordinators. We will focus only on those items that were initiated by the conference participants themselves. By deleting the institutional offers and requests we are left with 48 offers and 55 requests, representing a total of slightly more than 10 items per conference, or an average of 4.8 offers and 5.5 requests, per day.

It is evident that the two weeks of the study appear to be quite different. During the week in February 59 items were dealt with while in June only 44 items were brought up for discussion. Moreover, in February 60 per cent of the items were offers and 40 per cent were requests whereas in June only 43 per cent of the items were offers and 57 per cent were requests.

Looked at in a different manner, during the two weeks the contacts themselves brought up 70 per cent of the items dealt with in the conferences (103 of the 144 items). As for offers, the participants initiated only 57 per cent of the offers with the others coming from the agencies and Eurovision in New York. At the same time, the contacts were responsible for initiating 86 per cent of all the requests with the remaining ones coming from the June News Co-ordinator. Interestingly, the News Co-ordinator in February did not make a single request of her own. In fact, this is one manifestation of the difference in style of the work of the two News co-ordinators which we closely observed. In February the News Co-ordinator did not seem to encourage many requests from the services whereas the June News Co-ordinator not only sought to stimulate requests but, as noted, made quite a number of her own.

Table 1. Offers made by services and agencies

Date	Topic of item	Initiator	Decision
16 Feb	Shamir arrival in Washington	EBU-NY	Get from London
	Resignation of Contra leader	EBU-NY	No action taken
	Hazards of gypsum dump	BRT	Accepted w/o poll

	Italian carnival	RAI	Accepted by poll
	Murdered Italian policemen	RAI	Rejected by poll
	German tax evasion trial	ARD	Accepted by poll
	Thatcher meeting Gemayel	ITN	Accepted w/o poll
	Supplies for Palestinians	WTN	Accepted by poll
	Visiting Demjanjuk in prison	VISNEWS	Accepted by poll
17 Feb	Shamir in Washington	EBU-NY	Get from London
	Confirmation hearing on Gates	EBU-NY	No action taken
	Discussion on *Amerika* series	EBU-NY	No action taken
	Senate committee hearings	EBU-NY	No action taken
	Iraqi bombing of Tabriz	ZDF	Accepted by poll
	Irish elections taking place	RTE	Accepted by poll
	French planes in Cyprus	CyBC	Accepted by poll
	Spanish farmers demonstrating	TVE	Rejected by poll
	Columbian guerrilla killed	TVE	Rejected by poll
	NATO and Warsaw Pact talks	ORF	Accepted by poll
	BBC journalists on strike	BBC	Accepted by poll
18 Feb	Shamir in Washington	EBU-NY	Get from London
	Gates CIA hearings	EBU-NY	No action
	Senate foreign aid committee	EBU-NY	No action
	US assistance to El-Salvador	EBU-NY	No action
	Twilight Zone trial testimony	EBU-NY	No action
	Greek Cypriots held by Turks	CyBC	Rejected by poll
	Statement on EEC policy	FR3	Accepted by poll
	Counting votes in Ireland	RTE	Accepted by poll
	Ali Acga's mother asks pardon	RAI	Accepted by poll
	Greek students support Arabs	ERT/WTN	Accepted by poll
	Rome sanitary workers strike	RAI/WTN	Rejected by poll
19 Feb	Shamir in Washington	EBU-NY	Rejected by poll
	End of Spanish student unrest	TVE	Accepted by poll
	Declaration by Basque leader	TVE	Accepted by poll
	Protest for Begun in New York	EBU-NY	Get from London w/o poll
	Vranitsky visits Yugoslavia	JRT	Rejected by poll
	Students vs. police in Lima	WTN	Accepted by poll
	Trouble in West Bank	JCS/WTN	Rejected by poll
	Russian fleet in Adriatic Sea	RAI	Rejected by poll
20 Feb	Reagan talks to conservatives	EBU-NY	Rejected by poll
	Investigation of arms to Iran	EBU-NY	Rejected by poll
	Spanish protests of prices	TVE	Accepted by poll
	Carnival in Tenerife	TVE	Rejected by poll
	Archbishop Glemp in Brussels	BRT	Accepted w/o poll (RAI wants item)
	Norwegian protest in London	ITN	Rejected by poll
	Berlin film festival opens	ARD	Accepted by poll
	Iran builds air shelters	WTN/WTN	Rejected by poll
15 June	Reagan meets reporters	EBU-NY	No action
	Jury deliberation in Goetz trial	EBU-NY	Wait for next day

33

	Departure ceremony for army chief	EBU-NY	No action
	50th anniversary of writers' meeting	TVE	Accepted w/o poll
	Iranian PM visits Turkey	TRT	Rejected by poll
	Greece beats USSR in basketball	ERT	Rejected as irrelevant
	Visit to Hungarian Parliament	Intervision	Rejected by poll
	Italians vote in local places	RAI	Accepted w/o poll
16 June	The Neckar arrives in Kiel	ZDF	Accepted w/o poll
	Interview with Vietnamese leader	ARD	Rejected by poll (1 wanted)
	Network feeds from Seoul & Moscow	EBU-NY	Get from London w/o poll
	Reagan goes to Capitol Hill	EBU-NY	No action taken
	Suarez visiting in Geneva	SRG	Rejected by poll
	Shipping traffic on the Rhine	ARD	Accepted w/o poll
	Yemeni report of sabotage	?	Rejected by poll
	Philippine-US relations	VISNEWS	Reluctantly accepted by poll
	Land reform in the Philippines	VISNEWS	Rejected by poll
17 June	Reagan meeting President of Costa Rica	EBU-NY	Already scheduled for EVN-1
	Russian space walk	Agencies	Accepted by poll if available
	Artists and actors elected in Italian elections	RAI	Accepted by poll
	Black box found from crashed plane 8 years ago	RAI	Accepted by poll
	Khaddafi meets Sudanese delegations	LJB	Rejected by poll (ITN wants item)
	Killings in Santiago, Chile	TVE	Accepted w/o poll
	Aftermath of explosion in Lima bank	Agencies	No action
	Cocaine raid by Columbian police	VISNEWS	Accepted by poll (for EVN-2)
	Attack by drug dealers on police in Venezuela	VISNEWS	Accepted by poll (for EVN-2)
	Press conference of US arms control negotiator	Agencies	Rejected by poll
	Tamil refugees arrive in southern India	Agencies	Accepted by poll
18 June	Cicciolina fans cause disturbance in Rome	WTN	Accepted by poll
	Replica of ancient Portuguese ship launched	RTP	Accepted by poll
	Jews protest Waldheim's invitation to Vatican	EBU-NY	Accepted by poll
	Corpus Christie celebrations in Toledo, Spain	TVE	Rejected by poll
	Ascot Ladies' Day	ITN	Rejected by poll
	Conflict between Venezuela and Columbia	TVE	Accepted w/o poll
19 June	Soviet Foreign Minister visits Yugoslavia	JRT	Accepted by poll
	Rajiv Ghandi's party looses in election	WTN	Accepted by poll
	Interviews with friends of kidnapped Glass	WTN	Get from London

Table 2. Requests made by services

Date	Topic of item	Initiator	Outcome
16 Feb	Pictures of Palestinian camps	BBC	Conditional
	Strike in Greece	SVT	Accepted by poll
17 Feb	Spoiled mussels in Germany	TDF	Accepted w/o poll
	French test driver killed	RTL	Referred to Sports
	Plane crash in Mulhouse	RTL	To be checked out
	Car crash in Australia	SRG	Need unilateral
18 Feb	German comic on Khumeini	TVE	Not available
	Amnesty Int'l on death penalty	BRT	If available in time
	British soccer hooligans	BBC	If event happens
	Live executions in Libya	BBC	Not available
	WHO conference on AIDS	ITN	Accepted w/o poll
	Car crash in Australia	SRG	Need unilateral
	Bardot and Greenpeace	NRK	Referred to TDF
19 Feb	End to Spanish student unrest	DR	Offer made by TVE
	Testimony in Demjanjuk trial	NOS	Will provide if available
	British fans hurt in crash	BBC	TVE will check availability
20 Feb	Press conference on Channel	BBC	Checking availability
	First Basque parliament session	SRG	Accepted w/o poll
	ETA attacks Renault showroom	NOS	Material scheduled for EVN-0.
	Police protect German comedian	RTL	No coverage available
15 June	Demonstration in East Berlin	NCORD	Mistaken information
	Beatles' statue erected in London	NCORD	Checking availability
	Shipping in the Rhine blocked	NOS	No material available
	Agricultural ministers meet	NCORD	Accepted by poll
	Austerity measures in Brazil	NCORD	Request annulled
16 June	Bangladesh students want to cheat	RTL	No material available
	Parents to visit German pilot	NCORD	Will provide if possible
	Farm prices talks in Luxembourg	RTE	Rejected by poll
	EEC parliament in Strassbourg	ITN	Will check possibility
	Bomb blast in Spain	ITN	Accepted by poll
	Sikhs killed in Punjab	NCORD	No material available
	Strikes in S. Africa commemorating Soweto	NOS	Rejected by poll
	Cypriot foreign minister in Vienna	CYBC	ORF will check availability
17 June	Gunter Grass speaking in East Berlin	NCORD	No material available
	Nottinghill Gate incidents in London	NCORD	Will check availability
	International conference on drug abuse in Vienna	ITN	Accepted by poll
	Farm talks in Luxembourg	ITN	Accepted by poll
	Auction of Brigit Bardot artifacts	NOS	Will offer if material arrives
	Greek PM policy speech on investment in Greece	CyBC	Accepted by poll

35

	Draw for European volleyball championships	CyBC	Referred to sports co-ordinator
	Question and Answer session at EEC parliament	CyBC	Will check availability
	Radioactivity problem in French nuclear station	NOS	No material available
	Photo opportunity of new British government	NCORD	Will provide for EVN-1
	India's PM meets with opposition leaders	SVT	No material available
	Floods in China	NOS	Will check availability
18 June	Flooding in Swiss lakes	RTL	Accepted by poll
	Placido Domingo sings in Central Part,	NYRTV	Will check availability
	Oliver North saying 'no comment' in testimony	SVT	Rejected by poll
	Cocaine raid the previous day in Columbia	NOS	Outcome unclear
	French AIDS workers to Sri Lanka	ITN	Will check availability
	Meeting of EEC agricultural ministers	ITN	Rejected by poll
	Harayana elections	NOS	Accepted by poll
	Clashes between Columbian army and Leftists	NOS	Outcome unclear
	Vietnamese parliament meeting of new leaders	NOS	No action
19 June	Senator Kennedy suggests sanctions against Korea	SVT	Accepted by poll
	Pictures of US Marine to be court martialled	RTL	Request rescinded, no pictures
	Kafka auction at Sotheby's	NOS	Rejected by poll
	Dutchman tried for selling arms to Iran & China	NOS	Material not available
	Officer held hostage in Gloucester	RTE	Will check availability
	Murder of Briton and Dutchman in Corfu	NOS	Will check availability
	Government meeting	TVE	Accepted by poll
	Commemoration of murders in Lima last year	SVT	Item was selected already by NCO
	China's Ziao visits Bulgaria	NOS	Grudgingly accepted by poll
	South African crash killing 70 people	RTE	RTE will take it unilaterally

Of the 29 offers made in our February sample, 20 were accepted by the News Co-ordinator. Of these 20 items, 17 were accepted following a poll of the conference participants and only 3 offers were accepted without the News Co-ordinator polling the member services for their interest in them. The remaining 9 offers (31 per cent) were rejected. In June, on the other hand, of the 19 offers made, 11 (58 per cent) were accepted by the News Co-ordinator – 5 with and 6 without a poll of the participants – and relatively more (42 per cent) of the offers were rejected.

By their very nature, offers are items that have been judged newsworthy by the country whose service presents them for consideration. Requests, on the other hand, can but do not necessarily have anything to do with the country whose service asks for them. Thus in the case of the requests we coded the items into three categories: (a) requests for information on an event directly concerning the country asking for the material or directly concerning its nationals and which took place in the country from whom the request was made (e.g. a British service asking the Spanish service for material on British soccer fans rioting in Spain); (b) requests for material on events of clear relevance to the requesting service's country although the event did not involve its nationals (e.g. a request by the Dutch service from the German services on traffic blockage on the Rhine river); and (c) requests for information on events that have nothing specifically to do with the country whose service made the request – i.e. an item of potentially more universal interest – (e.g., a request by the Dutch service to the French services for material on an auction of artifacts owned by movie actress Brigitte Bardot).

The analysis clearly reveals that most (70 per cent) of the requests are of the third category, namely, universally interesting items. An additional 17 per cent were items directly relevant to the country requesting them, and only 13 per cent were of the remaining category (those only of relevance to the country making the request but not involving that country's own nationals).

We also analysed the arrays of offers and requests in terms of the specific countries and services initiating them. This was done since it appeared to us that there was much variance in terms of the contribution of the various services to the conferences. Table 3 presents a list of the countries making offers and/or requests during the conferences, ranked from the highest total number of contributions to the lowest. Before reporting on these findings we must point out that we do not have an exact count on the number of services that participated in each of the 10 conferences that we monitored as some of our recordings do not include the attendance checking but only began when the actual conference started. Therefore we cannot be absolutely sure whether most or only few of the services actually attending made offers or requests on any given day. But we do know that on the days that we did record the roll call non-attendance was limited to between three and five of the service contacts. Thus we can safely assume that there were indeed quite a number of services whose contact listened in on the conferences but made neither offers nor requests.

During the course of the 10 days, 24 services made at least one offer or request. Eight services brought up a total of five or more items (which amounts to at least one item every other day). By contrast, 9 of the services only brought up one item. Of the leading participants, the Netherlands is clearly in first place, followed by Spain, the United Kingdom, Italy, Luxembourg and Cyprus. Despite the possibility that our two week sample was affected by factors of item specificity – which is always an issue in news research – it seems clear that both big and small countries are major participants in the conferences. Thus along side with both services in the United Kingdom as well as Spain and Italy, we find the Netherlands, Luxembourg and Cyprus.[8] As for the lowest contribu-

8. Nevertheless some degree of frustration was expressed by the French A2F co-ordinator in her report following her co-ordination week in March, 1991: 'I wish to say that I am surprised that some big services make so few offers of foreign reports which they offer immediately when asked for. I am therefore always thankful when members come on the circuit to ask for items seen on the vast European network. The

tors including those that made no contribution at all, we also find large countries such as France and small countries such as Denmark, Portugal and Norway, as well as countries on the periphery of Eurovision such as Turkey and Libya.

Table 3. Offers and requests by national services

Country and services	Total	Offers	Requests
The Netherlands (NOS)	15	0	15
Spain (TVE)	12	10	2
United Kingdom (ITN)	10	3	7
Italy (RAI)	8	8	0
Luxembourg (RTL)	7	0	7
United Kingdom (BBC)	6	1	5
Cyprus (CYBC)	6	2	4
Sweden (SVT)	5	0	5
Switzerland (SRG)	4	1	3
Ireland (RTE)	4	2	2
Germany (ARD)	4	4	0
Belgium (BRT)	3	2	1
Germany (ZDF)	2	2	0
Greece (ERT)	2	2	0
Yugoslavia (JRT)	2	2	0
Austria (ORF)	1	1	0
France (FR3)	1	1	0
Libya (LJB)	1	1	0
Portugal (RTP)	1	1	0
Turkey (TRT)	1	1	0
Denmark (DR)	1	0	1
France (TF1)	1	0	1
Norway (NRK)	1	0	1
Slovenia (RTV)	1	0	1

What is more striking, however, is that among the services contributing the most, there is a clear distinction between those who may be termed 'sellers' and those whom we will refer to as 'buyers'. For example, Spain, Italy and to some extent Germany (ARD), made relatively many offers but made few if any requests, whereas the Netherlands, Luxembourg, Sweden and to some extent the United Kingdom appeared to make relatively many requests but few offers. Thus while all these stations make use of the Exchange, they do so in different ways.

Finally, we attempted to determine which services are most likely to express interest in the various items that are discussed during the conferences. Making this determination

News Co-ordinator is too busy to keep an eye on all these channels. Once more I ask services to make more offers. They may be rejected but at least the conferences would be more lively. It gets very boring to hear one's own voice pleading: "any more offers? any requests? any suggestions?" I wish services could learn how to sell better their own material, which is often turned down because it is badly explained at the conference'.

was not easy, first because News Contacts use their service codes rather than their full designation when indicating their interest, and second because two or more Contacts often simultaneously attempted to indicate the interest of their respective services thus making it difficult to hear who is actually responding. It should be pointed out that this difficulty is encountered from time to time by the News Co-ordinators themselves and not only by the researchers.

Using the computer to scan the complete set of conference transcripts we found that two small services, SRG (Switzerland) and RTL (Luxembourg), responded most heavily to the offers (20 and 19 affirmations, respectively). Next in line with 16 mentions was NOS (the Netherlands), followed by TVE (Spain) with 11 mentions, ITN (United Kingdom) with 10 mentions, BRT (Belgium) with 9 mentions, and TF1 (France) with 8 mentions. Several services were never heard to support any offer: FR3 (France), ERT (Greece), and CyBC (Cyprus).

Consensus and the right to differ

An analysis of the text of the conferences seems to reveal a dynamic culture of a global newsroom where different points of view try to find a common ground for negotiation and agreement. And yet, despite the common denominator which the newsroom promotes, time and again we find moments of tension and disagreement among the participants who must mobilise their best argument to achieve harmony. Let's listen carefully to this 16 February interchange:

NCORD	And RAI?
RAI	Coming in. I have one light item to suggest for EVN-0, still. It is at Viareggio, the carnival, to have the decorated cars which are huge, very nice images. Also President Reagan is depicted. It is quite nice.
NCORD	OK, who would be interested in this item?

At least three members say 'yes' and the offer is accepted. Consensus is readily achieved, so we find time and again, when 'light', 'colourful', items are offered. Trying to characterise a typical 'good argument' in the context of the conferences we would suggest the recurrent 'it is quite nice' and/or 'there are very nice images'. But often consensus is not that easily achieved. Let's listen to what immediately follows.

RAI	OK. And then I have another item still. The funeral of the two murdered policemen by the Red Brigades takes place this morning and we can offer that if there's interest.
NCORD	Who is interested in this material for EVN-0? It's the funeral of the two people who were killed; it was last Saturday?
RAI	Right! Two policemen murdered by the Red Brigades.

The offer was rejected. Nobody was interested. Or as the News Co-ordinator puts it: 'I am afraid there is no real interest for EVN-0. Thank you'. Was the item rejected because of the way the News Co-ordinator translated the vernacular of the offer to a more universal, neutral one? RAI speaks of a funeral that takes place *this morning*, which seems to be a good argument for newsworthiness and to justify highlighting the story. The News Co-ordinator's mediation, referring to *last Saturday* (this discussion takes place the following Monday) seems to undermine the argument. Timeliness is, to be sure, a most significant criterion of newsworthiness, but what is even more telling is the difference – or distance – of points of view. For RAI the story is of the two policemen *murdered* by the Red Brigades while for the News Co-ordinator it is of the two *people* who were *killed*. The tension between the two points of view is heightened by RAI's repetition emphasizing the Italian point of view. To the News Co-ordinator's question: 'It was last Saturday?' he (the RAI representative) replies affirmatively, but to her detached, neutral: 'the two people killed' he responds by repeating his version: 'two policemen murdered by the Red Brigades'.

For us this is a telling illustration for the limits of consensus in the global newsroom or for the uneasy dialogue we encountered during the conferences. The various participants in the daily conferences seem to be at the same time engaged in two kinds of dialogue. One is an amicable, professional negotiation very much like the discussion by academics during an international gathering where a universal culture is celebrated. The second is a somewhat competitive, belligerent bargaining session on particularistic meanings and images. Here participants may find themselves in situations where they must insistingly present their particular interpretation and at times even defend the interests of their nation and service.[9]

Human interest stories and 'very nice pictures'

As noted, stories of universal appeal: the bizarre, the remote, the exotic, the emotional, raise little if any resistance. The services usually say 'yes' to one or two such items, like a carnival, a natural disaster, a 'human story' where children, animals, melodramas and romances are involved. For example, on 18 June:

RTL	RTL would be interested if SRG can make an offer on the too high level of the water in the Swiss flood which is due to heavy rain.
NCORD	Calling SRG
SRG	Yes, well I could offer it for EVN-0. We had the maximum last evening but at the moment everything is OK again.
NCORD	Is it very alarming?
SRG	It's not very serious, but the pictures are quite good.

9. In his weekly report, following his Co-ordination, the Flemish News Co-ordinator in April, 1991 seems to express these tensions in a down-to-earth and less academic tone: 'Should the news Co-ordinator regard himself as Europe's editor? I don't think so. News Co-ordinators should function more as news organisers and less as news editors'. What he is rejecting here is the notion of institutionalised and authoritarian central editing in favour of peer-group authority.

NCORD	Is there any interest for this item for EVN-0, the lake over-filling?
RTL	[expresses interest]
ITN	[expresses interest]
NCORD	Anybody else?
ARD	[expresses interest]

This 'not very serious' item but one with good pictures was accepted. Such items are usually perceived as colourful or emotional. They seem to be judged beyond particular contexts of politics, culture, ideology and beyond serious journalistic criteria. They are readily accepted.

At the same time, however, it is recognised that these light elements of universalistic appeal are and should be marginal and few.[10] It is also noteworthy that in the context of the Eurovision conferences the dominant tone of the discussion is serious and matter-of-fact. Only very rarely can one detect irony and cynicism, which are not that foreign to television newsrooms in general. It seems that the very context of the international gathering slightly colours the conference with reverence and solemn professional responsibility.

There might be one interesting exception to this seeming consensus. RTL, the Luxembourg service, presents a particular case. As Nick Jacob (RTL's foreign news editor, 17 February) told us: 'Luxembourg is different! We almost have no domestic news, only foreign news. Yes, one can argue that we try to be more "popular" than the other European stations'.[11] The RTL representative seems to be interested, more than anyone else, in the conference, in human-interest stories 'with good pictures', even two at a time (17 February):

NCORD	Any other offers or requests?
RTL	RTL has two requests.
NCORD	Yes.
RTL	The first one is to TVE. There was the French driver Arnu who had an accident on a test race. Is there some pictures about that?
NCORD	I think you can maybe wait for the Sports conference.

10. In his weekly report following his co-ordination in February 1990, the Norwegian News Co-ordinator suggested: 'In this era of hard news it is nice to be able also to include some soft items now and then. Two such highlights this week were an NOS piece on restoration of Van Gogh paintings and an item from BBC with children swimming and playing with dolphins in the Bahamas'.

11. When we interviewed Jacob in 1987 most European stations were still non-commercial and RTL was the exception. Moreover, for the Luxembourg economy RTL has always been an important exporter who tries to make a hard sale. In addition, RTL broadcasts in Belgium, France and Germany compete with the bulletins (and programmes) of the members there. It also operates on a small budget with few staff. RTL therefore relies on coverage from its competitors to produce a bulletin with which it will in turn compete with the original supplier of the coverage.

RTL	OK, then I have a second one to SRG. There has been a military plane crash in Mulhouse this morning.
NCORD	Is SRG with us? OK, we will do the request to them, RTL.
RTL	OK.

It seems that the other services were quite indifferent to these requests.

Pictures: necessary but not sufficient

When serious, high-news-value items are considered, that is, when public-interest issues are raised, the Eurovision members seem to be somewhat skeptical referring to the value of pictures. In such cases they don't seem to subscribe to the commonplace notion that 'a picture is worth a thousand words'. 'Good' or 'nice' pictures are not always a relevant argument for the acceptance of an item. For example (19 February):

RAI	We can offer images, interesting ones, of a Russian fleet that is moving in the Adriatic sea. There is one aircraft carrier, one helicopter carrier, there are assisting ships, and they are being watched by Italian ships and by Italian aircraft. The film images are taken from an aircraft. The images are interesting.
NCORD	Any interest? [A few seconds of silence] Sorry, Albert, and thank you.

Thus, despite the unusual pictures, shot from an aircraft, there was no expressed interest among the members. On the other hand, a BBC request for pictures, was treated somewhat differently (16 February):

BBC	Good morning, Marine. If you're taking a satellite from ORTAS we would quite like to see some fresh pictures from the camps even though they're probably going to show the same as yesterday.
NCORD	Yes, I got some offer this morning, Rhona, but it was more or less the same pictures. But if I have new material, of course I will take something.

Thus the request was only tentatively honored provided the pictures would truly meet the timely criterion of newsworthiness. Furthermore, sometimes the value of the picture is measured against the value of the background sound without which the pictures become diminished (17 February):

ZDF	Marine, concerning the story requested by Alfriede, we had some pictures in our main bulletin last night but it was not very much material, I think only a few seconds. We had a more important item in another transmission but I have to find out whether I could get the international sound version. It was approximately 3 minutes. Would it be OK to get it to EVN-1 as well? I doubt that we can get it to EVN-0.
NCORD	If you can get the international sound that will be very good for us.

Finally, some items of hard news, which are no doubt of much importance in the European context, are readily accepted without any concern expressed about the nature of the pictures. For example (17 February):

ORF	Good morning, Marine. We can make an offer for EVN-1 about talks between NATO and Warsaw Pact countries in Vienna on the reduction of conventional weapons.
NCORD	OK, thank you, is there any interest?
BRT	[expresses interest]
LJB	[expresses interest]
SRG	[expresses interest]
RAI	[expresses interest]
NCORD	OK, in this case that will be accepted.

While no mention is even made in the offer concerning the nature of the footage, the satellite feed later on indicated what could easily have been presumed by the participants, namely, that the pictures were quite boring: a large table, delegates shaking hands, etc. Nevertheless at least four services unhesitatingly confirmed their interest in the story.[12]

New York is not Europe

The conference participants tend time and again to express a Eurocentric rather than a truly universal point of view. They quite easily dismiss New York because of logistical inconveniences, presumed excessive costs and differences in time zones. However, as we suggest, it is very much the sense of community that the Eurovision newsroom creates which places New York on the fringe. Several times in our sample we encountered a 'thanks, but no thanks' attitude on the part of the News Co-ordinator following her discussion with the New York representative. For example, on 20 February:

---

12. On the other hand, complaints are sometimes made about excessive offers of boring pictures such as talking heads. Thus the ZDF News Co-ordinator lamented in June 1991, following his week on the job: 'Member services are also offering more and more talking heads, sometimes giving the really good picture for the same story only on special request. In my view we should try to get more picture and fewer heads'. What he seems to be saying is that he prefers good pictures even when the boring talking heads are the essence of the story.

> NCORD   OK, thank you Kevin. Are there any questions for New York? [silence] OK, I'm afraid, nothing for you. Thank you Kevin. Bye bye.

And another example from 15 June:

> NCORD   For the trial we will probably wait for EVN-0 tomorrow. And are there any questions to Tony in New York? [silence] No ... well ... we've seen that it's very quiet unfortunately, or fortunately, I don't know. So thank you very much, Tony.

Since this seems to be the general attitude towards New York, no wonder that the man in New York is somewhat apologetic and seems to lack confidence in presenting his unwanted 'merchandise' (16 June):

> NCORD   OK, so what else have you to tell us for today?
>
> NY   I've got very little for today. Just informationally there are network feeds coming in from Seoul and Moscow a little later, which would be in time for EVN-1. If you wanted something new turned around you can get it in London. Additionally, President Reagan is going to Capitol Hill for lunch; that will be too late for EVN-2, I'm afraid; otherwise I don't see much going on at all today outside.
>
> NCORD   So what do you expect from Moscow?
>
> NY: Parents of the pilot going to visit the boy [the boy is Mathias Rust, a German who flew a light plane into Red Square].
>
> NCORD   Oh yes, OK, thank you. We'll probably get that from our side, I hope. Thank you very much. Are there any questions to New York? No, well, thank you very much Heather. Have a good day.
>
> NY   Thank you, bye for now.
>
> NCORD   Bye bye.

Nevertheless, some stories out of New York do find their way into the Eurovision system. These would typically be stories that are predominantly of European interest, even if they have an American peg. For example (18 June):

> NY   New York has a late offer.
>
> NCORD   Yes, Heather?
>
> NY   Referring to the invitation from the Vatican to President Waldheim.
>
> NCORD   Can you speak up please?

NY	Yeah. Jewish leaders in the United States reacting negatively, of course, to the invitation from the Vatican to President Kurt Waldheim. We have a soundbite of Tannenbaum, one of the Jewish leaders here, saying they are mind boggled by the invitation and he may even consider canceling a meeting with the Pope when he visits the United States in September. If there's any interest in that.
RTL	[expresses interest]
NCORD	Anyone else?
ITN	[expresses interest]
NCORD	Yes, I think we can include that coverage. Right. Anything else for New York and Zero? No? *Merci*, Tony ...

Another example of an accepted story was a breakfast which Secretary of State Schultz had with Yitzhak Shamir, the Israeli Prime Minister. However, on the same day three other American-related stories were not accepted: the CIA director's testimony in the Senate; the Senate debate on aid to El Salvador, Guatemala, Costa Rica and Honduras; and the trial of the producer of the film 'Twilight Zone' in which two people were killed. Could it be that the Schultz-Shamir story was accepted because Israel is a member of the Exchange?

While the role of the New York bureau may not be central for Eurovision operations – and perhaps it never truly was – it seems that the relatively new Moscow bureau is gaining prominence. This can clearly be explained by the changes that took place in Eastern Europe. Thus, in March 1992, the Cypriot News Co-ordinator, in his weekly report, tells his colleagues: 'The EBU bureau in Moscow was very helpful and is becoming as important as EBU-NY, given the situation in the CIS. I appreciate the fact that our colleagues in Moscow are starting to function as advisers to the News Co-ordinators as well'.

This new European reality may also be creating a new Eurocentric outlook. Russia and the other former members of the USSR are today active members of Eurovision. As an expression of this development we note the call of the Dutch News Co-ordinator in his report during July 1990, to expand Eurovision's map of Europe: 'At NOS most of the time we have an interpreter in-house, enabling me to judge whether we had the right quotes. However, it is essential that at ORF [the Austrian link-point to Moscow] somebody is also available who can understand Russian and who can advise which parts of the speeches are of relevance [given at the 28th Congress of the Soviet Communist Party]. During this week this was the case, I am happy to say.'

The universal and the particular

Initially we assumed that offers made by services would tend in most cases to represent particularistic points of view typically based on stories taking place within their borders. We also assumed that requests would reflect particular interests and news value judge-

45

ments from the initiator's point of view. The data in Tables 1 and 2, however, suggest that these assumptions should be modified.

As for offers, it seems that members are also socialised into proposing stories that have at least some element of universality, and when doing so they draft good arguments in order to persuade their colleagues. For example, on 17 February the BBC offers a story on a strike by its own journalists which has universal appeal to all Western journalists and presumably also to Western audiences.

BBC	BBC coming in with an offer.
NCORD	Yes, Rhona.
BBC	It's for EVN-1, maybe cancelled and re-offered for EVN-2. Members of the national union of journalists throughout the country today are taking part in a 2-hour protest stoppage over the treatment of the BBC during the 'Secret Society' programme affair, the so-called 'satellite affair'. What we expect to see: the London journalists lobbying in Parliament, a protest march and rally in Glasgow, and journalists of BBC Glasgow. If you remember, it was BBC Glasgow that was raided.
NCORD	Yes, and you said it was EVN-1 or EVN-2?
BBC	Yes.
NCORD	Thank you, Rhona. Who would be interested?
PARIS	[expresses interest]
LJB	[expresses interest]
SRG	[expresses interest]
BRT	[expresses interest]
RTP	[expresses interest]
NCORD	OK, so we'll try for EVN-1.
BBC	OK.

Requests represent another tension between the domestic and universal interests and values. In most cases, however, it is not the particularistic but rather the shared interest which seems to be the motivation for a service Contact to initiate a request and for various services to accept it. For example, on 19 February Denmark requests of Spain:

DR	DR [Denmark] has a question to TVE Madrid.
TVE	TVE is listening.
DR	Would you be able to offer anything on the agreement between the student organizations and the government?
TVE	Yes, I was just coming with that for the conference.
DR	Sounds good.

Later on in this conference the Spanish contact actually offered this story and four services (Portugal, the Netherlands, France and Austria) joined in supporting the acceptance of the item. For all these countries the end of the conflict between the students and the Spanish government is a clear example of foreign news with no domestic involvement. Could it also be that student unrest, wherever it may be, is likely to receive relatively high attention? In fact, interest was expressed for another story on the same day by Spain, Italy and the Netherlands, involving students fighting police in down town Lima, Peru – very far from Europe.

Another example (18 February) is the Irish elections story offered by RTE in Dublin and readily accepted by 5 services: the Netherlands, Sweden, Norway, Belgium and Switzerland. These services did not need any seductive arguments for the story to be appealing and acceptable.

RTE	RTE coming in.
NCORD	Yes, Kathy.
RTE	The counting of the votes in the Irish general elections takes place today. The results won't be known until the early hours of the morning, but I can give you 'wallpaper' shots, meaning just people counting votes, if you want it for EVN-1.
NCORD	Thank you for the offer. Is there any interest for that in EVN-1 today?
NOS	[expresses interest]
SVT	[expresses interest]
NRK	[expresses interest]
BRT	[expresses interest]
SRG	[expresses interest]
NCORD	OK, in this case this is accepted.
RTE	OK.

From the British point of view, however, the counting of the Irish vote is far from being conceived as a foreign story; it is in fact almost-domestic news. That is why the BBC uses its own Dublin reporter to present the story. As we know from the analysis of the actual newscasts, the British coverage of this event is much broader than in any other European country and is highly domesticated (see Chapter 3).

The right to differ can also be reflected in several other ways. A case in point is the Swiss (SRG) request (17 February) where the distinction between domestic and foreign news becomes blurred.

SRG	Good morning, Marine, good morning, everybody. As you know, perhaps, there was a bus accident in Australia, with four people killed and 34 injured, most of them Swiss. I wonder if we could get pictures of the accident or aftermath.
WTN	WTN coming in.
NCORD	Yes, there was a satellite offer for this morning. Can you give us some more details?
Geneva	The item was shot yesterday. Three woman passengers and the driver died when a bus packed with Swiss tourists collided with a car and rolled down a hill on Monday. 34 others were injured in the accident. Three are regarded as critical. The group had arrived in Melbourne on Sunday for a 14-day tour operated by a hotel plan in Switzerland. The bus left the Melbourne hotel for Philip island, 20 km to the south. On its return 7 hours later, the coach clipped a small car, rolled down an embankment, and crashed into a line of trees. The item is expected to show the smashed bus and the injured being loaded into ambulances and taken to hospital. Offer via satellite ex Sydney.
NCORD	Apart from SRG, who would be interested?
RTP	[expresses interest]
NCORD	What about SSR? [French-Swiss Television]. [A brief silence]. I think, SRG, you can make your own arrangements.

Interestingly, French-Swiss Television in Geneva does not join its sister service in Zurich in supporting the request. It should be noted, however, that Swiss Television co-ordinates all requests from its different language newsrooms in Zurich. SSR Geneva is not an active participant in the conference. SRG Zurich was therefore requesting on behalf of Swiss Television and the News Co-ordinator should have realised that SSR could not respond. The support of Portuguese Television alone could not 'universalise' this story: in the eyes of German-Swiss Television, Swiss tourists from the Zurich region of the country – while killed in Australia – makes it a domestic story.

Finally, the Gorbachev speech delivered in Moscow at the Peace Forum on 16 February provides two additional examples where domestic and foreign news become truly blurred. First, in the ZDF newsroom on 16 February we were told that West Germany's main interest in the story was the reaction of the East Germans. Indeed, in the ZDF newscast that evening there was lengthy coverage from East Berlin. And second, at Israel Television the main focal point in covering Gorbachev's speech was the fate of Joseph Begun, the Jewish dissident who for many years was prevented from immigrating to Israel and whose release was promised on that same day but was not materialised. Thus the speech by the Soviet leader was somewhat discredited in the Israeli bulletin where the definition of domestic news often includes the Jewish world, particularly when it directly relates to the Jewish State.

Small countries are different

As noted in Table 3 there is much variability among the services in making requests. It seems that most of the requests came from the smaller countries: the Netherlands, Cyprus, Luxembourg, Sweden and Switzerland. Just as the RTL Contact told us about Luxembourg being a country with little news, we can assume that the situation in these other relatively small countries is somewhat similar. Thus these services tend to seek more foreign news to supplement their meagre domestic supply of television stories. In contrast, the larger countries have sufficient news of their own and require fewer supplements.

According to our data, the United Kingdom seems to be an exception. Could it be that its relatively high demand for foreign stories can at least partially be explained by Britain's historical global orientation from the old days of its empire compounded with its world-wide radio service? It should be noted that today both the BBC and ITN have institutionalised their contribution to worldwide television in the form of the BBC's World Service Television and ITN's involvement in the Super Channel.

Rejecting Attempted Manipulation

One more illustration of the common journalistic culture in the Eurovision newsroom is the rejection of a Greek-Cypriot offer on 18 February.

Geneva	Geneva coming in. We've received an offer from CyBC Cyprus. They are offering out of ERT Athens, without satellite charges. The item is as follows on the telex: Parents, wives, and children of 1,320 Cypriots missing since the Turkish invasion of 1974 have made a dramatic appeal to the international community to pressure Turkey to cooperate in efforts to trace the fates of their relatives. Spokesmen said that after the invasion not one single missing person has been traced by the UN. Many have been seen alive in the hands of the Turkish army after the invasion. Relatives of the missing, clad in black and holding photos of the missing, gathered on the outskirts of the Turkish-occupied town of Famagusta, demanding an end to the human drama. The item shows relatives gathered near a UN outpost, holding photos and crying; a woman fainting; a wife of a missing saying she lost traces of her husband ten months after their marriage; and the daughter of a missing person praying for the safe return of her father. Duration approximately two minutes, offered from ERT Athens.
NCORD	Any interest? [Brief pause]. No?!

No action was even taken on this offer. It seems to us that the distinction between news and propaganda was brought to the fore in defending the demarcation lines between legitimate reporting and illegitimate manipulation. The offer, made 'without satellite charges', making it even more suspicious, unanimously and almost instinctively activated professional norms of Western journalism.

49

From self-serving to self-irony

Our final set of observations concerns two extreme nationalistic points of view which help demarcate the limits of consensus.

The first example concerns Libya, an authoritarian regime within the generally liberal Eurovision community. On 18 February we hear the following:

	Text	Commentary
BBC	Marine, apparently, LJB [Libyan Television] have covered some live executions on television.	
NCORD	Yes, I know this, but so far we have no offer.	
NRK	NRK [Norwegian Television] is also very interested in that item.	
NCORD	Yes, we will do our best.	
		The Libyan contact does not initiate any response thus far.
[A few moments later...]		
NRK	What do you think the realistic chances are to have the pictures from Libyan TV on the execution last night?	
NCORD	We are going to ask them, it's all that we can do.	The Libyan contact remains silent.
Geneva	Geneva coming in. Is LJB on the circuit? LJB for Geneva! [brief pause]. Apparently not. I'll send them a telex.	The Libyan continues to ignore the effort to reach him.
[Two minutes later ...]		
Geneva	Is there any interest in the Greek 'rally' offer?	Suddenly the Libyan contact is heard from. He interrupts Geneva and expresses interest in the Greek story.
LJB	LJB [Libya expresses interest]	
Geneva	That's the students demonstrating in support of the lifting of the siege on the Palestinian refugee camps.	
NCORD	Any interest for demo today in Athens?	
ITN	[expresses interest]	
TVE	[expresses interest]	
LJB	[repeats his expression of interest]	
NCORD	So we'll accept this.	

Libya can be described as a pocket of resistance to whatever is considered as a European, secular, liberal and open belief system. The LJB Contact is so threatened by the request to provide footage of the executions in his country, that he prefers to totally 'disconnect'. He suddenly surfaces, however, when an offer is made which supports the Palestinian cause which clearly supports his interest and ideology.

Our final example comes from the same day. Here the BBC contact asks her Spanish colleague for material on British football:

BBC	BBC coming in, Marine.
NCORD	Yes, Julie.
BBC	Good morning. I've got a couple of things we're interested in. First, England is playing Spain in a friendly international in Madrid. We are wondering what our little football fans are going to get up to and wondering if TVE were covering anything?
TVE	We are covering the match, but what do you mean?
BBC	Our hooligans!
TVE	Oh sure, if there is some incident, be sure I will offer it for EVN-1.
BBC	Lovely!

While the Libyan's self-serving attitude excludes himself from the dialogue, the British self-irony helps him remain one of the pack despite the embarrassing circumstances.

Thinking about the conferences

The Eurovision contacts and News Co-ordinators interact on a daily basis. Many thousands of news items are discussed each year. There are several opportunities for the News Contacts and News Co-ordinators to discuss the conferences and reflect upon them. One of these occasions are the formal semi-annual meetings of the Contacts and Co-ordinators at which they consider problems of the Exchange. As noted, the News Co-ordinators also file a report following their duty week which is distributed to all the Contacts. Indeed, we presented some of the comments made in these reports in several footnotes in this chapter.

In addition, in our own questionnaire which we sent to all the News Contacts, during the spring of 1994 (see Chapter 1), we also asked some questions about their attitudes and feelings regarding their work in general and the conferences in particular. We now report on some of these sentiments.

By and large most of the Contacts felt quite satisfied with their work. Of the 40 Contacts who responded to the questionnaire, 33 said they were 'very satisfied' or 'somewhat satisfied'; five said they were 'not very satisfied' and only two said they were 'not satisfied at all'. It should be noted that there was essentially no difference between the 20 contacts who also serve as News Co-ordinators and the 20 Contacts who do not.

Furthermore, when we asked about three specific facets of the role of being a Eurovision

Contact, we found what we consider a high degree of satisfaction. Specifically, 31 contacts felt very rewarded and nine felt somewhat rewarded by 'interacting with colleagues from other countries'. Also, 15 of the 40 contacts felt very rewarded and 18 felt somewhat rewarded by 'helping to shape the news agenda of many countries' with only one contact not being rewarded at all by this facet. The third facet of the work we asked about was its intellectual challenge. Here 16 said they felt very rewarded and 15 somewhat rewarded by the challenge while seven were not so rewarded and two not rewarded at all.

We also tried to get some sense of personal involvement of the contacts in their work. We put this to them in the following question: 'When you make an offer to the Exchange and it is not accepted, how do you generally feel?' Seventeen respondents said that it doesn't bother them at all; 17 said they get a little upset; and only five said they get quite annoyed. This seems to indicate that more than half of the contacts have a personal stake in their work and express some degree of sentiment about it.

In order to determine what the contacts thought about the substance of their work and the decisions that they make, we asked them to rank six typical categories of foreign news. We asked them to rank the categories based on how they perceived the interest that viewers in their own country might have in them. Table 4 presents the mean scores based on the ranking of the six categories for all the Contacts. We also divided the contacts into those who served as News co-ordinators and those who did not.

Table 4. Mean rankings of news categories by Eurovision contacts

	Total (n=40)	NCORD (n=20)	Non-NCORD (n=20)
Conflicts between nations	1.5	1.7	1.6
Accidents and disasters	2.5	2.7	2.3
Internal politics of foreign nations	3.4	3.8	3.0
Advances in science and medicine	4.1	4.4	3.8
Ceremonial events	4.5	4.4	4.7
Artistic events	4.8	4.6	5.1

We found that the first category by far was 'Conflicts between nations' followed by 'Accidents and disasters', 'Internal politics of foreign nations', 'Advances in science and medicine', 'Ceremonial events', and culminating with 'Artistic events'. While the mean rankings differed slightly between the Contacts who were and were not News Co-ordinators, the overall rankings of the two subgroups was the same.

We also asked the respondents, using open ended questions, to indicate which topics they felt were offered too much and which were not offered enough through the Exchange. Exactly half of the respondents could not indicate any topics which should have more or less presence in the Exchange. While 'Conflicts between nations' was ranked first in the overall rankings, four contacts felt that there were too many war and conflict stories and three additional contacts said there were too few non-war stories. There also seems to be a demand for more universal stories. This is reflected in that seven Contacts thought there were too many 'country-specific' items and four felt that there were too few 'Area-specific' stories. Also, six Contacts wanted to see more 'Feature or soft' news items which can also be considered more universal.

This tendency to be interested in more universal stories, which go beyond national borders and the specifics of a single country, is in accord with the notion of an international news organization and its global newsroom. Moreover, this might suggest that the Eurovision concept of news is closer to the quality end in the traditional distinction between the popular- versus quality-press continuum.

We also asked a series of questions concerning the offers and requests made during the conferences. First, we asked who usually initiates the requests? One third of the respondents said they take the initiative; one fifth said that the foreign news editor takes the initiative; and nearly half of the respondents said that the decision is taken jointly by the contact and the foreign news editor.

As for the frequency of making offers and requests, we asked how often each of the services makes requests and how often requests are made of each of the services. We feel that the replies to these questions are best presented by looking at three categories of services: the eight services from large (Western) countries.[13], the 21 services from small countries.[14], and the 11 services from Eastern European countries.[15] As for making requests, the large countries say they do so quite often whereas the East European services make relatively few requests.

Among the 21 smaller western and peripheral services, however, some make many requests and some hardly ever do so. We have not systematically explored why this might be the case. However, it is possible that some News Contacts, particularly from smaller nations, may be less facile in English and thus be reluctant to speak on the circuit. It is also possible that in some, smaller nations women, even women journalists, are not supposed to be outspoken, so female News Contacts from those countries would not make many requests of the exchange.

As for the reciprocal, namely, requests being made from the different services, we found that the large countries say that requests are often made of them whereas there is a tendency for fewer requests to come from the smaller countries and from the East European countries.

---

13. France (TF1, FT2 and CPF), Germany (ARD and ZDF), Italy (RAI), Spain (TVE) and United Kingdom (BBC).

14. Algeria (ENTV), Austria (ORF), Belgium (BRT and RTBF), Cyprus (CYBC), Denmark (DRKTV and TV2), Egypt (ERTU), Finland (YLE), Ireland (RTE), Iceland (RUV), Israel (IBA), Jordan (JTV), Luxembourg (RTL), Monaco (RMC), Norway (NRK and TV2), Portugal (RTP), Sweden (SVT), Switzerland (SRG) and Turkey (TRT).

15. Czech Republic (CT), Croatia (HRT), Estonia (ETV), Hungary (MTV), Latvia (LTV), Macedonia (MRT), Moldavia (MNTV), Poland (TVP), Russia (RTR), Slovenia (RTV) and Ukraine (DTRU).

The view expressed by the Contacts in 1994 is important as it speaks in more direct and contemporary terms compared with the findings presented above in Table 3 which represent a two-week period in 1987. The replies of the Contacts from the large countries seem to indicate that they are dominant players in the Exchange, compared with the smaller countries, both Western and Eastern. This is noteworthy especially since it could be suggested that it is the smaller countries that are more likely to benefit from the Exchange whereas the larger ones are less dependent upon it for obtaining foreign news stories.

Finally, in connection with the conferences, we asked those Contacts who were also News Co-ordinators several questions about how they relate to the formal rules of the Exchange. Thus, for instance, we wanted to know whether or not they decide to accept or reject an item based on the needs of the News Co-ordinator's own service. Of the 19 relevant respondents, 12 said they almost never do so, while six said they sometimes do it and one News Co-ordinator admitted to doing it frequently.

The contacts were also asked 'Please imagine a situation in which you are the News Co-ordinator and no service is interested in a particular item being offered; Would you nonetheless decide to accept the item?' Only 31 per cent said they would not accept the item given these are the rules; 46 per cent said they would accept it hoping that some service would ultimately use it; and 23 per cent said they would accept it assuming that their own service would use it. In other words, more than two-thirds of the Contacts say they would not adhere to the letter of the rule. Here, once again, is an expression of tension between professional and bureaucratic authority. These contacts seem to prefer collegial authority in voicing their personal view and thus enabling their colleagues to have a second chance to consider the item when it arrives.

Finally, the respondents were asked if they read the weekly reports submitted by the News Co-ordinators summing up their week in that role. Of the 40 Contacts, 25 said they read every report; 10 claimed to read some or few of them; and five don't read any of the reports.

3   What's in the News?

With this chapter, we shift our focus from newswork on a global scale to news *content*, both globally and within a sample of nations. We begin in the Global Newsroom with an examination of *what* kinds of raw news materials are transmitted on the daily EVN feeds. Then we report our findings regarding *which* EVN items are picked up for use by national services, and finally we conclude by considering *how* broadcast journalists in different countries shape the EVN footage into finished news stories.

During the two week fieldwork period in 1987, we managed to videotape almost all EVN-0's and EVN-1's, transmitted Monday through Friday. The week's twenty EVN's contained 186 news items. A log which briefly describes each item now follows in Table1.

Table 1. Log of items transmitted on the Eurovision News Exchange

Date	Item name[1]	Subject
16 February 1987		
EVN-0		
	Begun(Visnews)	Soviet refusnick's wife on husband's release.
	Demjanjuk (WTN/Visnews)	Scene-setter for opening of Demjanjuk trial.
	Oath (Asiavision)	Philippine army induction ceremonies.
	Son (WTN)	Reactions by Demjanjuk's son as trial opens.
	Protests (WTN/Visnews/CBS)	Demonstrations against TV programme *Amerika*.
	Obeid (CBS)	Aide to Lebanese president released by gunmen.
	Tiger (CNN)	Zoo tiger undergoes dental surgery.
	Carnival (RAI)	Parades and costumes in Viareggio, Italy.
	Traffic (RAI)	Automobile traffic banned in centre of Rome.
	Gorbachev (TSS)	Gorbachev et al. speak at Moscow peace forum.
EVN-1		
	Forum (TSS)	Other speeches during Moscow peace forum.
	Agriculture Prize (EEC)	Common Market agricultural ministers meet in Brussels.
	Shamir (WTN)	Israeli Prime Minister arrives in New York City.
	Gemayel (ITN)	Lebanon's Gemayel sees Thatcher and Archbishop.
	Trial (ARD)	Verdict in 'Flick' tax evasion trial in Bonn.
	Radioactive (BRT)	Illegal dumping of radioactive waste in Belgium.
	Shelling (WTN)	West Beirut shelling kills six.

Date	Item name[1]	Subject
	Sakharov (WTN)	*Ex-dissident Sakharov at Gorbachev's peace forum.*
	Trial (WTN)	Demjanjuk trial opens in Jerusalem.

17 February 1987

EVN-0

	Strike (ERT)	Demonstration by striking workers in Athens.
	Dublin (RTE)	Voting in Irish election.
	Security (SLRC)	Government forces maneuvering in north of Sri Lanka.
	Begun (CNN)	New York demonstration to free Joseph Begun.
	Calero (Visnews)	Nicaraguan rebel leader resigns from US-backed group.
	Fighting (Visnews)	Aftermath of fighting in Beirut.
	Berri (Visnews)	News conference with Nabi Berri about refugee camps.
	Sakharov (TF1)	More footage of ex-dissident Sakharov at peace meeting.

EVN-1

	Talks (ORF)	NATO and Warsaw Pact talks in Vienna.
	Mussels (ZDF)	Spanish toxic mussels withdrawn from sale in Germany.
	Crash (FR3)	Mirage bomber crashes in Mulhouse, France.
	Planes (CyBC)	French planes bring supplies to Palestinian camps.
	Shamir (Visnews)	Israeli Prime Minister arrives in Washington.

18 February 1987

EVN-0

	Runcie (ITN)	Archbishop of Canterbury asks release of Terry Waite.
	Reagan (WTN)	President Reagan praises state of US economy.
	Train (WTN)	Passenger train crashes in Brazil.
	Dead Fish (WTN)	Contaminated fish and birds in Nevada lake.
	Gates (CNN)	C.I.A. nominee testifies before US Senate committee.
	AIDS (CBS)	Abortion policy for AIDS-positive pregnant women.
	Columbia (Visnews)	Columbia wages publicity campaign against cocaine.
	Parachutist (CBS)	Para-glider jumps from New York skyscraper.

EVN-1

	Agca (RAI)	Mother of Papal-assailant arrives to meet Pope.
	Delors (FR3)	Budget of European parliament presented in Strasbourg.
	Gorbachev (TSS)	Soviet leader tours Riga, Latvia.
	Train (SSR)	Sixteen injured in Swiss train crash.
	Tabriz (Visnews/IRIB)	Aftermath of Iraqi air raid on Iranian city.
	Camp (WTN)	Conditions in Beirut militia camp.
	Shopping (Visnews)	Lull in fighting allows shopping in Beirut.
	Fighting (WTN)	Aftermath of West Beirut fighting.
	Tamils (BBC)	Tamil immigrants blocked at London airport.

19 February 1987

EVN-0

	Chernobyl (WTN)	Russian documentary on Chernobyl nuclear disaster.
	Fighting (Visnews)	Patrols, street fighting, aftermath in Beirut.
	Sharansky (Visnews)	Natan Sharansky news conference on Russian Jewry.
	Nablus (WTN)	Aftermath of terrorist attack on taxi in West Bank.
	Gates (Visnews)	C.I.A. nominee appears before Senate committee.

Date	Item name[1]	Subject
	Cooperatives (CBS)	New economic forms developing in Russia.
	Shamir (CBS)	Israel to work with Senate Iran-Contra investigators.
	Avalanche (WTN)	Search for survivors of Colorado avalanche.
	Elections (RTE)	Irish politicians react to election results.
	Fleet (RAI)	Soviet fleet holds maneuvers in Adriatic.
EVN-1		
	Students (TVE)	Spanish students sign agreement with government.
	Statement (TVE)	Speech by leader of Basque separatists.
	Gorbachev (TSS)	Gorbachev visits Riga and Tallin.
	Clashes (WTN/CBS)	Student demonstrators clash with Lima, Peru police.
	Bomb (Visnews)	Aftermath of bomb blast in Lima, Peru.

20 February 1987

EVN-0

	Demo (WTN)	Demonstrators in Teheran protest German TV programme.
	Bilbao (TVE)	Bomb attack on Renault distributor.
	Fire (ORF)	Large fire in centre of Vienna.
	Begun (Visnews)	Russians confirm release of dissident Begun.
	Syrians (Visnews)	Syrian troops patrol streets of Beirut.
	Demjanjuk (WTN)	Continuing coverage of Demjanjuk war crimes trial.
	Volcker (Visnews/WTN)	Federal Reserve bank head testifies to US Senate
	Schultz (WTN)	US Secretary of State on Russian internal politics.
	Afghanistan (CBS)	Impact of Soviet troops on daily life in Afghanistan.
	Alzheimer (Visnews/CBS)	Advances in treatment of Alzheimer's disease.
	Poland (WTN)	Reactions by Poles to lifting of US sanctions.
EVN-1		
	Agca (RAI)	Mother of Papal-attacker visits with Pope.
	Glemp (BRT)	Roman Catholic Cardinal Glemp arrives in Brussels.
	Damage (Visnews)	Aftermath of heavy fighting in Beirut.
	Deployment (Visnews)	Syrian troops stationed in Beirut.
	Jumblatt (Visnews)	Lebanese leader Jumblatt arrives for Beirut talks.
	Push Ups (Visnews)	World record set for push-ups.
	Aircraft (Visnews)	French relief flight arrives in Chad.

15 June 1987

EVN-0

	Bolzano (RAI)	Scenes of voting in picturesque Italian village.
	Election (RAI)	Italian parliament candidates, including Cicciolina, vote.
	Students (Visnews/WTN)	Students demonstrate in Seoul, South Korea.
	Page (Visnews/WTN)	File footage for actress Geraldine Page obituary.
	Wedding (WTN/Visnews)	Thousands attend wedding of rabbi's son in New York.
EVN-1		
	Meeting (RTL)	Agriculture ministers meet in Luxembourg.
	Onassis (ERT)	Ceremonies awarding 'Onassis Prizes' for 1987.
	Results (RAI)	Italian election results.
	Helicopter (ARD)	Arrival of American witnesses in TWA terrorist attack.
	Plane (ARD)	Polish pilots flee to US air base.
	Neckar (ZDF)	Collision between NATO-Warsaw Pact ship in Baltic.
	Congress (TVE)	Fiftieth anniversary of writer's conference.

Date	Item name[1]	Subject
	AIDS (ORF)	*Meeting hears about possible new anti-AIDS vaccine.*
	Strike (TF1)	French postal workers strike.
	Terrorist (A2F)	Terrorist arrested.
	Rommel (WTN)	Rommel's son honored by mayor of Jerusalem.
	Demo (Visnews)	Civil service workers demonstrate in Paris.
	Israel (Visnews)	Israeli peace activists meet illegally with PLO.

16 June 1987

EVN-0

	Panama (TVE)	Interviews with Panamanian general Noriega.
	Minicow (TVE)	Genetic research creates improved cow.
	Bomb (TVE)	Aftermath bomb explosion in Barcelona.
	ASEAN (AVN)	Conference of ASEAN nations opens.
	Procession (AVN)	Demonstration against Indian ambassador to Sri Lanka.
	Floods (Visnews)	Floods in Argentina.
	Peace (WTN)	Rally for world peace held in Moscow.
	Demonstration (WTN)	Students demonstrate in Seoul.
	Tender (ZDF)	German and Polish warships collide.
	Reagan (US Pool)	President Reagan speaks about US foreign policies.
	Stark (WTN)	US warship Stark repairs begin in Bahrain.
	Bond (WTN)	Exhibit of James Bond movie memorabilia.
	Seoul (WTN/Visnews)	More student demonstrations in Seoul.
	Reax (RAI)	Reactions to Italian parliamentary elections.

EVN-1

	Strasbourg (FR3)	Seminar of European parliament.
	Blockade (ARD)	Barges block Rhine at Karlsruhe.
	Record (WTN)	Car driven on two wheels for 4 hours fifteen minutes.
	Neckar (ZDF)	Damaged NATO ship returns to Kiel.
	Rust (ZDF)	Mathias Rust's parents visit him in prison.
	Schultz (WTN)	US Secretary of State trip to Philippines.
	Reactions (RAI)	Italian politicians comment on election returns.
	Cicciolina (RAI/WTN)	Pornographic movie star elected to Italian parliament.
	Soweto (WTN)	Strike and events on anniversary of Soweto massacre.

17 June 1987

EVN-0

	Boatfire (AVN)	Twenty-five die in ferry fire in Japan.
	Assassinate (FR3)	Corsican anti-separatist killed in Ajaccio.
	Cuellar (ORF)	U.N. head meets with Kurt Waldheim in Vienna.
	Seoul (Visnews)	Students clash with Korean police.
	Election (WTN/Visnews)	Elections in India.
	Ships (WTN)	US and Soviet warships in Persian gulf.
	Goetz (CBS/Visnews/WTN)	Bernard Goetz has hearing on subway shootings.
	Persian (CNN)	European reactions to Reagan speech on Gulf.
	Chinese (WTN/Visnews)	Pinnochet meets with Chinese diplomats.
	Actors (RAI)	Actors elected to Italian parliament.
	Korea (WTN)	Demonstrators gassed in Seoul.

EVN-1

	Farm (RTL)	Meeting of agriculture bureaucrats in Luxembourg.

Date	Item name[1]	Subject
	Papandreou (ERT)	*Greek prime minister's speech on farm policy.*
	Drugs (ORF)	International conference on anti-drug strategies.
	Space-walk (TSS)	Soviet cosmonauts walk in space.
	Refugees (WTN)	Tamil refugees flee to India.
	Cocaine (TVE)	Columbian-Venezuelan police raid drug laboratories.
	Killings (TVE)	Twelve political radicals killed in Santiago, Chile.
	Pasqua (FR3)	French interior minister on political killing in Corsica.
	Bomb (Visnews/WTN)	Guerilla group bombs bank in Lima, Peru.
	Black Box (RAI)	Italian officials retrieve 8-year old flight recorder.

18 June 1987

EVN-0

	Ministers (AVN)	Meeting of Asian non-aligned nations.
	ASEAN (AVN)	Meeting of ASEAN diplomats.
	Bardot (TF1)	Auction of actress's collectibles.
	Fire (FR3)	Fires in Var region of France.
	Seoul (Visnews/WTN)	Students demonstrate in Seoul.
	Kafka (Visnews)	Auction of Franz Kafka memorabilia.
	Ortega (WTN)	Ortega interview.
	Presidents (WTN)	Latin American economic summit.
	Crash (ITN)	One killed in collision between UK military planes.
	Floods (Visnews)	Flooding in China.
	Korea (Visnews)	More student demonstrations in Seoul.
	Cicciolina (RAI)	Porn star-member of parliament and admirers.
	Drugs (WTN)	Raid in drug-growing region of Columbia.
	Reax (Visnews)	Jewish reaction to Waldheim visit to Pope.
	Ships (RTP)	Reproduction of sailing ship christened in Lisbon.

EVN-1

	Submarine (NRK)	Russian submarine discharges wastes into North Sea.
	Sheik (Visnews)	File footage sheik ousted by brother in U.E.R. coupe.
	Haryana (WTN)	Election day scenes in Haryana, India by-election.
	Attack (SIN)	Funeral of Venezuelan soldiers killed in anti-drug raids.
	Parliament (European Parliament)	Armenians protest outside European Parliament.
	Bokassa (RFO)	African economic leaders discuss development plans.
	Journalist (ABC)	File footage kidnapped US TV journalist Charles Glass.
	Santiago (WTN)	Demonstrations against crackdown on Leftists in Chile.
	Arrest (RAI)	Terrorists arrested, arms cache seized in Rome.

19 June 1987

EVN-0

	Reaction (Visnews/CBS)	US reaction to kidnapping of journalist Charles Glass.
	Cholesterol (Visnews)	News conference about fat in diets.
	Demos (CNN)	Students demonstrate in Seoul.
	Arias (Visnews/WTN/CBS)	Costa Rican president's news conference in Washington.
	Kennedy (Visnews)	Senator blasts US support for Seoul government.
	Guerillas (Visnews)	Guerillas ambush military convoy in Columbia.
	Eiffel (FR3)	Eiffel tower wrapped in rainbow-coloured cloth.
	Glass (Visnews)	Friends of Charles Glass react to his kidnapping.
	Clashes (Visnews)	More student demonstrations in Seoul.

Date	Item name[1]	Subject
	Games (WTN/Visnews)	*Background on preparations for Korea Olympic games.*
EVN-1		
	Shevardnadze (JRT)	Russian leader visit to Zagreb.
	Pusan (WTN)	Korean students clash with police in Pusan.
	Funeral (WTN)	Burial of dozen persons killed by police in Chile.
	Zao Zyang (BT)	Chinese Party Secretary Zao Zyang visits Bulgaria.
	Reactions (TRT)	Statement about Armenia at EEC meeting in Turkey.
	Meeting (WTN)	Sri Lankan and Indian officials meet about Tamils.
	Congress Party (WTN)	Wins by-election, calls for Gandhi resignation.
	Sendero Rally (Visnews)	Lima demonstrators mark anniversary of prison deaths.

1 Each EVN item is given a one or two-word 'slug' to make it easier for the journalists to refer quickly and unambiguously to it. This use of slugs is common in all forms of journalism. Originating service or agency appears in parentheses. Sports items are excluded.

The average EVN-0 contained 10 items, excluding sports; while the EVN-1 transmitted about eight as a mean. The average length of all EVN items for the sample period was just under two minutes (116 seconds). Materials ranged from 20 seconds (for footage of pornographic movie star Cicciolina greeting her admirers after her election to the Italian parliament) to 310 seconds (for aftermath footage of a raid by police in Santiago, Chile in which twelve members of a radical group were killed). Some 22 per cent of EVN items ran between 20 and 79 seconds; just over half (51 per cent) were between eighty and one hundred thirty-nine seconds; one-fifth (nineteen per cent) were between one hundred forty and one hundred ninety-nine seconds in duration; while only eight per cent of EVN materials were two hundred seconds or longer.

Having watched the sample EVN's over and over again, we would offer several generalizations about those materials. First, it is obvious that the EVN feed almost always offers far more stories than most member services are likely to use in their news, and those stories transmitted by the Eurovision News Exchange generally seem longer in duration than the typical 'foreign' news story on most national evening bulletins. This over-abundance of stories and footage is no doubt intended to allow national broadcasters the greatest possible latitude in their choice of what to air. However, as we will show later in this chapter, national newscasters are remarkably consistent in their story selections and choice of shots to use. It is also clear that while broadcast journalists in different countries often choose the same stories and the same footage, the stories they tell by their narration voiced over that footage may be dramatically different.

Second, there is substantial variation in EVN footage with regard to how much, if at all, it has been edited, that is to say how much structure has already been imposed on the images by the originating service. It is possible to think of this phenomenon as a rough continuum, ranging from 'raw' to 'fully cooked' news stories. Some EVN materials, the 'rawest', looked as though they had come directly from the journalist's video camera. The tell-tale sign of little or no editing was the presence of what was clearly unusable footage (e.g. dizzying pan shots; rapid tilts, up or down; extreme close-ups without contextuating medium or long shots), mixed in with the usable visual elements. Far more EVN items, it seemed, were lightly edited, and offered chunks of action in real time, joined together in a progression of scenes, vignettes, or sound-bites. This footage had then a rough story-line, expressed as visual narrative. Even without knowing the details of these items, it was possible for us to derive some understanding of the action. Finally, at the most 'cooked' end of the continuum, we occasionally observed EVN offerings which in fact *were* completely edited stories. However, since Eurovision policy stipulates that EVN materials must carry only 'international' or ambient sound, the voice of the originating service's anchor or reporter had been removed. In a handful of fully-edited stories, however, this requirement for international sound was violated; a 'foreign' anchor or reporter was clearly heard narrating the fully-structured story, while the 'local' journalist was voicing his or her own script. We can only wonder what this polyglot audio track does to audience comprehension of the news.

Our third observation about EVN content is this: many EVN items were simply sound bites of speeches or news conferences. These video quotations present obvious choices for national broadcasters. For one thing, if the sound bite is not in the native language of the national service on which it airs, then the local journalists might feel free to ignore the precise content of the quotation and use the sound bite as little more than a moving illustration. Alternatively, a national newscaster may decide to subtitle the sound bite in the language or languages spoken by local viewers. Either way, 'talking heads' rarely make for visually provocative or engrossing television journalism.

Indeed, extending on this point about visual impact, we would suggest that overall relatively few EVN items could be characterised as exciting or dramatic television. Even footage whose news peg involves violence (terrorist bombings or urban civil war, for example) is more likely than not to show either the *aftermath* of the violence or violence from a distance, rather than capturing the action when it happens or close-up. Moreover, a large part of the materials transmitted by the news exchange portray the highly routinised, visually boring comings, goings, and doings of various political elites: pictures, for example, of distinguished and not-so-distinguished men, arriving in sleek black limousines at large, ornate public buildings; technocrats sitting behind long, linen-covered conference tables, listening, more or less attentively, to each other speak. These comings-and-goings, these conferences and debates are no doubt often of great political and economic significance. But the pictures scarcely make for exciting television footage. Indeed, the footage itself generally does not directly show the 'what' or 'why' behind the activities which are accessible to the television cameras. There is, of course, often no easy way to take pictures of complicated matters of international relations or domestic policy. And so, these boring visuals become an easily obtained fall-back for the television newscast. In and of itself, footage of this type is largely uninformative. But for journalists whose professional norms require them to have pictures whenever possible, it serves a purpose – providing what newscasters call 'B-roll' or 'wall-paper', that footage which can be shown while the 'real' news, the invisible or non-tangible news, is presented in the audio narrative.

Fourth, we were struck by how repetitious much of the EVN footage seemed for continuing or 'running' stories (e.g. the student demonstrations in South Korea, the civil war in Lebanon, or even demonstrations or protest marches in general). We do not wish to sound cynical, nor do we wish to demean the importance, particularly in human terms, of these continuing stories. But there is little doubt that one student demonstration *looks* much like any other student demonstration, particularly if it is in the same country; and that the aftermath of a terrorist bombing in one urban centre or sectarian fighting around a refugee camp is visually not all that distinct from a 'similar' event. Thus, in a sense, the news contained in an item about a continuing event is more likely to be found in the narration, which cannot avoid interpretation and contextualization.

Finally, we noticed how event-driven much EVN coverage is. To personify the exchange just a bit, we would say: EVN goes to an event when it happens – or soon thereafter. In other words, EVN items are generally *today's* news, and rarely *tomorrow's*, in the sense that the Eurovision News Exchange only very infrequently provides what working journalists call 'backgrounders', 'scenesetters', or 'advancers' for upcoming events. During our sample week, for instance, several regular and associate EBU members did stories about the upcoming Irish parliamentary elections (see the discussion of 'The Irish Elections' later in this chapter). But none of those pre-election stories had EVN materials in them, because, as best as we can determine, the news exchange had not transmitted any advance or background materials.

There are at least three reasons for the EVN's present-tense outlook. First, and this is a limitation that the EVN shares with all television journalists, it is difficult, but not impossible, for the EVN or its contributing services to take pictures of something that has not yet occurred, say, for example, the Irish voting. But EVN's reluctance to offer preview stories, scenesetters, or background 'analysis' items may also reflect two other factors. Stories in advance of events can be told, *if* they are packaged with an anchor/reporter voice-over or a reporter's piece-to-camera (stand-upper). From EVN's perspective, a story constructed with such narration would have limited appeal, because viewers might not understand the language used. Secondly, and both more subtly and perhaps more importantly, scene-setters or advancers typically require some speculation on the part of the presenting journalist. Thus, even if the language barrier could be overcome, it is possible that the EVN would be hesitant to transmit 'analysis' materials, that is to say items which may or may not successfully negotiate the thin line between what journalists believe to be 'objective' or 'subjective' reporting.

What the EVN's offer

Using a content coding scheme developed by Cohen, Adoni, & Bantz (1990), in which each item was coded to determine which of twenty-four categories best characterises the item, we analysed all EVN items by general topic or subject matter (Table 2). This reinforces our observations presented above. Almost three quarters of all EVN items fell into three categories: Some thirty-four per cent were coded as dealing primarily with 'internal law and order', more than one-quarter (26 per cent) focused basically on 'international relations', and eleven per cent centred on 'internal politics'.

Table 2. Topics of EVN transmissions[1]

Topic	Percentage (N=186)
Internal law and order	34.3
International relations	26.3
Internal politics	11.3
Transportation	3.2
Cultural	3.2
Natural disasters	2.7
Social relations	2.7
Other human interest	2.7
Domestic economics	2.2
Health-medicine	2.2
Housing	2.2
Labour relations	1.6
Ceremonial	1.6
Science-technology	1.1
Agriculture	1.1
Sports	1.1
Education	0.5
Total	100.0

[1] Based on EVN-0s and EVN-1's for 16–20 February and 15–19 June 1987;
Includes two sports items which were considered to be hard news.

Typical stories coded 'internal law and order' included footage of government troops on maneuvers in the north of Sri Lanka; aftermath of a terrorist attack in Nablus, the West Bank; the appearance in court of Bernard Goetz, who was accused of shooting black teenagers in the New York City subway; and coverage of a raid by Columbian and Venezuelan police on drug laboratories. Common examples of 'international relations' footage would include: NATO and Warsaw Pact talks in Vienna; the visit of the US Secretary of State to the Philippines; a news conference in Washington by the president of Costa Rica; and the Archbishop of Canterbury calling for the release of Terry Waite. Materials coded 'internal politics' focus almost exclusively on elections or their consequences. Exemplars would include footage of a by-election in an Indian state with implications for the Ghandi government, scenes of early voting in the Irish parliamentary elections, and reactions of Italian politicians to a national election.

'Soft' or human interest stories made up a comparatively small proportion of EVN materials. Depending on which categories of materials one includes in this more feature-oriented super-cluster, the percentage may not exceed twelve or fifteen per cent of items transmitted. This is somewhat surprising, since several EVN journalists with whom we spoke jokingly suggested that 'animal stories' and especially items about panda bears were much favoured by the news exchange.[1] Indeed, one might expect a higher percentage of feature or human interest stories, since such items might be expected to more readily

1. In fact, during our field observations, a news editor summarily turned down an agency offer of footage showing twin, new-born panda bears at a US zoo. So much for journalistic self-awareness!

transcend political and language barriers and thus more easily tap into globally-shared concerns, stereotypes, icons, myths, etc. (For a more systematic examination of how EVN journalists feel about 'soft' news and for a more detailed review of global newsroom criteria of newsworthiness more generally, see Chapter 2.)

EVN exemplars

In order to provide readers with a richer understanding of EVN materials, we have prepared a shot-list of EVN footage for four news events. These four events represent the three most common subject categories of EVN feeds (Internal Law and Order; International Relations; and Internal Politics).

South Korea unrest

A prototypical EVN item dealing with internal law and order is the story of student protests against the government of South Korea, which dominated our sample week in June (see, Table 11 later in this chapter). The basic story each day was similar: against the backdrop of the upcoming Olympic games, the students demonstrated for democratic reforms and their protests were met with brutal responses by the South Korean police. The EVN-0 item ('Students') was the most widely used of the week's EVN materials on the unrest in South Korea and exemplifies the other items.

Table 3. Descriptive shot list for South Korea unrest item ('Students') from EVN-0, 15 June 1987

1	Establishing shot of crowd in front of Seoul cathedral (4 seconds).
2	Student in baseball cap, rhythmically thrusting his fist into the air and leading a small group of students in chanting (5 seconds).
3	Panoramic view of avenue leading up to Seoul cathedral, showing crowd in general and including the student group from Shot #2 (2 seconds).
4	Group of men, dressed in white shirts, ties and jackets/suits, squatting, clapping, and chanting (2 seconds).
5	Long shot of undifferentiated throng walking down avenue, away from camera (4 seconds).
6	Same general shot as #5, but closer, so that individuals can be seen shaking fists (5 seconds).
7	Crowd running back toward camera. Individuals clearly identifiable. Runners split into two streams, with camera panning to follow one stream down side street (7 seconds).
8	Riot police, with helmets and shields, pursue demonstrators, chasing them to the end of the street. Clouds of tear gas hang in the air (9 seconds).
9	Students continue to flee down street, while police stop and regroup (6 seconds).
10	Students, standing in front of cathedral holding flags, with some wearing surgical face masks (4 seconds).
11	Riot police lined up, shield to shield, completely blocking street (3 seconds).

12	Closer shot similar to #10 above (5 seconds).
13	Long shot of milling crowd, riot police massed at edge (5 seconds).
14	Medium shot of riot police marching (5 seconds).
15	Closer shot, slightly different angle, of riot police marching (3 seconds).
16	Students being loaded on to police bus. Some give V-for-victory sign (4 seconds).
17	Medium shot of students on police bus. Most are waving (2 seconds).
18	Slightly different angle of waving students on police bus (5 seconds).
19	Police bus begins to pull away; students wave rhythmically out windows (5 seconds).
20	Police bus pulls away from crowd with Seoul cathedral in background (8 seconds).
	TOTAL: 93 seconds

In 93 seconds and 20 shots, this EVN item offers a relatively complete *video* story, a tale in two acts, each with a beginning, a middle, and an end. The first third of the feed establishes the location (near to Seoul's well-known cathedral) and shows the protestors (mostly students, but some older persons) speaking, chanting, and marching in a relatively orderly fashion. Suddenly, in Shot #7, the calm is broken. The protestors now flee away from the cathedral, back toward the camera. In pursuit, riot police, dressed in 'Darth Vader'-style helmets, lobbing tear gas, and waving batons. The students run off. End of Act I. Then police regroup and march toward a crowd which has formed near the cathedral. The police move in and make arrests. Protestors are loaded on busses and are taken off into custody waving and chanting to well-wishers. Denouement.

It is interesting to note how the visual structure of this item so clearly indicates a story-line, a progression of events, easily understood by any viewer, even without the benefit of a detailed narration. This item seems to be an instance of where the pictures 'speak for themselves'. A voice-over narrative will, of course, provide additional context for even such seemingly obvious images, and we discuss how this material is packaged by several different national services later in this chapter.

One final point here. Compared to the subsequent day's coverage, 'Students' is relatively non-violent. It contains no scenes of physical contact between police and demonstrators, no beatings by the police, no retaliation by the demonstrators, no water canons, and not much tear gas. Indeed, the protestors seem almost happy as they climb willingly on to the police buses and from which they continue to cheer and chant. Thus, one has to wonder why these relatively innocuous images received as much global news-play as they did, while far more vivid footage from later in the week was less frequently used.

Civil war in Beirut

Given the large proportion of the EVN feeds devoted to materials about internal law and order, we thought it would be apposite to include a second example of this kind of news story. Here, we examine EVN items dealing with the sectarian fighting in Beirut. As Table

11 shows later in this chapter, the struggle between the rival militias, factions, gangs, and religions captured the attention of the EVN during our sample weeks. In fact, if usage is taken as an indicator, then the civil war in Beirut was the biggest story in the global newsroom for three days in a row.

Table 4. Descriptive shot list for Beirut civil war items, EVN-1, 18 February 1987: 'Camp', 'Shopping' and 'Fighting'.

'Camp'

1   Long shot of road leading to militia camp (2 seconds).

2   Pan along stockade wall, blocking street and made of tires (9 seconds).

3   Two militiamen standing near stockade wall (6 seconds).

4   Militiaman climbs ladder to guard tower which has skull-crossbones decoration (9 seconds).

5   Three militiamen enter bunker area (5 seconds).

6   Armed militiaman walks toward/away from camera, climbs to guard tower (22 seconds).

7   Four militiamen sitting, relaxing in day-room (8 seconds).

8   Militiamen leave day-room, walk into courtyard (10 seconds).

9   Several militiamen peer over sandbagged, tire-wall (14 seconds).

10 Long shot militiamen sitting in former storefront shelter (9 seconds).

11 Militiamen posing with weapons while sitting in living room chairs (17 seconds).

12 Militiaman looks out through his rifle sight (3 seconds).

13 Medium shot group of militia peer over stockade wall (8 seconds).

14 Long shot, group of militia crouched at stockade wall (12 seconds).

15 Slightly closer shot, group of crouching militia (5 seconds).

TOTAL: 139 seconds

'Shopping'

1   Medium shot, women and children waiting outside store (4 seconds).

2   Medium shot, woman wrapping a package (4 seconds).

3   Long shot of man walking down middle of street, carrying bread (3 seconds).

4   Long shot of small crowd waiting outside store (5 seconds).

5   Zoom out from hairless store mannikin, lying on ground behind fence (12 seconds).

6   People walking near street vendors and pushcarts (8 seconds).

7   Medium close-up newspaper vendor, with zoom out to newspaper reader (11 seconds).

8   Teenagers standing around in candy store (10 seconds).

9   People walking by butcher shop, looking at meat (9 seconds).

10 Militiaman waving flag in middle of street, walks off (12 seconds).

TOTAL: 78 seconds

'Fighting'

1   Zoom in to building (factory?) with many broken glass windows (12 seconds).
2   Medium shot of burned out automobile (5 seconds).
3   Zoom out from extreme close-up different burned-out car (18 seconds).
4   Long shot of man walking casually down street (5 seconds).
     TOTAL: 40 seconds

We have created shot-lists for the three Beirut-related stories from the second day, 18 February 1987. The most intriguing point about this raw news material is despite the fact that the fighting in Beirut had been fierce the day before and would resume in earnest the very next day, the three stories transmitted do not convey an impression of a continuing civil war. Indeed, the EVN footage actually suggests a sense of calm, a feeling of relative normalcy, and even a certain attitude of boredom. In the EVN item, 'Camp', for example, we are shown a militia base and a small number of fighters, who lounge about, occasionally peer over their make-shift stockade fence, and assume what can only be judged as poses, brandishing their weapons or pretending to be on the look-out for the 'enemy'. To carry this theme even further, we would point out that the core idea of the EVN item, 'Shopping', is that a lull has taken place in the fighting, and that has allowed Beirut's beleaguered populace a brief moment to come out, shop for food, and stroll around. And finally, with unintentional irony, the third EVN item of the feed, 'Fighting' offers pictures of shattered glass windows and burned out cars, but despite its title, this short piece of video does *not* show any combat.

Gorbachev's peace conference

We shift gears now, moving from our shot-by-shot analysis of internal law and order news to a focus on international relations items, transmitted by the news exchange. Our in-depth example of international relations materials from the EVN is three items, fed on 16 February 1987. All deal with a Peace Forum in Moscow, initiated by Mikhail Gorbachev. Considered by some to be a landmark event in the process of Glasnost (and ultimately in the break up of the Soviet Union), this international conference was attended by several thousand foreign dignitaries, writers and celebrities. As Table 11 shows later in this chapter, footage of this meeting was one of the two most widely used EVN items of the day.

Table 5. Descriptive shot list for Gorbachev peace conference from EVN-0 ('Gorbachev') and EVN-1 ('Forum', 'Sakharov'), 16 February 1987.

'Gorbachev'

1   Medium shot of Gorbachev speaking at podium, pauses to take drink from glass (24 seconds).
2   Cut-away with Gorbachev's voice continuing over picture of part of audience, listening through earpieces to translation. Applause (5 seconds).

3   Medium close-up of Gorbachev speaking (52 seconds).

4   Cutaway to two men listening to Gorbachev's speech (9 seconds).

5   Medium close-up of Gorbachev speaking (48 seconds).

6   Cut-away to bushy-bearded man in audience listening 'attentively' (19 seconds).

7   Medium close-up of Gorbachev speaking (24 seconds).

8   Cut-away to two, 'distinguished'-looking men, listening pensively to speech (6 seconds).

9   Medium close-up of Gorbachev speaking (18 seconds).

10   Cut-away to section of audience. Scattering of applause (8 seconds).

11   Cover shot from balcony, showing stage, podium, etc. (6 seconds).

12   Cut-away to Russian Orthodox cleric and a woman, listening (4 seconds).

13   Medium close-up of Russian Orthodox bishop, speaking at podium (6 seconds).

14   Cut-away to several rows of audience, including one with Russian Orthodox clerics (12 seconds).

15   Speaker from Shot #13 presents Gorbachev with plaque (8 seconds).

16   Cut-away to audience applauding (7 seconds).

     TOTAL: 256 seconds

'Forum'

1   Long-shot of audience applauding (2 seconds).

2   Medium shot of Gorbachev and President Velikhov of Soviet Academy of Sciences. Gorbachev applauds (5 seconds).

3   Floor-level pan of audience. People standing, applauding (6 seconds).

4   Long-shot of podium (3 seconds).

5   Velikhov standing, speaking. Gorbachev seated to his right (4 seconds).

6   Cut-away to part of audience (2 seconds).

7   Academy President Velikhov speaking (2 seconds).

8   Cut-away to close-up of young man in audience (3 seconds).

9   US scientist speaking (4 seconds).

10   Medium long-shot of audience (3 seconds).

11   Head, Italian-Soviet Chamber of Commerce speaking (4 seconds).

12   Cut-away to part of audience (4 seconds).

13   German Social Democrat Egon Barr speaking (4 seconds).

14   Cut-away to members of audience wearing turbans (3 seconds).

15   Russian Orthodox leader (same as Shots 13 and 15 in 'Gorbachev') speaking (4 seconds).

16   Cut-away to part of audience (3 seconds).

17   British author Graham Greene speaking (4 seconds).

18   Cut-away to audience (4 seconds).

19   Retired British general speaking (4 seconds).

20   View of audience from side of hall (3 seconds).

21   Bulgarian Academy of Sciences magazine editor speaking (4 seconds).

22   Cut-away to audience (4 seconds).

23   Gorbachev speaking (5 seconds).

24   Long-shot of stage as cut-away (2 seconds).

25   Cut-away of audience, with zoom-out (3 seconds).

26   Velikhov speaking, perhaps in news conference setting (30 seconds).

27   Cut-away to medium shot of Asian couple (5 seconds).

28   Velikhov seated, speaking (3 seconds).

      TOTAL: 127 seconds

'Sakharov'

1   Long-shot of Gorbachev at podium (8 seconds).

2   Medium close-up of Gorbachev speaking (7 seconds).

3   Cut-away to audience applauding (3 seconds).

4   Cut-away to different part of audience. Sakharov visible in background (4 seconds).

5   Cut-away to yet different part of audience (5 seconds).

6   Medium shot of Gorbachev speaking (14 seconds).

7   Cut-away to medium shot of Sakharov listening, turning to companion (7 seconds).

8   Cut-away to row of Russian Orthodox clergymen (5 seconds).

9   Reverse shot, looking at audience from perspective of stage (9 seconds).

10   Gorbachev speaking (4 seconds).

11   Cut-away to Sakharov, with zoom out to surrounding audience (12 seconds).

12   Cut-away to close-up of bearded man in audience (2 seconds).

13   Cut-away to medium shot of two men in audience (4 seconds).

14   Gorbachev speaking (16 seconds).

15   Cut-away to medium shot of US actor Kris Kristofferson (5 seconds).

16   Cut-away to Egon Barr listening and then laughing (11 seconds).

17   Cut-away to long-shot audience applauding, laughing (6 seconds).

18   Gorbachev speaking (9 seconds).

19   Cut-away to actor Marcello Mastroianni. Zoom out and pan audience (14 seconds).

20   Gorbachev speaking (4 seconds).

21   Cut-away to three men listening to speech (12 seconds).

22   Gorbachev speaking (3 seconds).

      TOTAL: 164 seconds

The first item transmitted ('Gorbachev') ran 257 seconds, five-eighths of which consisted of Gorbachev delivering his speech to the assembled audience. Virtually all of the remainder of the transmission consisted of cut-away shots to various individuals and/or sections of the auditorium.[2] The audience is shown as being generally attentive, if not wildly enthusiastic. Few, if any, of the persons appearing in the cut-away are well-known. Thus, the clear focus on this first EVN item is Gorbachev himself and his prepared text. It is impossible, of course, for a non-Russian speaking journalist or viewer to know whether the sound-bites presented in this item represent important elements from Gorbachev's speech, or whether they were selected more or less at random. Neither Moscow State Television, which was the initial supplier of the pool footage, nor the Eurovision News Exchange provided translations of these video quotations.

Since the Peace Forum was billed as an international gathering of VIPs, the second EVN item seeks to show some of the personages present. In 'Forum', also from Moscow State Television and running 126 seconds, upwards of nine, different individuals are shown addressing the meeting. Among those whom we could identify were: the head of the Soviet Academy of Sciences, author Graham Greene, and German Communist Egon Barr. Each speaker appears on camera for no more than four seconds, while an announcer gives their names in Russian. The remainder of this item is made up mostly of long-shots of the hall and medium long-shots of the audience, all of which seem designed to aid tape editors in assembling a news story from the 'raw' EVN footage.

The final item related to the Gorbachev Peace Forum was called 'Sakharov'. Titling this story 'Sakharov', is a bit misleading, since only 23 out of its 163 seconds show that the long-time Soviet dissident was sitting in the audience. Almost three times more footage is devoted to yet additional sound-bites of Gorbachev's speech and in fact, several additional celebrities, including movie stars Kris Kristofferson and Marcello Mastroianni, are also shown listening to Gorbachev. Obviously, however, the title of this item ('Sakharov') represents an attempt to play up this somewhat ironic 'meeting' between the dissident physicist and the Soviet leader who kept him in internal exile.

Interestingly, given the overall somber tone of the Peace Forum and the serious implications of Sakharov's presence for a new openness in Soviet society, it is surprising to see that this EVN item actually shows Mikhail Gorbachev telling a joke as part of his speech. The audience in return smiles, laughs, and claps in harmonious response. Although Sakharov's reaction is not shown, Germany's stony-faced leader Egon Barr is captured breaking out into gales of laughter over Gorbachev's light comments.

In summary, then, the Eurovision News Exchange offered its members three different story threads about the Gorbachev Peace Forum: (1) Footage of Gorbachev's fairly routine foreign policy speech; (2) Pictures of invited celebrities whose presence was thought by

---

2. In editing television news stories, cutaways are inserted to allow narration, spoken words and/or actions to be edited (i.e. shortened). The visual is said to 'cover' the point at which the audio/video is edited and cut)away thus provide what appear to the viewer as a seamless flow of audio and/or 'real', i.e. non-compressed, time.

some to give political and moral support to the Soviet leader, and (3) Some footage of Andrei Sakharov, whose presence personified the new ways. How the EVN national services and associates chose to use these items will be discussed later in this chapter.

Italian elections

The June, 1987 Italian parliamentary elections represent a typical EVN story about 'internal politics'. The five-party coalition which had governed Italy virtually uninterrupted since 1981 was coming apart due to a power struggle between the Socialists and Christian Democrats. Italy's Communist party was hoping to make major gains and thus win a place in a new leftist coalition. The 'problem' for the Eurovision journalists in covering the actual election itself was a common one for broadcast reporters, namely what pictures to show while the votes are being counted and how to present the election returns in a form that will be readily understood by viewers.

EVN-0 on 15 June carried a story, 'Election', which one might have expected to show scenes of prominent politicians (e.g. Prime Minister Craxi, Communist party head Alessandro Natta) casting voting by placing their ballots in the traditional wooden voting boxes. Instead, however, almost half of 'Election' showed a most unusual candidate for parliament, La Cicciolina, the blonde pornographic movie star with a penchant for publicly displaying her bosom.

Table 6. Descriptive shot list for Italian elections items, 'Election' from EVN-0, 15 June 1987 and 'Reax' from EVN-0, 16 June 1987.

'Election'

1	Long shot of Cicciolina walking in courtyard toward camera (3 seconds).
2	Medium shot of Cicciolina holding teddy bear and ballot (10 seconds).
3	Cut-away of man and woman looking at Cicciolina (2 seconds).
4	Close up of Cicciolina exposing her right breast (7 seconds).
5	Medium shot of several police waiting outside polls (4 seconds).
6	Medium shot of female police office outside polls (3 seconds).
7	Long-shot of Cicciolina entering polling area, hands ballot to official (8 seconds).
8	Medium close-up of Cicciolina voting, baring right breast, exits polls (9 seconds).
9	Cut-away sign, 'Voting here' (2 seconds).
10	Cicciolina returns to poll area, puts second ballot in box, exposes right breast (22 seconds).
11	Cicciolina standing in front of election poster, shows right breast (4 seconds).
12	Cut-away to woman on-looker (5 seconds).
13	Long-shot distinguished-looking man enters polling place (6 seconds).
14	Close-up of ballot in hand (2 seconds).
15	Man from Shot #13 waiting to vote (7 seconds).

16   Cut-away to election clerk with list of voters (4 seconds).

17   Man from Shot #13 votes; woman with him votes next (21 seconds).

18   Various people voting (12 seconds).

19   Medium shot woman voting (21 seconds).

20   Medium shot various voters (15 seconds).

TOTAL: 167 seconds

'Reax'

1   Animated graphic of vote for Christian Democratic party (9 seconds).

2   Animated graphic of vote for Communist party (9 seconds).

3   Animated graphic of vote for SPI (9 seconds).

4   Animated graphic of vote for MSI-DN (9 seconds).

5   Animated graphic of vote for PRI (8 seconds).

6   Animated graphic of vote for PSDI (4 seconds).

7   Political partisans celebrating, hugging, kissing (11 seconds).

8   Pan from celebrating crowd to party flag being waved (8 seconds).

9   Medium shot man waving party flag (4 seconds).

10   In-studio comments by politician (12 seconds).

11   In-studio comment by different politician (8 seconds).

12   Journalist in studio reading newspaper headlines about election (10 seconds).

13   Close-up of various newspaper front pages about election (6 seconds).

TOTAL: 107 seconds

The first 12 of the total 18 shots in this story revolve around Cicciolina and in 4 of the 12, the would-be parliamentarian is shown pulling back her halter top to reveal her right breast. Once Cicciolina has cast her vote, the EVN item continues with more traditional shots of men and women, including one very distinguished-looking gentleman who might well have been an Italian political figure of some standing (although we did not recognise him).

Central tendencies and variability

At this point in the chapter, we switch our focus from the content of EVN transmissions to the content of news presented by national services that are part of the news exchange. This section presents some of the main attributes of the news items that appeared on national newscasts. In the next section we shall return to the above EVN exemplars and show how they were used in some of the newscasts.

For this quantitative analysis we used copies which we obtained of the main evening newscasts from 16 services in 8 Eurovision member countries: three major European countries (the United Kingdom, France and Germany); three less dominant countries (Luxembourg, Belgium and Spain); and two peripheral EBU-member countries (Israel and Jordan).[3]

The sampling and coding of the materials involved two stages. First, we did a general coding of the main attributes of all the material which we obtained. This initial sample consisted of 2,527 items. We then proceeded to do additional and more detailed coding on a composite two-week period. This was done in order to take into account the different number of television services in each of the countries. Thus in the case of countries that have two services in the country's dominant language (the United Kingdom, France and Germany) we randomly selected one week for each of the two services.[4] In the case of the bilingual countries, we decided to use the newscast of the dominant language. Accordingly, for Luxembourg we used its German service RTL-Plus; for Belgium we used the RTBF French speaking service; in Israel we used the Hebrew newscasts of the IBA, and in Jordan we used the JTV Arabic news.

Obtaining all the newscasts was a difficult task strewn with problems. Some of the video recordings turned out to be technically problematic, in some cases there were labour strikes at the television studios, and in still other cases we simply missed one or two days. Thus for Israel we have only seven of the 10 newscasts and only eight of the 10 from Jordan (when necessary we take account of this fact in the analyses that follow).

This final sample, on which most of what we report below is based, consisted of 1,142 news items. Table 7 presents the complete details of the sample of this analysis.

Table 7. Number of news stories per day by country.

Date	UK	FRA	GER	LUX	BEL	SPA	ISR	JOR	Total
Monday, 16 February 1987	14	15	9	20	12	14	19	17	120
Tuesday, 17 February 1987	18	14	10	18	14	9	19	13	115
Wednesday, 18 February 1987	12	16	11	19	15	11	14	21	119
Thursday, 19 February 1987	14	13	12	20	20	17	17	26	139
Friday, 20 Friday 1987	11	14	12	20	12	12	–	–	81
Monday, 15 June 1987	14	16	11	15	13	15	19	19	122
Tuesday, 16 June 1987	15	21	11	15	19	18	–	–	114
Wednesday, 17 June 1987	15	19	9	10	19	14	21	21	18
Thursday, 18 June 1987	14	18	12	12	13	16	21	21	106
Friday, 19 June 1987	11	20	15	18	16	16	12	12	108
Total	138	166	112	167	153	142	114	150	1142

3. The following services were included: BBC and ITN in the United Kingdom; TF1 and A2F in France; ARD and ZDF in (West) Germany; the Hebrew and Arabic news from IBA, Israel; the Arabic and English news from JTV, Jordan; the German (for Luxembourg and Germany), French (for France) and French (for Belgium) newscasts from RTL, Luxembourg; BRT and RTBF in Belgium; TVE, Spain.

4. The week in February included Britain's ITN, France's A2F and Germany's ARD; the week in June included Britain's BBC, France's TF1 and Germany's ZDF.

Domestic vs foreign news

The key discriminating variable which we used is the *generic location* of the item, which distinguishes between items that are *domestic* from the point of view of the country of broadcast, *foreign* to the country of broadcast, and items which we determined to be a *combined* entity, namely, items that involve the country of broadcast and at least one other country. Domestic items are those that take place in the country of broadcast and have nothing to do with any other country. Foreign items are those which take place outside the country of broadcast and have nothing to do with the country of broadcast. Combined items are those which take place either in the country of broadcast or abroad and are relevant to the country of broadcast and to at least one other country. Thus, for example, a combined foreign and domestic item would be the visit of the head of state of the country of broadcast to another country, or conversely, the visit of a foreign dignitary in the country of broadcast.

As can be seen in Figure 1, across all eight countries,[5] nearly half of the items (46.7 per cent) were domestic, exactly one third were foreign and one fifth were of the combined (domestic and foreign) category. Among the countries there was some variance, however. Jordan and Israel were polar opposites: only 36 per cent domestic stories in Jordan and 65 per cent in Israel, and conversely, 18 per cent foreign stories in Israel and 49 per cent in Jordan. The European scene was somewhat more balanced: from 24 per cent foreign stories in France to 41 per cent in Belgium, and from 38 per cent domestic stories in Luxembourg to 57 per cent in France. Finally, regarding combined stories, the range was from 16 per cent in Spain to 30 per cent in Germany.

Salience

Nevertheless, for the moment we continue using the above trichotomy of domestic, foreign and combined stories. In doing so we examined several attributes of salience of the items: length, position in the newscast line-up, and being mentioned in the headlines. The assumption is that items that are considered by journalists as important will receive more broadcast time, a higher position in the line-up, and special recognition by being mentioned in the headlines.

Length of news items

As could be expected, there was much variability in the length of the news items. In fact, of the 1,142 items, 24 lasted 10 seconds or less, while 22 items were longer than five minutes. Moreover, the distribution of length was quite skewed: the overall mean length was 86 seconds, the median length was 67 seconds and the modal length was 30 seconds.

Figure 2 indicates that the shortest items were in Luxembourg (mean of 57 seconds) and the longest items were Spain (124 seconds). The figure also shows that there was relatively

---

5. It should be noted that in all the figures presented below we grouped the three major Eurovision members (the United Kingdom, France and Germany) together on the left, the less dominant members (Luxembourg, Belgium and Spain) in the centre, and the peripheral Eurovision members (Israel and Jordan) at the extreme right hand side of the figures.

little variability among the three generic locations in Luxembourg, Israel and the three major countries, and relatively high variability in Belgium Spain and Jordan. Moreover, across the board, the domestic items (and sometimes the combined items) were longer than the foreign items, except in the case of the United Kingdom.

Position in line-up

In examining the data in Figure 3 one must not pay much attention to the absolute mean position since this depends on the number of items in each newscast, which varies from country to country.[6] Instead, the main focal point should be on the relative difference among the means of the items in the three generic locations.

The overall albeit not entirely consistent pattern indicates that there is a tendency for the foreign items to be presented later in the newscasts, and for domestic and combined stories to be presented earlier. In the United Kingdom the mean position in the line-up was identical for the three generic locations, in France, Germany and Belgium there were very small differences, and a slightly larger difference was found in Spain. In the other three smallest countries there was much variability among the generic locations with no clear and consistent pattern among them.

Mention in headlines

As noted above, the assumption underlying this variable is that items considered by journalists to be more important will also be more likely to appear in the headlines of the newscast. Across the eight countries (see Figure 4) there was much variability in terms of percentage of items mentioned in the headlines of the newscasts: in Germany only seven per cent of the items were mentioned while in Spain 35 per cent were mentioned.

Regardless of the overall level of reference in the headlines, there was a tendency, although not in all the countries, for foreign items to be mentioned in the headlines less frequently than domestic and combined stories. Moreover, in the three major countries and Luxembourg, there were little differences among items of the three generic locations. In the other four countries, however, there was more variability.

News topics

Each of the news items was coded to determine its general topic. As noted earlier, we used the two-level scheme developed by Cohen, Adoni and Bantz (1990) which allows the coders to determine which of 24 major categories best characterises the item.[7] However, since some of the items could not easily be coded into only one topic, we permitted an item to be coded into as many as three codes.

---

6. The newscast with the greatest number of items in Germany was 15; in the United Kingdom and Spain, 18 items; in Israel, 19 items, in Luxembourg and Belgium, 20 items, in France 21 items, and in Jordan there was one newscast with as many as 26 items.

7. The coding scheme also allows for finer coding into as many as ten subtopics per major category. This was done here as well but not reported because of the large number of cells and hence the many empty or nearly empty ones.

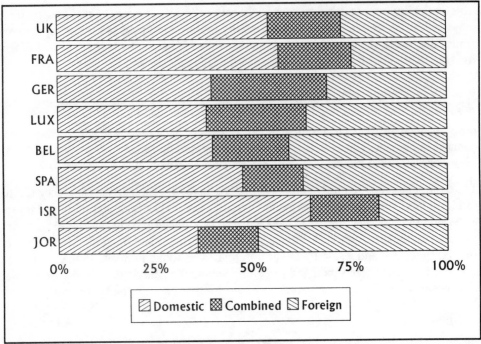

Figure 1. Generic location of news items by country (in %).

Table 8. General topics* by generic locations (in per cent†).

Topic code	Domestic	Combined	Foreign	n
International politics	3.0	44.7	29.3	226
Internal law & order	17.9	11.9	29.0	226
Internal politics	14.1	4.9	14.6	137
Economics	7.4	4.4	2.4	56
General human interest	6.4	2.2	3.7	51
Business/commerce	5.4	5.8	1.3	45
Labour relations	7.6	0.0	0.3	39
Defence	2.6	2.7	5.1	38
Transportation	3.2	3.5	2.7	34
Cultural events	4.4	2.2	1.3	32
Ceremonial events	4.4	0.9	0.5	26
Health/medicine	4.0	0.9	0.8	25
Social relations	1.4	3.1	2.9	25
Communication	4.0	0.0	1.1	24
Population/immigration	1.6	5.3	0.3	21
Education	3.4	0.4	0.3	19
Energy	1.8	0.9	1.3	16
Sports	1.2	2.2	0.8	14
Agriculture	1.2	2.7	0.5	14
Welfare/social services	1.8	0.9	0.5	13
Natural disasters	1.2	0.0	0.3	7
Environment/ecology	0.8	0.4	0.5	7
Housing	1.2	0.0	0.0	6
Science/technology	0.4	0.0	0.5	4
Total	100.0	100.0	100.0	1105

*Each item could be coded into three topics. For the sake of brevity, however, we present only the first topic coded for each item (n = 1105) since its distribution and that of the combined codes were virtually identical.
†Ordered from highest to lowest overall coding.

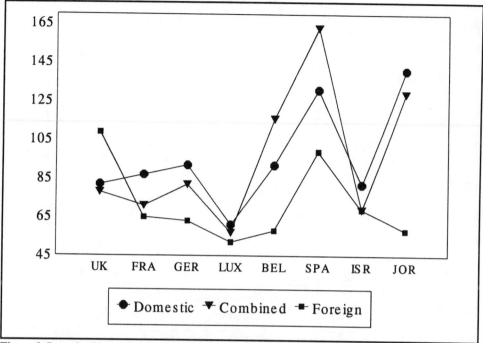

Figure 2. Length of items by country and generic location (in seconds)

In the current analysis the first code was done for 1,105 of the 1,142 items (37 items could not be coded at all). The second and third topics, when pertinent, yielded an additional 1,008 codes for a total of 2,113 coded topics, or an overall mean of 1.85 coded topics per item. However, since the distribution of the codes for the first topic was virtually the same as for the combined three codes, we present in Table 8 only the first topic code. The data are presented for all eight countries.

Most noteworthy is the fact that nearly half (44.7 per cent) of the combined stories dealt with international politics. In other words, these stories dealt with relations between the country of broadcast and at least one other country. Of all the foreign stories, 29.3 per cent dealt with the same category, which in this case refers to events in countries other than the country of broadcast.

Items concerning internal law and order appeared just as frequently as international politics. Interestingly, they were significantly more prevalent in foreign stories than in domestic stories. Also, stories on internal politics were just as prevalent among foreign stories as they were among domestic stories.

It is important to note that some of the seemingly typical stories in the 'classic' repertoire of foreign news events, such as natural disasters and health and medicine appeared in relatively very low frequencies in our two-week sample. Also, stories on science and technology, as well as cultural and ceremonial events, appeared in relatively low frequencies and were predominantly domestic stories.

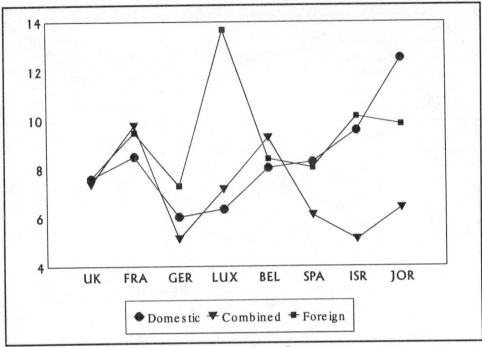

Figure 3. Mean position in line-up by generic location and country.

Economics, business, commerce as well as stories concerning labour and industrial relations were also relatively high on the agenda but mainly as domestic news (20.4 per cent) compared with only 4.0 per cent among the foreign news items and 10.2 per cent in the combined category. Finally, general human interest events, either positive or negative,[8] were also found more prevalent in the domestic column compared with the combined and foreign categories.

Where the news happens

The final descriptive attribute which we present are the country locations of the events. While the domestic events are, by definition, events that take place in the country of broadcast, the foreign and combined stories are related to other countries. Table 9 presents the eight distributions of the locations of the *foreign* events and Table 10 presents a comparable set of distributions for the *combined* events. We present these data in complete detail in order to be able to speak of the extent of variability in the newscasts. At the top of both tables we present the co-occurrence of events in the eight countries of the study, followed by an alphabetical listing of all other countries mentioned.[9]

---

8. These included animal stories, obituaries, 'records' achieved, stories on celebrities, etc.

9. In coding the country locations, it was possible to indicate one or two countries. The data in the tables take into account all mentions of countries. Also, in some cases, which appear at the end of the tables, reference was made to groups of countries, such as EEC countries, NATO countries or Arab Gulf States.

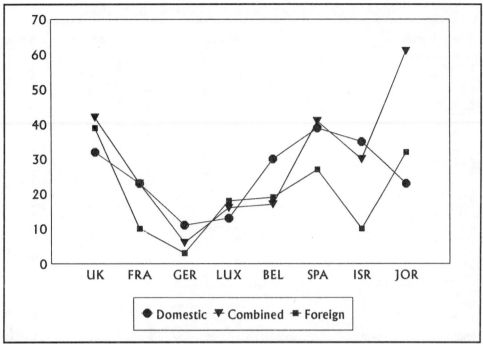

Figure 4. Mentioned in headlines by generic location and country (in %).

Table 9 makes reference to 448 mentions of a foreign country, in a total of 52 individual countries and two compound groups of countries (the EEC and the UN). Of the 52 countries, 14 were mentioned at least 10 times: 69 references were made to the United States, 60 to the Soviet Union, 47 to Lebanon, 30 to Israel (including 16 by Jordan), 24 to South Korea,.and 18 each to Italy and France. On the other hand, 19 countries were mentioned only once.

The table also indicates that RTL-Plus in Luxembourg and RTBF in Belgium reported on events in six of the other seven countries of the study (neither reported on events in Jordan). The other six countries of the study reported on events in fewer countries of the study, while Jordan, as noted, is outstanding in having reported on 16 stories taking place in Israel. Moreover, across all countries mentioned, both the United Kingdom and Israel mentioned only 13 countries each,[10] Jordan mentioned 30 countries,[11] and the other five countries mentioned events having taken place in 18–23 countries.

---

10. Since these data refer to absolute numbers, it should be recalled that there are no data for Israel Television on three of the 10 days, hence this alone could possibly explain part of the relatively low number of countries referred to in its newscasts.

11. This is an extremely large number of countries especially since the Jordanian sample had no data for two of the 10 days.

Table 9. Country locations of *foreign* events by services.

Country location	UK	FRA	GER	LUX	BEL	SPA	ISR	JOR	Total
United Kingdom	–	–	–	3	2	2	1	3	11
France	2	–	1	6	6	1	1	1	18
West Germany	–	2	–	2	3	2	1	1	11
Luxembourg	–	2	–	–	3	2	1	1	9
Belgium	–	–	–	2	–	–	–	–	2
Spain	1	2	1	1	2	–	–	–	7
Israel	1	3	2	4	4	–	16	16	30
Jordan	–	–	–	–	–	–	–	–	–
Afghanistan	–	–	–	–	2	–	–	1	3
Argentina	–	–	–	–	–	1	–	–	1
Austria	–	3	1	1	–	2	1	2	10
Brazil	–	–	2	3	1	3	–	1	10
Canada	–	–	–	1	–	–	–	–	1
Chad	–	1	–	–	–	–	–	1	2
China	–	1	–	–	–	–	–	3	4
Columbia	–	–	–	–	–	4	–	–	4
Costa Rica	–	–	–	–	–	1	–	–	1
Cyprus	–	1	–	–	–	–	–	–	1
Egypt	–	–	–	–	–	–	–	4	4
El Salvador	1	–	–	–	–	–	–	–	1
Greece	–	1	–	–	–	–	–	–	1
Honduras	–	–	1	–	–	–	–	–	1
Iceland	–	–	–	–	–	1	–	–	1
India	3	–	–	1	–	–	–	3	7
Iran	–	1	–	2	2	2	1	8	16
Iraq	–	1	–	–	1	1	–	9	12
Ireland	3	–	2	1	5	2	1	–	14
Italy	–	1	2	4	4	4	1	2	18
Japan	–	–	3	1	–	–	–	1	5
Kuwait	–	–	–	1	–	–	–	2	3
Lebanon	3	5	2	9	5	5	5	13	47
Libya	–	1	–	–	–	–	–	–	1
Nicaragua	–	–	1	–	–	2	–	–	3
Paraguay	–	1	–	–	–	–	–	–	1
Peru	–	–	1	–	–	1	–	–	2
Philippines	–	–	–	–	–	–	–	1	1
Poland	1	2	1	1	1	–	1	–	7
Saudi Arabia	–	–	–	–	–	–	–	3	3
South Africa	3	–	1	–	1	–	–	–	5
South Korea	6	3	3	3	3	4	1	1	24
Sri Lanka	–	–	–	–	–	–	–	1	1
Sudan	–	–	–	–	–	–	–	1	1
Switzerland	–	–	–	–	–	–	–	1	1
Syria	–	1	–	–	–	–	–	1	2
Turkey	–	2	–	–	–	–	–	–	2
USSR	6	9	6	9	13	6	5	6	60
USA	7	6	8	16	7	10	5	10	69
Venezuela	–	–	–	–	–	–	–	1	1
Vatican	–	2	1	–	–	–	–	–	3
Vietnam	–	1	–	–	–	–	–	–	1
Yugoslavia	–	–	–	–	–	–	–	1	1
Zimbabwe	1	–	–	–	–	–	–	–	1
EEC countries	–	–	1	–	–	–	–	–	1
United Nations	–	–	–	–	–	–	–	2	2
Total number of items	38	52	40	71	65	56	25	101	448
Mean number of foreign items per newscast*	3.8	5.2	4.0	7.1	6.5	5.6	3.6	12.6	
Number of other countries mentioned	13	23	19	20	18	20	13	30	

*Corrected because of the missing data for Israel on 3 days and Jordan on 2 days.

Table 10. Country locations of *combined* events by services.

Country location	UK	FRA	GER	LUX	BEL	SPA	ISR	JOR	Total
United Kingdom	26	2	1	1	–	1	–	1	32
France	3	28	1	2	8	–	–	–	42
West Germany	–	1	26	–	–	2	–	–	29
Luxembour	–	–	–	35	–	–	–	–	35
Belgium	–	–	1	1	15	–	–	–	17
Spain	–	1	–	1	1	21	–	2	26
Israel	–	–	–	–	–	–	16	1	17
Jordan	–	–	–	–	–	–	–	23	23
Algeria	–	3	–	–	–	–	–	–	3
Austria	–	–	1	1	3	–	–	–	5
Brazil	–	–	–	–	–	5	–	–	5
Canada	1	–	–	–	–	–	–	–	1
China	–	1	–	–	–	–	–	–	1
Congo	2	–	–	–	–	2	–	–	4
Czechoslovakia	–	–	–	1	–	–	–	1	2
East Germany	–	–	6	2	–	–	–	–	8
Egypt	–	–	–	–	–	–	1	–	1
Iran	3	–	4	4	–	–	–	–	11
Iraq	–	–	–	1	–	–	–	3	4
Ireland	2	–	–	–	–	–	–	–	2
Italy	–	2	–	–	–	–	–	1	3
Japan	–	–	–	–	1	–	–	–	1
Lebanon	3	1	–	7	–	–	1	–	12
Libya	–	–	–	1	–	–	–	–	1
Netherlands	3	–	–	1	–	–	–	–	4
Nigeria	1	–	–	–	–	–	–	–	1
Norway	–	–	–	1	–	–	–	–	1
Oman	–	–	–	--	–	–	–	1	1
Panama	–	–	–	1	–	-1	–	–	2
Poland	–	–	2	–	1	–	–	–	3
Portugal	–	–	1	–	–	–	–	–	1
Rumania	–	–	–	–	–	–	–	3	3
Saudi Arabia	–	–	–	–	–	–	1	–	1
South Africa	–	3	–	–	–	–	–	–	3
South Korea	6	3	3	3	3	4	1	1	24
Sri Lanka	1	–	–	–	–	–	–		1
Sudan	–	–	–	–	–	–	–	1	1
Switzerland	–	–	–	–	3	–	1		4
Syria	–	–	–	–	–	–	–	1	1
Togo	–	–	–	–	–	–	2	–	2
USSR	2	3	8	7	1	–	4	–	25
USA	–	5	2	8	1	1	8	1	26
Yemen	–	–	–	–	–	–	–	4	4
EEC countries	–	–	3	4	4	4	–	–	15
Arab Gulf States	–	–	1	–	–	–	–	–	1
NATO	–	–	1	–	–	1	–	–	2
Warsaw Pact	–	–	–	1	–	–	–	–	1
United Nations	–	1	1	–	1	2	–	–	5
Total number of items	53	54	62	83	42	44	35	44	417
Mean number of foreign items per newscast*	5.3	5.4	6.2	8.3	4.2	4.4	5.0	5.5	
Number of other countries mentioned	11	12	15	19	11	10	8	13	

*Corrected because of the missing data for Israel on 3 days and Jordan on 2 days.

Table 10 reports on references to 417 mentions of combined stories, in a total of 43 individual countries and five compound groups of countries. The top portion of the table indicates the number of countries mentioned among the countries of the study. The only noteworthy point is Belgium's RTBF which reported on eight stories which took place in Germany. Among the remaining countries, five were mentioned ten or more times: 26 references to the United States, 25 to the Soviet Union, 24 to South Korea, 12 to Lebanon, and 11 to Iran. Thirteen countries were referred to only once.

As for the specific countries of the study, whereas with regard to the foreign stories the range of different countries mentioned was from 13 (in the United Kingdom) to 30 (in Jordan), with regard to the combined stories the range was from 8 different countries mentioned in the Israel news to 19 different countries mentioned in the news from Luxembourg. Among the other six countries of the study only 10–13 different countries were mentioned.

Thus, while the reporting of foreign news spanned a relatively large number of countries, the reporting of combined stories, which concern the country of broadcast and another country, dealt with far fewer countries. This clearly indicates that while national services quite often refer to stories taking place in foreign countries, they have a much smaller 'circle' of countries on whose bilateral and mutual interests they report.

Using EVN footage

The most important variable of interest in this context is whether or not the EBU services used EVN material in their nightly news. To begin examining this point we first determined for which items broadcast in each of the eight countries was there any EVN footage actually available for the service to use. This was determined entirely on the basis of the items that the services decided to include in their respective newscast, but regardless of whether or not the service in fact chose to use any such EVN material. Figure 5a presents separate percentages of foreign and combined items aired by each service that *could have used* EVN material.[12]

For foreign stories the range was from 35 per cent in Jordan to 100 per cent in Israel (i.e. in Israel, all foreign items broadcast could have used EVN footage). Furthermore, as could be expected, in all countries but Belgium, the availability of EVN footage was higher for foreign stories compared with combined stories (the range for combined stories was 0 per cent in Jordan and 67 per cent in Belgium).

The next step in the analysis was to determine which items shown by the various services clearly *used* EVN footage. In most cases it was very simple to determine this fact, although we also had a coding option for footage that was only possibly of EVN origin. Because of our desire for a conservative estimate we do not include those items in this analysis. Figure 5b presents the data separately for the eight countries and for foreign vs. combined stories.

Across all countries there was naturally higher use of EVN footage for foreign stories

---

12. There is a touch of irony here in that in many instances a service decides to present a story only because it has footage available. Nevertheless at this point we simply want to know for how many of the items broadcast was there EVN footage available.

compared with combined stories. For combined stories EVN footage was used in up to 20 per cent of the items, in Luxembourg and Israel (for example, footage of a visit by Israel's Prime Minister Shamir to Washington was used by Israel Television, in combination with footage from its Washington correspondent). As for foreign items, the French services had the lowest usage level of EVN footage (10 per cent) as opposed to 78 per cent use by Israel Television.

The most poignant indication of the use of EVN footage, however, was determined by computing for each country the ratio of the percentage of the clear use of such footage based on the availability of the footage for those particular items. Figure 5c presents these findings.

As we have seen above, the use of EVN footage was clearly higher for foreign items compared with combined items. The French and British services were the lowest users of EVN footage (24 per cent and 30 per cent, respectively). The German, Spanish and Belgian services used EVN footage to a larger extent (61 per cent, 72 per cent and 86 per cent, respectively) while the Jordanian, Luxembourg and Israeli services were extremely dependent upon EVN footage (92 per cent, 96 per cent and 100 per cent, respectively). As for combined stories, here we found no use of EVN material in the United Kingdom, France, Spain and Jordan; moderate use in Spain and Germany, and a relatively high level of use in Israel (50 per cent) and in Luxembourg (58 per cent).

Using Your Own Pictures

In one respect the obverse of the use of EVN footage in news items is the use of local station material.[13] This can be of three specific kinds: (a) local station footage taken by the station crew itself in order to cover the specific event, usually during the day of broadcast or shortly before it; (b) local file material, by which we mean footage shot by the station on some previous occasion, in connection with the same or a similar event and kept in the station's video files; and (c) archive footage, which is distinguished by its historical nature. The findings indicate that there was relatively high use of local station footage, moderate to low use of local file footage, and very low use of archive material.

As can clearly be seen in Figure 6a, in all the countries there was more usage of local footage in combined stories compared with foreign stories. With regard to foreign stories, the highest level of local station footage was in the United Kingdom and France, apparently because these countries have many correspondents serving abroad who provide their own reports; Germany and Spain follow suit while Luxembourg, Belgium and Israel have very little usage of local footage in foreign stories, probably because these services have very few correspondents serving abroad. The case of Jordan is interesting and requires some explanation: While that country does not have many foreign correspondents, a reporter from Jordan Television does go to various Arab countries when important events take place there, hence the 20 per cent figure of local station footage for foreign news.

---

13. It should be noted, of course, that not all news items have visual footage, hence local footage is not necessarily the statistical complement of EVN footage yielding a total of 100 per cent.

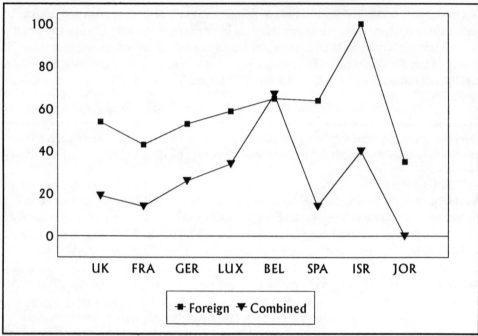

Figure 5a. Availability of EVN footage for foreign and combined stories by country (in %).

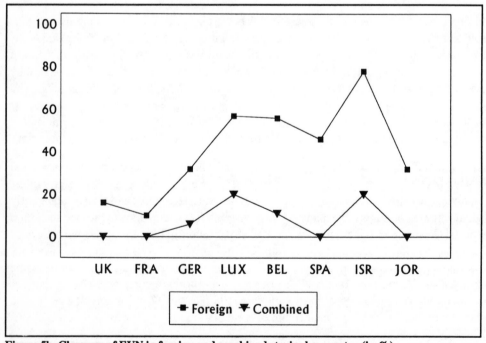

Figure 5b. Clear use of EVN in foreign and combined stories by country (in %).

As for combined stories, the United Kingdom, Spain and Jordan are quite high in usage, which can be the result, among other things, of relatively many visits by heads of state abroad or visits to the country of broadcast. France and Germany are relatively lower, while Belgium, Israel and Luxembourg have the least amount of local footage.

The use of local file material was generally quite low in all the countries except for a relatively high level in Spain and moderate use in the United Kingdom and France, for both combined and foreign stories. It should be noted that in five of the eight countries there was no use at all of local file material in foreign stories.

Finally, there was very little use of archive (historical) footage and hardly any difference between foreign and combined stories (except in Israel). In the United Kingdom, France, Germany and Luxembourg there was some use of archive material in foreign items, but in the other four countries virtually no such footage was used.

Quantifying domestication

The final set of variables we examined concerns the extent to which journalists at member services 'domesticate' foreign news. By domestication, we mean that journalists some-times construct foreign news stories in ways which attempt to create links of meaning between the stories and the history, culture, politics, society, etc. of the viewers. Thus, domestication may be thought of as part of the working-theories that journalists bring to their jobs, one of many craft guidelines for helping journalists 'know' how to tell stories. Moreover, foreign news stories which are created using this journalistic rule-of-thumb and which are given a special domestic or localised slant can be said to be domesticated news items.[14]

Later in this chapter we will present several qualitative analyses of domesticated news. In this section we report on our search for four discrete and clearly defined attributes which we believe are indicators of domesticated news: (a) instances in which implications or consequences to the country of broadcast are spelled out; (b) instances in which it is specifically reported that people from the country of broadcast are involved in the story or at least mentioned in it; (c) instances in which local figures are quoted or interviewed; and (d) instances in which visuals such as maps are presented thereby connecting the foreign country to the country of broadcast.

The coding of these variables was done in the course of determining the availability and usage of EVN materials. Thus, if an item was reported by the news reader in the studio without any accompanying news footage, it was not coded for these domestication variables. Therefore the findings in Figures 7a–d may be conservative underestimates of the true parameters. In fact, it might be that foreign items without footage would be even more domesticated in the text of the news reader since only the text, and not the pictures, would be the justification for the presentation of the items in the first place.

---

14. Domestication, as we shall see in Chapter 4, is also something that members of the audience do, when, in trying to decode television news stories, they often seek to make sense of them by applying symbols and narratives from the local culture.

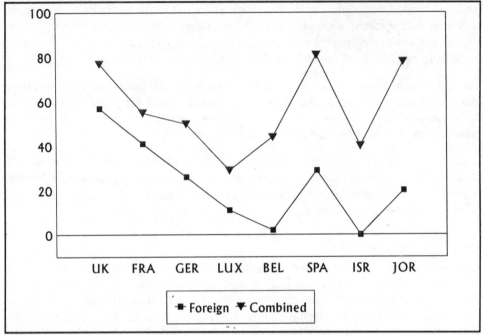

Figure 5c. Clear use of AVAILABLE EVN footage in foreign and combined stories by country (in %).

In any event, we found vast differences between the items based on the criterion of generic location. What is striking is the extremely low level of domestication of the foreign items using all four attributes. In Germany there were some modest indications of domestication, especially with regard to implications to the country of broadcast and visual maps linking the two countries. In the United Kingdom, France, Luxembourg and Spain there were only minuscule hints at domestication, and in Belgium, Israel and Jordan there were absolutely no indications of domestication. But as noted, these may be underestimations.

While it may initially appear strange to consider the domestication of combined items, that is, of stories dealing with the country of broadcast and another country or countries, we nevertheless coded and presented the findings for combined items as well. We did so since in many cases the mere juxtaposition of the two countries implies some measure of relationship between the two.

Convergence and diversity

The tension between consensus and particularism to which we referred in our analysis of the conferences also seems to resonate when we study the news output. Studying the newscasts of the services during our two-week sample we found quite a strong convergence on the top stories which included hard international news, while on stories of lesser international significance there was more diversity.

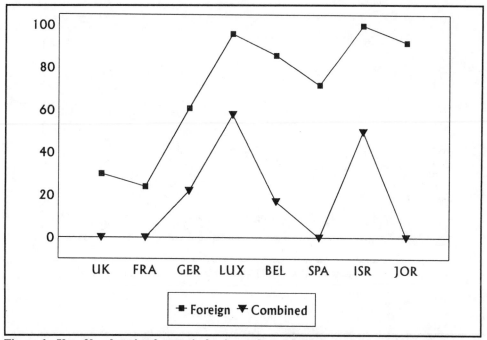

Figure 6a. Use of local station footage in foreign and combined stories by country (in %).

We begin our presentation of the convergence and diversity in the patterns of usage with Table 11. The table reflects the extent to which the news stories transmitted by the Exchange actually appeared on the various services' newscasts. We added to this table the relevant items from the three American networks since we will be using some of them for the analyses which follow. Therefore, we included in the table the two stories which appeared in the greatest number of services of our sample during the 10-day period. Thus the most heavily aired story could be viewed in a minimum of 9 services and in as many as 19 services.[15]

The table shows that for some big or rather 'appealing' stories there is substantial consensus across the 19 services. On two of the ten days, the story of the Korean riots and a speech by President Reagan appeared in the newscasts of all the services. The two next most dominant stories appeared in 17 newscasts (the siege of Beirut and the Italian elections), and Gorbachev's Peace Forum in Moscow as well as the opening in Jerusalem of the Demjanjuk trial appeared in 16 of the newscasts. However, this quantitative perspective provides only one angle on the processes at work. Another way of looking at

15. For the in-depth case-study analyses of some of the top stories reported in the news of the various services, we reverted back to the larger array and selected our examples from the complete data set of 19 services regardless of whether or not these services were included in the 8-country composite 2-week period which we used for the detailed quantitative analysis. This also includes the three American networks, ABC, CBS and NBC. We did so in order to take advantage of a greater number of renditions of the same stories.

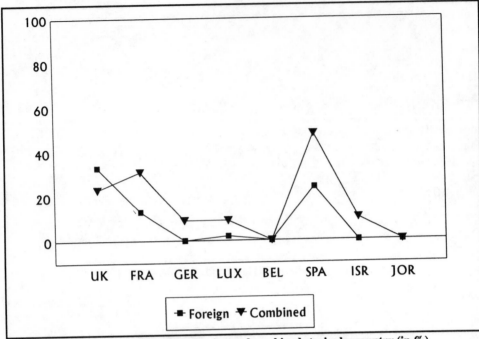

Figure 6b. Use of local file material in foreign and combined stories by country (in %).

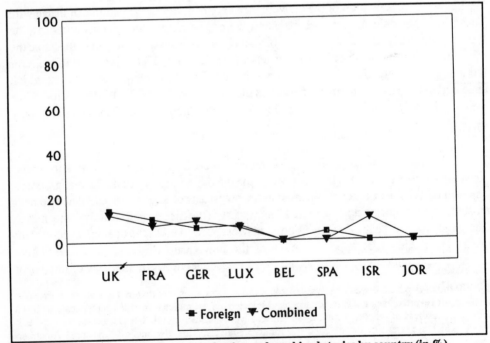

Figure 6c. Use of local archive footage in foreign and combined stories by country (in %).

this phenomenon is to analyse in depth the ways in which a variety of broadcasters treat the same topics. It is perhaps worth reiterating that the Exchange offers its members only unedited raw visual footage, mostly with natural sound and rarely with spoken words, and usually it is long enough to enable the creation of a brief or a long piece by the various services. Thus it is clear that different national broadcasters may frequently produce quite different stories out of the same material. An important assumption here is that visual materials are more open than verbal texts. Raw visuals can be edited and contextualised more easily. In other words what we have here is an on-going demonstration of the process of journalistic construction of reality: a display of how identical visual accounts are edited and packaged to give different meanings to different audiences.

Table 11. Most frequently reported stories by day.

Date	Story	Services airing
16 February	Gorbachev Peace Conference	16
	Demjanjuk trial opens in Jerusalem	17
17 February	Beirut Siege	17
	Impending release of Soviet dissident	9
18 February	Beirut Strife	14
	Irish elections results	9
19 February	More Beirut Fighting	15
	Irish election results	9
20 February	Soviet dissident released	13
	Archbishop Glemp visits Brussels	13
15 June	South Korean unrest	19
	Italian elections	17
16 June	Reagan speech	19
	German flies to Red Square	15
17 June	Corsican terror	15
	NY subway vigilante sentenced	11
18 June	South Korean unrest	13
	Auction of Bardot's artifacts	10
19 June	South Korean unrest	16
	Bomb blast in Spain	12

Roeh and Dahlgren (1991) suggest that for a foreign news item to appear on a national television bulletin it must be culturally translated. Every single EVN clip is at least minimally packaged, localised or domesticated in order to make sense to the local audience. Here again is the tension between news-from-nowhere (to use Epstein's 1973 ironic formulation) and news from 'our' point of view.

We now return to the four 'EVN Exemplars' discussed earlier in this chapter; and with

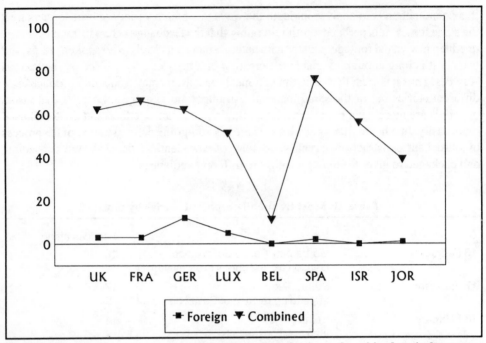

Figure 7a. Implications or consequences to local country in foreign and combined stories by country (in %).

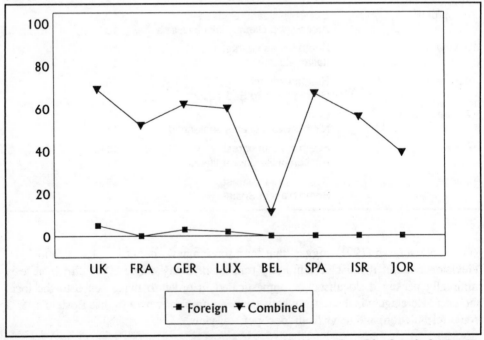

Figure 7b. Implications or consequences to local country in foreign and combined stories by country (in %).

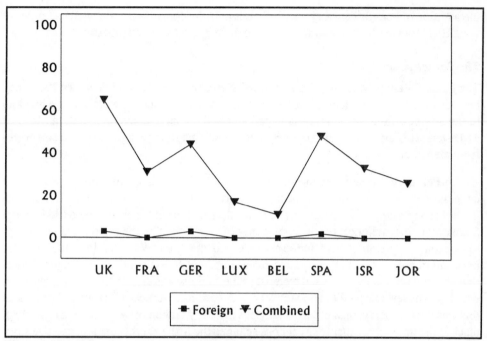

Figure 7c. Local figure quoted or interviewed in foreign and combined stories by country (in %).

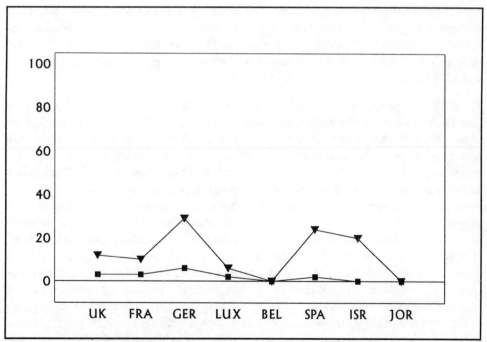

Figure 7d. Visual link between local and foreign country in foreign and combined stories by country (in %).

the addition of one further story ('Irish Elections'), we consider five detailed examples of what EVN footage looked and sounded like once it had become domesticated news.

The Soviet peace forum

The Peace Forum in Moscow, initiated by Mikhail Gorbachev, in mid February 1987, may be considered a landmark event in the process of Glasnost, and ultimately in the breakup of the Soviet Union. Several thousand people filled the large convention hall in Moscow and listened to numerous speeches by Soviet and visiting foreign dignitaries and celebrities from many countries.

On 16 February, 16 services in our sample reported on this event. An analysis of the coverage revealed five major themes: (a) the growing openness in Soviet society as seen in Gorbachev's emphasis on human rights; (b) the presence of the up-to-then exiled Andrei Sakharov in the audience; (c) the applauding of Gorbachev by the impressive gathering; (d) Gorbachev's criticism of the arms race and the 'Star Wars' programme; and (e) uncertainty concerning the impending release of Jewish dissident Joseph Begun. More-over, the bulk of the footage used by most of the stations was clearly Eurovision material, which was nevertheless edited by each service according to its needs. In four of the services this was the lead story, in another six services the story ranked between second and fourth place in the line-up, another four versions spanned the fifth to eight position, and one story each appeared in the tenth and the fifteenth place.

Israel Television was the only service which began its report with the story of Begun. In the report, Begun's wife complains on camera (Eurovision material) that despite Gor-bachev's promises her husband is still in prison. The story that follows – the celebration of peace – is to be read in the Israeli version with skepticism: How can one take Gorbachev seriously if he doesn't stand by his own words.

The CBS story opens with a tabloid-like pun suggesting that Gorbachev is combining an 'arms offensive with a charm offensive' and points out immediately that 'his latest move to be taken seriously and sincerely by the West may have been blunted by his own KGB secret police'. His deceit is implicit in that while Gorbachev is all smiles, his secret police continues its dirty work. Begun is introduced early as a foil to Gorbachev. Following Dan Rather's introduction, CBS's Moscow correspondent prefaces the Soviet leader's state-ment on nuclear arms with a warning that this is an 'unusual speech, full of flowery language ... as if he wanted to convince the world that he means it when he says he wants no nuclear weapons'. The dubious character of the speech, already established by Rather, is thus restated by the reporter. After the clip from the speech the reporter makes a transition from the intent of the conference to its effectiveness. Gorbachev, he tells us, was speaking to a 'collection of one thousand of the world's most influential writers, business-men and scientists' and 'if Gorbachev was working on impressing them he succeeded'. In fact Rather had set up the function of this audience with his very first words: 'A star studded group of international movers and shakers was in Moscow today'.

After the intent of the conference is made clear its authenticity is further questioned by inserting the story about Begun's continued imprisonment. 'Mr. Gorbachev's speech concludes a week of contradiction', the CBS reporter tells us, 'while there have been releases of political dissidents, Begun is still not free ... Gorbachev seemed to be fighting hard for the respect and understanding of his powerful audience. In short, trying to earn from one thousand influential private citizens what he has not earned from the Reagan administration'.

That the CBS story is driven by shared American narrative frameworks can be seen in its commonalities with the ABC and NBC stories. All three are stories sceptical of Gorbachev's motives and both Sakharov and Begun serve to strengthen this general tone. Like Begun, Sakharov functions to some extent as an instrument of the narrative's aim to create distrust of Gorbachev's intentions. They serve to invoke another staple of American narrative of the Soviet Union, namely, the representation of opposition to communism and to the Soviet government by heroic and charismatic personalities to whom the American notion of commitment to freedom and democracy is attributed. It can even be argued that both Sakharov and Begun represent the fundamental American empowerment of the individual who singlehandedly and heroically fights oppression and big government.

We now turn to the two British stories. Unlike their US counterparts, both are essentially appreciative of Gorbachev's policies and his leadership and somewhat critical of the American response by President Reagan. The BBC begins its story with a statement: 'Mr. Gorbachev has accused the United States of making a secret move at the Geneva arms talks which, if true, breaks a promise made to both the American Congress and the NATO alliance'. Reference to the scrapping of the ABM Treaty is framed in bold accusatory terms against the United States. (In the American stories, by the way, the ABM accusations were given only marginal play.)

The focus on the US role in the arms race serves as a lead-in for the two intertwined themes in the narrative of the British stories. Gorbachev's efforts – the dominant element in the story are portrayed approvingly. The BBC story ends with Gorbachev's call to dispose of all nuclear weapons while the Soviet Union is 'willing to renounce its nuclear power status and reduce all other armaments to a bare essential'. America's secret moves over the ABM treaty and the continued efforts on the 'Star Wars' are seen as endangering the Soviet initiatives.

The ITN lead sentence is: 'Even by the standards Mr. Gorbachev has himself set, this was a most extraordinary event; five years ago with Lenin's statue looking on, the idea of Leonid Brezhnev turning up for the same event as Gregory Peck, Kris Kristofferson and Andrei Sakharov would have been unthinkable. Yet that precisely is what Mikhail Gorbachev chose to do.' It should be noted that the presence of these foreign visitors as well as Sakharov were presented as merely mute medium-shot visual frames in which they are seen sitting among the audience and applauding along with the others.

In the British stories Begun and Sakharov function differently. Compared with the US Begun's role is marginalised while the presentation of Sakharov is largely neutral and referential and does not compete with Gorbachev's central position. In fact, in the ITN story Sakharov's approval of Gorbachev is particularly noted: 'The freed dissident Andrei Sakharov was there to applaud him'.

'Beirut strife'

Stories about the fighting in Beirut in February 1987 between the Shiite Amal militia and the Palestinians residing in camps in Beirut (and other areas in Lebanon), were broadcast on almost all the European services. Many, though not all, were accompanied by EVN-supplied footage. One possible reading of these stories offers an alternative meaning, which actually is opposite to our previously explicated notion of 'domestication'. If the concept of 'domestication' is taken to imply an establishment of some *connection* between the story and the audience, many of the stories on the fighting in Beirut (with one major exception, to be discussed below) may have served to *distance* the audience from the events in Lebanon. This is not to suggest however that the concept of domestication fails here. Rather, it alerts us to the possibility that domestication may be conceptualised as some sort of rough continuum, ranging, at one pole, from news stories (and their antecedent creation) which bring viewers psychologically 'closer' — to the other extreme, where news stories (and the journalistic work which goes into their creation) psychologically distances viewers from the story. Where any given news item would fall on this domestication continuum is, of course, open to empirical investigation.

The Beirut Strife stories, for example, contain two different themes: the first, portraying the actual fighting in Beirut, serves to distance the audience by portraying the situation as a sequence of almost random, confusing and incomprehensible destruction; the second, dealing with the plight of the Palestinian refugees besieged in their camps, invokes sympathy and compassion for the human suffering portrayed, and thus may serve to connect the audience to the event.

Most of the stories we examined were told in a straightforward, factual mode, citing the number of casualties and the plight of the Palestinians besieged in their camps. Images of street fighting and random shelling reinforce a story of random, incomprehensible carnage. For European viewers the stories may have been doubly incomprehensible. First, sorting out the confusing array of combatants would have been highly difficult for those not familiar with the convoluted political/military situation in Beirut, in which Amal militiamen, PLO and Druze fighters, and Syrian soldiers were entangled in a struggle whose meaning is difficult to decipher. Who is on whose side? Who are the 'good guys' and who are the 'bad guys'? What is the fighting about? Compounding this confusion and uncertainty is the 'alien' nature of the combatants and the terrain. Lebanon's geographical proximity to Europe notwithstanding, images of destroyed buildings, burnt cars and gunmen scurrying back and forth, firing their guns in an apparently aimless fashion must have appeared quite strange and remote to viewers in Europe's relatively stable societies.

A point of connection between the stories and the audience is established via the compassion invoked by tales of the plight of the Palestinian refugees, who have been besieged in camps and were running out of food, water and medicines. The stories tell that the refugees have been reduced to eat dogs, cats and even rats. An EVN-footage provides pictures of the distribution of fresh bread when the siege on one of the camps has been lifted.

The BBC's stories, on the other hand, stand out as the most elaborate and comprehensive offerings on these dates. On 16 February a three-part story about the fighting in Beirut is the lead story on the *Nine O'clock News*. The first part, reported from Cyprus by the BBC's own correspondent tells the tale of a U.N. relief convoy heading toward one of the refugee camps with supplies of food, after it was given permission to do so by the Amal militia. However, the reporter tells us, as the convoy approached the camp, gunmen opened fire on it, and blocked its progress. We see a picture of one of the trucks with its tires shot out. The convoy was forced to stop a short distance from the camp, but for the residents of the camp, who could not get to the stalled convoy because of sniper fire, the 'convoy might as well have been on the moon'. That reference appears to be apt to describe the entire Beirut story which, for the viewers (in that case a British audience), might be as remote as the moon.

The second part of the story tells the tale of life in the refugee camps. Both the text and the pictures portray a moon-like place: piles of rubble; destroyed dwellings; streets that are not streets but 'open sewage'. Some commentary is provided by a former resident of the camp, now living in London, further casting the story as one of human disaster, whose appeal to human compassion is universal.

Finally, in the third section the story is powerfully domesticated through the tale of Dr. Pauline Cutting, a young British surgeon, who is the only doctor still living in the camp and attempting to minister to the sick and the wounded. Still pictures of the young woman accompany the story which informs us that she, too, has been forced to eat 'the flesh of dogs'. Pauline's father is interviewed, saying that he is concerned about his daughter but feels that she is relatively safe. A British connection to the events in Beirut is thus firmly established, and it is strongly reinforced when at the end of the bulletin we are told that 'during the last half hour' Pauline's parents have succeeded in establishing telephone contact with their daughter. Mom and dad are seen talking to Pauline on the phone, expressing hope for quick reunification of the family.

Another BBC story on the following day again focusses on the refugees and on what the correspondent describes as 'the war of the camps'. Bleak pictures of the camps and of Palestinian gunmen rushing about and firing their weapons are followed by a 'background' text, retelling the story of the origins of the camps, populated by refugees who were driven from their homes, and pictures of Israeli tanks driving into Lebanon. The Palestinians, we are told, have for months now been subjected to heavy Israeli shelling, and now the Shiite Moslems want them out too. But, the correspondent concludes, 'they have nowhere to go'. On the screen is a picture of Palestinian refugees walking across a muddy, puddled road, possibly an open sewer.

An additional touch of 'domestication' appears in the story immediately following, in which we see Amin Gemayel, the Lebanese President, meeting with Margaret Thatcher and the Archbishop of Canterbury in London. Gemayel is quoted as saying that he will do everything in his power to free the British hostage, Terry Waite.

Taken together, the stories illustrate the complexity and the diversity of the coverage. Thematically, the 'Beirut strife' offers a number of alternative story lines: of street fighting, shelling and destruction; of a treacherous and lawless city ruled by innumerable war lords and their fighting forces, some recognised, others shadowy; and of women and children caught in a devastated shanty town, left without food, water or hope and a place to go. One European connection to the place has been the hostages, British and German. But otherwise the stories veer between the strangeness of this event and the instant connectibility with images of suffering. The news editors have made their choices.

'Korean unrest'

As an illustration of the struggle between convergence and diversity we present an analysis of the story which we refer to as 'South Korean Unrest' which so dominates our sample week in June. This story was a continuing one, which appeared every day during that week (including the two top stories on three of the five days). During that week, there were violent protests in South Korea's capital, mainly by students, against police brutality in the context of the students' demand for greater democracy and more civil rights. It should be noted that all this took place in the foreground of the forthcoming Olympic games scheduled to take place in Seoul the following summer. Our analysis repeatedly finds the same violent pictures in most of the versions: students throwing fire-bombs at the heavily armed policemen who use tear-gas and water cannons in an attempt to disperse the crowds; several policemen whose uniforms catch fire; and students at a sit-in near the city's main church. And yet, two clearly different frames were constructed, one by several of the European services and the other by the American networks.

Through European eyes

The central frame that appeared in the European versions of the story was the violent confrontation between student demonstrators and the police, a motif that seems to be widely prominent in European collective memory.

South Korean students and police dominate the British news on both the ITN and the BBC. Thus on the BBC: 'Ten thousand students defied the police ... while most of the citizens of Seoul watched and suffered the suffocating effects of tear-gas ... showed their anger at the methods of the police'. An explicit element of domestication can be heard in the continued voice-over: 'The growing wealth in Korea has generated large numbers of university students; there are proportionately more students in Korea than in Britain'.

France's TF1 similarly dramatises the confrontation between the students and the riot police, inviting the viewer to empathise with the suffering caused by police aggression. 'Look at the gas', exclaims the reporter, as we see pictures of people trying to cover their faces with pieces of plastic to avoid inhaling the gas. The emphasis is on the physical confrontation and its consequent victims, but not on the political circumstances surrounding the clashes.

As our sample suggests, the RTL service in Luxembourg seems to represent a particular case in European television journalism. Being an exporter of news to Belgium, France and Germany, RTL does not manifest a strong cultural particularism. Instead the tendency is towards news as popular journalism with an emphasis on human interest stories and melodrama. Thus the RTL story to France opens: 'The gas masks are scrambling for the gold medal in Korea. In ten days of demonstrations the price has doubled ... it is now 600 francs.' The story is told through a concrete metonymy and one cannot escape the almost jovial intonation. In the RTL story beamed at Belgium, the Olympic games threatened by the political unrest in Seoul are clearly foregrounded as compared to the other television stations. This can be seen as another instance of popularity seeking.

In the different European stations the dominant tone of coverage is of a remote and somewhat estranged point of view. There is no sense of any type of involvement in the Korean situation. Thus the European perspective allows for a different framing in each country without political closure within their respective narratives.

Through American eyes

By contrast, in the United States, with its heavy involvement in world politics and long history of commitment to South Korea, the political frame dominates over any other possible interpretation of the events. The major American networks of the day seem to reflect a strong communality in their presentations with shared emphasis of the US political interests and concerns. On 19 June, one of the days of rioting in Seoul, when huge demonstrations and violent confrontations were taking place with the armed police, the American stations adopted the point of view of the 'World Policeman'. Thus ABC's anchor begins: 'Another trouble spot overseas today has made president Reagan very concerned. In South Korea violent protests have now turned to deadly protests: A policeman was killed today, several others injured ...' CBS told its viewers: 'President Reagan said today that he was very concerned about the continuing crisis in South Korea. He reportedly has asked President Chun not to overreact to the demonstrations ...' Finally, NBC reported: 'President Reagan said today that he was very concerned about the violent challenge to the government of South Korean president Chun. The White House indicated that the president has written Chun urging him not to overreact to these protests'.

American political involvement is further intensified on American television. On all three networks Secretary of State Schultz is quoted, on camera, in a similar manner: 'Our advice is to somehow resume the process of dialogue between the government and the opposition in Korea'. A reporter who introduces Schultz expresses support. He says: 'Korea's friends are hoping the two sides can reason together before their split becomes too wide to bridge'. The three networks then go on to construct a common narrative reasoning which enhances the legitimacy of the opposition in South Korea and questions the legitimacy of the South Korean government policies. This is done by various rhetorical strategies and story patterns, that the American viewer in all likelihood would perceive favorably. The CBS reporter, for example, says: 'At the latest wave of protests marched middle-aged, middle-class South Koreans'. The visuals show the diversity of the marchers. We see men and women, young and old, giving the impression that this is indeed an authentic popular protest, not just rebellious students. It is also noted by the reporter that university professors have joined the demonstrators.

NBC creates a sense of particular empathy when it shows protestors pushing back the police. The reporter voice-over provides an interpretation: 'They say they are tired of being pushed and now they are pushing back'. The camera then moves from long and medium shots of crowds to a close-up on an individual inviting personalised compassion from the American viewer. The text goes on: 'Fifty years old, Lin Kee Ra, a mother of five, has never done this before. Lin's family lives in a quiet residential area of Seoul. Her husband is a vice president of a trading company. Lin now supports the students' protest. Her son was tortured while in police custody.'

The story portrays a respectable middle class, suburban, one-of-us protestor and evokes imagery which is very much in accord with the horizons of mainstream America. The woman goes on to say (in English) that she 'can't remain silent any longer'. She then addresses the camera directly with a seductive symmetrical rhythm: 'Wherever there are peaceful demonstrations, I will be there; whenever there are unjust arrests, I will be there too; wherever I am needed, I will be there'. Completing the interpretive closure of the story the reporter adds: 'Others are also stepping forward'.

On all three American networks the demonstrators are presented as people with whom one (an American in particular) can easily identify; on the other hand, the Korean government is faceless, personified by the masked dehumanised police force. Also, it is underscored that the demonstrators want 'democracy, free elections and civil rights' and that the government is not providing any of these. Moreover, 'The political opposition vows not to disrupt the next year's Olympic games', concludes the reporter, with a one-liner popular appeal.

The networks generate essentially the same story inviting some identification with the opposition. The demonstrators are accorded legitimacy via moral implication and cultural affinity. Yet the narratives reflect the US entwinement in South Korean affairs and the American stories close on an optimistic note that the crisis can be resolved once the two sides sit down and talk. One can argue, then, that the three American networks tell very much the same story while the Europeans tell something quite different. Different perspectives breed different television reporting.

The Italian elections

The story of the Italian elections provides a different perspective on our use of the notion of domestication. The story appeared on four days in our materials: Election day, 15 June and the following three days. Election day stories consisted, in ritualistic fashion, of images of party leaders and political celebrities casting their vote, posing for the photographer holding their ballot about to be dropped into the voting box. The following day the stories focused, again in a familiar fashion, on a presentation and discussion of the election results.

While the story appeared on most of the European screens, our materials contain stories from only six services: JTV (Jordanian television), IBA (Israeli Broadcasting Authority – Hebrew Language), Belgian television, ARD and ZDF, the two German national networks, and RTL from Luxembourg. This rather narrow range may be due to the fact that most other services presented only brief 'tell' stories, not worthy of recording. In fact, and significantly, the story does not appear in the BBC's Evening News, and shows up only briefly on ITN's early evening news. It did not appear on ITN's flagship news programme 'News at Ten'. The US networks did not report it either.

Hence the possibility of explaining this rather lopsided and limited appearance of the story in terms of 'domestication'. With the exception of Jordanian television, whose use of the story can be explained in terms of its sheer availability, and Israeli television, whose usage we discuss below, the story appeared primarily on the screens of Italy's 'neighbours'. The notion of 'neighbours' need not be taken to mean purely geographical proximity or contiguity, but also cultural and political closeness. The Italian political spectrum, i.e. the range of the parties contesting the elections, resembles that of other European countries, and the contest between the Communists, the Socialists and the Christian Democrats in Italy echoes electoral contests in some other European societies. Thus, the audience in these countries is already attuned to similar political contests.

Support for this argument comes from a brief story which appeared on ARD on 16 June. After confirming the election results (which by then must have been familiar to the audience) the story adds – with the aid of a map – that 'In South Tyrol the Neo-Fascists gained votes in a landslide manner. In the province of Bozen they gained almost 7 per cent, and in the city of Bozen the Neo-Fascists, who fight against autonomous rights for Germans, gained almost 27 per cent'. Geographically, politically and ethically that brief glimpse at the results in a small province in the northern edge of the country was of special relevance to a German audience.

A couple of reasons may explain the relatively low profile of the story (if indeed we can describe it this way): first, government changes in Italy have been so frequent as to be regarded as a rather common occurrence. Second, the results of this election were not earthshaking. The Communist lost about 3 per cent; the Socialists gained about 3 per cent; the Christian Democrats gained 2 per cent. One result noted was the vote of 2 per cent for the 'Greens', who thus gained some representation in Parliament.

How did the various services report these results? RTBF opened by stating that 'the Italian political landscape has changed'. ZDF, on the other hand, claimed that 'everything seems to have remained the same'. Under these circumstances, judgements that the Communists' loss was a 'big' one (RTL), or that the mood of the Christian Democrats was subdued, because their win was lower than expected (ARD) are clearly in the eye of the beholder. The commentary provided by the various services is quite similar, apparently because not much 'spin', domestic or otherwise, could be put on these results.

A comparison of the stories reveals one intriguing difference between the various services, testing their resolve to resist the temptation of 'tabloiding' the coverage of the elections. Whether the Italian political landscape has changed or not, the 1987 election were 'memorable' for the candidacy of Cicciolina, the Italian 'porn queen', who carried a teddy bear and displayed her bosom at every cameraman's invitation. News editors around Europe had to decide whether or not to use these images (duly provided by EVN) in their stories.

The only two services which did 'succumb' to the temptation were IBA and RTL. In the case of Israeli television, the Italian elections story was carried on both 15 and 16 June. While the stories were rather brief, on both dates they included an account of the results of the elections, alongside a reference to the other theme of the elections stories: Cicciolina. The lead of the 15 June story reports the loss suffered by the 'powerful' Communist party, followed by computer projections of the rest of the results. The story then moves on to say that 'the show was stolen by the porno film star Cicciolina, who ran as a candidate of the Radical Party'. The news reader continues to tell the viewers that 'throughout her campaign Cicciolina exposed her body to the cameras' and the text is accompanied by EVN-supplied pictures of the 'star' casting her vote and baring her breast. Next day's story merely reports the results of the elections (confirming what has been reported the previous day), but again adds that the 'porn film star' won a seat in the Italian Parliament. This time, however, no pictures were provided.

One may ask why the news editors in Israeli television chose to use these pictures while their colleagues in most of the European services avoided showing them. We can only speculate about the answer. It might be that, like other resource-poor broadcasting services with little access to news footage, the Israeli editors are inclined to maximise usage of footage which arrives on the satellite from abroad and is available anyway. Another possible explanation might have to do with the fact that the porn star visited Israel some time before, and gave a couple of live performances before SRO audiences in Tel Aviv. She was thus familiar to the Israeli audience. In that case, familiarity could be assumed to breed keen interest.

RTL's coverage, or maybe un-coverage, of Cicciolina was even more unusual. Not only did they show pictures of Cicciolina 'in action', but the election day story picked up this brief segment of a few seconds, and repeated it seven or eight times in succession. This was very much in accordance with other aspects of RTL's story. The reporter began the story by saying: 'The election site closed at 2.00 this afternoon, but first I would like to invite you to that election site, where the most exciting candidate votes, and where she demonstrated her arguments once again'. The text is replete with double entendres, reinforced by the anchor's brief smirk as he introduced the story. RTL's analysis of the outcome of the election is also done tabloid-fashion. Thus, the discussion of who will head the government coalition, Craxi, the Socialist leader, or Andreotti, the Christian Democrat, begins with: 'two roosters are too many for the henhouse'. When the anchor returns at the end of the story he personalises it saying: 'in light of the continuing problems between

Craxi and Andreotti I am anxious to see how long it will take to form a new government'. But then he returns to the Cicciolina affair, and closes the story as follows:

> This woman, however, can celebrate. Illona Stalla (Cicciolina's real name) displayed her arguments quite freely. The former porno star will represent the Radical leftist party in Parliament. Hopefully, when it comes to making the decision on forming the government, nobody will forget to vote because they will be busy looking at Cicciolina, 'the small fat one', instead of listening carefully.

With the (trivial) exception of the 'Cicciolina affair' the Italian elections story did not offer the richness of imagery and text that characterised the other stories analysed here. Whether this is due to the rather mundane visuals of the election, or to results that augur little political change, this story did not supply much grist to our 'domestication' mill. The broadcasting organizations which did, however, devote time, effort and special correspondents to cover the story may have done so because of the proximity of the event and its potential relevance to their own political systems. Indeed, European stories may not need to be domesticated for European consumption. They are already 'domestic' stories.

The Irish elections

Our final example of how national services use EVN footage is from 17 February 1987 the day in which general elections took place in Ireland. Coverage of this event began before the results were in with some scene-setting stories. We present here several versions: from France, Belgium, England and America.[16] In this case it is the United Kingdom and the Unites States who present a similar perspective while France and Belgium chose a different point of view which is very particular.

Through Anglo-Saxon eyes

Both the BBC and CBS stories focus on Ireland's economic problems and more specifically on the high rate of unemployment among Irish youth. Both correspondents describe attempts by these young jobless to secure a better economic future outside Ireland, primarily in the US. The similarities between the stories are quite remarkable apart from the reporters' accents and occasional phrases such as the reference by the CBS reporter to 'the Irish sport of hurling which looks like hockey, played like baseball on a football field'. There are hardly any differences between the stories. And yet, different collective memories can be traced. Both the British and the American broadcasts express empathy towards the hardships of the Irish youth; both mention the famous potato famine of the nineteenth century, but for the Americans it seems more traumatic. The CBS presentation makes one feel that America is again threatened like back then by a wave of hunger struck immigrants. The BBC report is free from this historic wound.

---

16. We present these pre-election stories, based on the Eurovision feeds, because of their particularly interesting perspectives even though they did not appear as one of the top two stories of the day, based on the use of the Eurovision feeds. It should be noted that the following day, the results of the elections were reported and were highlighted in the EVN transmission.

Through Catholic eyes

The French (TF1) and Belgian (RTBF) versions domesticate the story by focusing the role of Catholicism and of the Catholic church in Irish politics. The story on the Belgian station focuses on the role of the Church. Images of multi-children families and of young mothers pushing baby strollers appear as a backdrop for a discussion of the resistance by the Church to contraception and abortion. The choice of this issue by the correspondent suggests an attempt to present the Irish election story in ways that would resonate among the home viewers who might be similarly preoccupied with the issue of the relationship between church and state.

The French station also focuses on the religious aspect strongly emphasizing that Irish Catholicism is 'different from ours'. The story creates an ambivalence towards the 'innocent' Irish who wish to preserve their religion while paying a heavy price for it: youth unemployment and painful emigration due to the restrictions on birth control. 'Amongst us' (*chez nous*) says the French reporter, 'even hard times do not result in emigration'. The story then implicitly contrasts the Irish and the French positions on limiting family size. Picture and text weave throughout the story to produce a rhetorical contrast between a kind of nostalgic 'authenticity' of the Irish society's preservation of traditional values (rural scenes, an old couple dressed in authentic village clothing, an accordion playing in the background) and images of the young unemployed struggling in a hopeless labour market.

4 Local Viewers in the Global Village

While much of our project on the globalization of television news has dealt with the various mechanisms by which foreign news stories are produced and delivered to audiences around the world, we also considered it important to study the global audience itself. We wanted to begin to answer several questions, including: what interest does the audience have in foreign news; how does it perceive the newsworthiness of different categories of foreign news; and is there in some sense a universal way in which audience members perceive foreign news?

Given the cross-national nature of the project, we hoped to investigate some of these questions in the largest possible number of countries. Budgetary constraints, however, and logistical problems kept us from studying audiences in all the countries represented in our content analyses. This part of the study was therefore limited to five countries: the United Kingdom, France, Germany, Israel and the United States. We included the American networks which hardly rely upon the Eurovision system, since we wanted to examine how Americans perceive non-American (i.e. foreign) news and to compare those perceptions with the ways European viewers deal with non-European news.

Rather than embarking on costly surveys of national audiences we chose to work with rather small, non-representative samples and to try to obtain in-depth and non-traditional information from these respondents.

In the autumn of 1990, we assembled in each of the five countries six groups of people consisting of 9–12 persons per group, for a total of 277 people. At all sites, about half of the participants were women and half were men. Five of the six groups in each country were composed by occupation (school teachers, bank clerks, sales people, factory workers, university professors), while the sixth group consisted of pensioners aged 65 or more with varied previous backgrounds. Thus the socio-demographic characteristics within each group were relatively homogeneous, while there was marked heterogeneity between groups. Participants in each group performed three tasks: (1) pretending to be a foreign news editor (role-playing); (2) completing a structured questionnaire; and (c) discussing their country's version of three foreign news stories which had been broadcast in all the countries some time earlier.

Playing foreign news editor

To learn how television news viewers perceive the newsworthiness of foreign news, we designed a special role-playing task. Each of the respondents in the focus groups was given a set of 18 index cards. On each card we printed the caption of an imaginary news item set in a foreign country. Table 1 lists the 18 items.

Table 1. Captions of news items in role playing task.

1 *International relations and conflicts*

 (a) Peru threatens to attack Bolivia after border incident
 (b) Presidents of India and Pakistan meet for talks
 (c) The kidnapping of a Turkish diplomat in Athens, Greece

2 *Foreign Artistic and cultural events*

 (a) A Dutch masterpiece stolen from a museum in Amsterdam
 (b) A Japanese sculpture garden opens in a town near Tokyo
 (c) The first International Film Festival opens in Peking

3 *Disasters or accidents in foreign countries*

 (a) Two trains crash in Finland killing over 100 people
 (b) A serious earthquake in Columbia leaves 20,000 victims
 (c) An avalanche traps 40 mountain climbers in the Himalayas

4 *Ceremonies and festivals in foreign countries*

 (a) The new king of Burma is crowned in an ancient ceremony
 (b) The annual Sicilian Wine Festival opens
 (c) Australia gives a royal welcome to the Sheik of Dubai

5 *Internal politics of foreign countries*

 (a) Guatemalans go the polls in their presidential elections
 (b) Students clash with police in Addis Ababa, Ethiopia
 (c) Anti-government riots in Tahiti because of rising prices

6 *Scientific or medical developments in foreign countries*

 (a) A new medication for migraine reported successful
 (b) Japanese reveal computer chip with triple speed capacity
 (c) New and cheaper technique developed for diagnosing AIDS

In order to simulate the repertoire of foreign news stories, the set of 18 items were based on six sets of three items each, derived from the major news categories which were commonly found in the EVN transmissions: international relations and conflicts among foreign countries, foreign artistic and cultural events, disasters and accidents in foreign countries, ceremonies and festivals in foreign countries, internal politics of foreign countries, and scientific and medical developments in foreign countries. In order to come up with a final selection of the stories to be presented to the participants, we developed a longer list of possible stories and then chose those stories which appeared to be of a similar level of newsworthiness. While the specific 18 items were made up especially for the study, they were modeled after well-recognised EVN items and could have appeared on a typical daily broadcast. All the items were 'foreign', that is, none of them were purported to have taken place in any of the five countries in which the study was conducted.

An identical set of index cards, carefully shuffled to ensure randomness, was given to each group member. Each participant was asked to imagine that he or she was the foreign news editor at his or her national television station and that the array of 18 items were all the foreign stories which occurred that day around the world and for which video material of broadcast quality was available.

Your task, participants were instructed, is to independently examine the cards and to select 6 items which, as editors, you would select for inclusion in the station's main evening bulletin. Participants were also told that since last minute changes requiring the deletion of news items often occur, they were to rank order the 6 items they chose, from the most newsworthy to the least newsworthy. Thus, if necessary the last item(s) could be dropped from the imaginary newscast. The respondents were not told that the 18 cards were designed as 6 groups of 3 items each. After the respondent indicated his or her selection of the 6 items on a special form, he or she was also asked to explain in her or his own words, in the space provided on the form, *why* each item had been selected. In addition to our desire to know why the respondents selected those particular items, through this procedure we perhaps also encouraged participants to invest some mental effort in thinking about the items and to take the task somewhat more seriously.

There were two main objectives for this task. First and foremost, we wanted to see which items the respondents would actually select, assuming that those selected would be considered relatively more newsworthy. Second, we wanted to know which, if any, of three possible 'strategies' were used by the respondents in selecting the items: (a) choosing one item from each of the 6 categories, thereby providing some balance in the newscast; (b) selecting all items from only two categories, which would clearly imply the dominance of those two categories; or (c) having no clearly discernable approach. In addition, we also wanted to be able to compare the perceptions of the respondents, representing news viewers, and the EBU Contacts' perceptions of their audiences using the questionnaires which the contacts completed (we report this comparison in the final chapter of this monograph).

Summary data for the news editor role-playing task are presented in Table 2. The 18 items are arranged from the highest overall ranking to the lowest overall ranking in the five countries. While there are some differences by country, there is a large degree of similarity among them. In fact, a computation of Kendall's Coefficient of Concordance resulted in a relatively high (W=0.74) coefficient.[1] Moreover, the top two items in the five countries were almost identical as were the bottom rankings, with most of the fluctuations in the middle range of rankings.

---

1. A correlation among n (where n > 2) independent rankings.

Table 2. Rankings of simulated news items by country[*].

	England	France	Germany	Israel	USA	Mean rank[†]
New diagnosis for AIDS	2	2	2	1	1	1.6
20,000 victims in Columbia Quake	1	1	1	2	3	1.6
Japanese computer chip	5	4.5	3.5	5	4	4.4
Medication for migraine	6	3	8.5	5	2	4.9
Train crash – 100 Finish victims	3	6	10	9	5	6.5
Peru threatens to attack Bolivia	9	4.5	3.5	12	8	7.2
Turkish diplomat kidnapped	10	14	5	3	12	8.8
Avalanche traps 40 in Himalayas	7.5	7.5	13	9	8	8.9
Indian & Pakistani presidents meet	4	10.5	17	5	8	8.9
Dutch painting stolen	7.5	10.5	6	11	14	9.6
Ethiopian students clash with police	13	13	7	7	10.5	10.1
Riots in Tahiti	14.5	7.5	12	14	6	10.8
Peking film festival	11	9	11	13	13	11.3
Guatemalan elections	16	12	8.5	9	10.5	11.9
King of Burma crowned	12	17	15	16	15	15.0
Japanese sculpture garden opens	17	15	14	15	16	15.4
Australia welcomes sheik of Dubai	14.5	18	18	17	17.5	17.0
Sicilian wine festival	18	16	16	18	17.5	17.1

[*]Based on number of mentions per item;
[†]Based on the separate rankings of the five countries.

From this point on we shall relate only to the overall ranking which appears in the right-hand column of Table 1. The overall rankings reveal a clear pattern: role-players selected news items according to the major categories, with stories on science-medicine in first place followed by news of accidents and disasters. The specific stories in an overall tie for first place in the five countries were 'a new diagnosis for AIDS' and 'earthquake victims'. The next two most highly ranked items were the 'discovery of a new high-speed computer chip' and a 'new medication for migraine headaches'. In the fifth place was the account of a train crash while in sixth and seventh place were stories on a threat of war on the Peru-Bolivia border and a kidnapped Turkish diplomat. The Himalayan avalanche item was in eighth place and closing out the top half of the list of items is the meeting between the Indian and Pakistani leaders.

The bottom half of the newsworthiness rankings also indicates that news selection was done according to the major news categories. Accordingly, the items in the ceremonies and festivals category appeared in the 15th, 17th and 18th place and the stories involving internal politics were in the 11th, 12th and 14th position. The only slight exception to this clear pattern were the items concerning artistic and cultural events which were ranked overall in the 10th, 13th and 16th spots.

In short, it seems possible that when participants pretended to be television news decision makers, they, knowingly or not, used a strategy of picking two major categories – science and medicine and disasters and accidents – instead of opting for a broader variety of news items and categories.

It will be recalled that the respondents were asked to select a total of six items, which would mean two 'complete' categories if they selected all the items from only two categories. In order to examine how solid were the mentions by category, we computed the mean number of selections that each of the six categories received. The highest ranked category – science and medicine stories – received a total of 509 mentions ;rom the 277 participants for a mean of 1.84 mentions of the possible 3 mentions. The second highest ranked category – disasters and accidents – received a total of 441 mentions for a mean of 1.59, which is still higher than one in two. However, in the remaining four categories there was a steep decline in the number of mentions and subsequent mean scores: for the third category – international relations and conflicts – 287 mentions and a mean of 1.04; for the fourth category – culture and art – 209 mentions and a mean of 0.75; for the fifth category – internal politics – 194 mentions and a mean of 0.70; and finally, for the sixth and last category – ceremonies and festivals – only 62 mentions and a mean of 0.22 mentions. These findings reinforce those based on the rankings and further demonstrate the overwhelming choice of science-medicine and disasters-accidents as the categories of greatest interest among foreign news items.

Questioning the audience

The second task in the audience part of the study was to have the respondents complete a questionnaire (see Appendix C). The questionnaires were completed individually by each respondent within the group setting. It took approximately 30 minutes to complete all the questions.

Interest in news

We began with a series of questions on the respondent's degree of interest in domestic and foreign news. We asked parallel sets of questions about interest in their home country and from abroad. In addition to general interest, we also asked about an array of 10 topics,[2] including: law and order; international conflicts[3]; meetings of leaders;[4] sports; culture and art; disasters and accidents; ceremonies; internal politics;[5] human interest; and science and medicine. For each question four response categories were provided 'Not at all interested',

2. In the role-playing task we presented the participants with items from only six news categories in order to keep the task manageable. In the questionnaire part of the study, however, we felt comfortable asking about the same six categories as well as four additional ones (sports, human interest, law & order, and leaders' visits. Moreover, asking about 'interest' in stories is different from choosing stories in the role-playing task. Among other reasons, the two procedures are different since in role-playing the participants were trying to imitate what they thought journalists did while in the questionnaire they were offering their own preferences.

3. In the case of domestic news these were defined as conflicts between the country of broadcast and other countries whereas in the case of foreign news these were conflicts between differe٦t foreign nations.

4. In the case of domestic news these were visits by foreign leaders in the country of broadcast, and in the case of foreign news these were visits by leaders of two or more nations taking place in a foreign country.

5. In the case of domestic news these were stories about the country of broadcast and in the case of foreign news these were stories of internal politics of foreign countries, such as foreign elections.

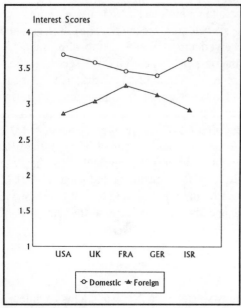

Figure 1. General interest in domestic and foreign news by country.

'Not very interested', Quite interested', and 'Very interested'. Thus the scores could range from 1–4.

Figure 1 shows general, overall interest in domestic and foreign news. As was expected, there was a tendency in all five countries for general interest in domestic news to be greater than general interest in foreign news. However, paired t-tests for each of the countries indicated that only in the case of the United States, the United Kingdom and Israel were the differences significant, whereas in France and Germany the differences were not significant. As for differences among the countries, we computed two separate one-way analyses of variance among the five countries, one for domestic and one for foreign news. Both were not significant, thus the overall levels of interest in domestic news in the five countries were the same, as was the case with foreign news.

We now present Figure 2 with the findings on interest in ten specific topics of domestic

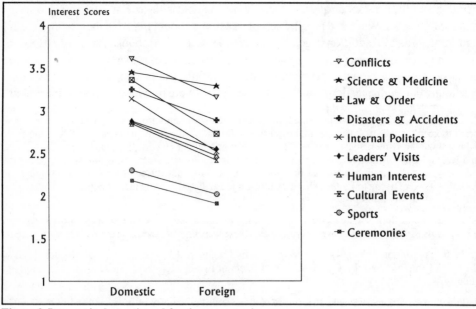

Figure 2. Interest in domestic and foreign news topics.

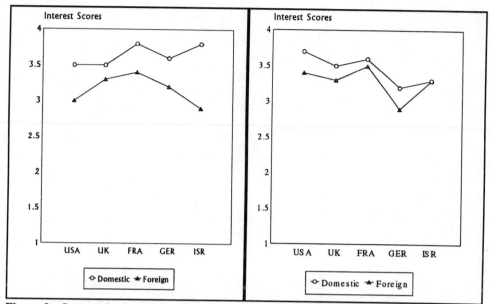

Figure 3a. Interest in domestic and foreign conflict news by country.

Figure 3b. Interest in domestic and foreign science and medicine news by country.

and foreign news. This figure reinforces what we saw in Figure 1, namely that domestic news was perceived as more interesting than foreign news. Moreover, looking at the 10 topic categories – with the focal point on foreign news – we find what appears to be four groups of news topics. Thus news about conflicts between nations and news about science and medicine are of highest interest; this is followed by news of law and order as well as items about disasters and accidents; next came news on internal politics, leaders' visits, human interest stories and cultural events; and in last place we found news about sports and various ceremonies.

The next series of Figures (3a to 3j) detail the differences in interest for each of the news topics between domestic and foreign news across the five countries. These figures are presented in the order corresponding to the overall descending interest levels in Figure 2. While Figure 2, which refers to *general* interest, indicates that there were no overall differences among the five countries, it appears that when dealing with specific topics there were many significant differences among the countries.

As for domestic news, in all news categories except for visits of leaders, the one-way analyses of variance among the countries were highly significant.[6] As for foreign news,

---

6. Post-hoc Scheffé tests yielded the following significant differences among the countries: interest in science & medicine news in the US and France was higher than in Germany; interest in news on disasters & accidents in Germany was lower than all the other countries; interest in news of internal politics in the US was higher than in the UK; interest in human interest news in the US, the UK and Israel were higher than in France and Germany; interest in news of culture & art in France was higher than in the US; interest in sports news in the US was higher than in France; and interest in news of ceremonies in the US, the UK and Israel were higher than in France and Germany.

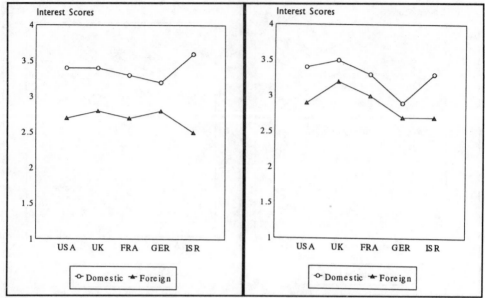

Figure 3c. Interest in domestic and foreign law and order news by country.

Figure 3d. Interest in domestic and foreign disaster and accident news by country.

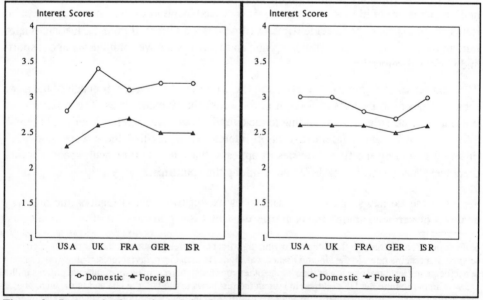

Figure 3e. Interest in domestic and foreign internal political news by country.

Figure 3f. Interest in domestic and foreign leaders' visits news by country.

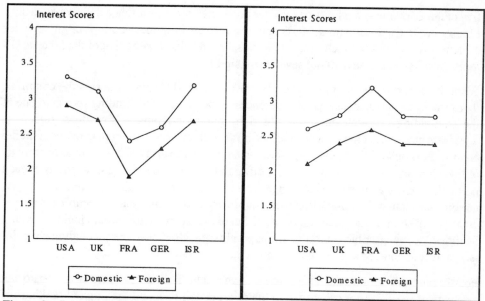

Figure 3g. Interest in domestic and foreign human interest news by country.

Figure 3h. Interest in domestic and foreign cultural news by country.

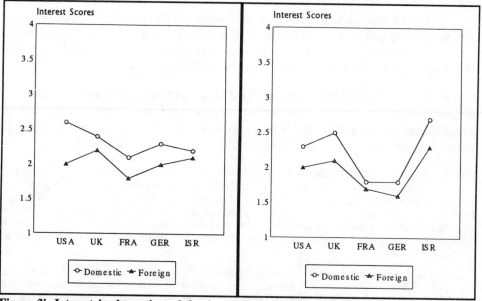

Figure 3i. Interest in domestic and foreign sports news by country.

Figure 3j. Interest in domestic and foreign ceremonial news by country.

five of the 10 one-way analyses of variance conducted were significant and five were not.[7] Finally, we carried out paired t-tests between interest in domestic and foreign news for each news topic and for each of the countries. The results showed that of the 50 tests (10 topics and five countries) all but seven were significant.[8]

What these findings seem to show is that despite overall similarity across the countries, there are indeed some meaningful differences among them. This finding speaks to one of the over-riding research questions posed by our monograph – how does globalised television news affect the viewing audience. We will return to that point in our concluding chapter. Suffice for here to say that, since our study uses an array of countries as exemplars of this process, it seems extraordinarily difficult to attempt detailed explanations of each particular instance of statistically significant difference in audience behaviors across nations. Obviously national differences in history and culture play a significant part in creating differential audience responses. Other explanatory factors would include, but not be limited to, geographic centrality or marginality; national character, including chauvinism; and economic power versus economic dependence.

For the purpose of internal consistency of the data, it is noteworthy to compare the rankings of the six news categories in the role-playing task and the implied rankings of expressed interest in the news topics reported in Figure 2. A rank order correlation between the six relevant news categories of Figure 2 and the role-playing data yields a correlation of $r = 0.89$ which is extremely high and clearly supports the reliability of the audience data.

The main source for foreign news

Next we looked at the consumption of foreign news, asking respondents what was their *major* source of information. They could choose only one source from among radio, television, newspapers, news magazines, and several foreign media sources. Figure 4 presents the data for viewer sources of domestic and foreign news.

As can be seen, television was clearly reported as the major source: in all five countries it was said to be the major channel for foreign events and in four of them also for domestic events. Israel was an exception: where radio was reported to be the major source of domestic news. Moreover, in all five countries, television was considered as more

---

7. Among the topics with significant differences, Scheffé post-hoc tests indicated the following: interest in news of foreign conflicts were higher in the UK and in France than in Israel; interest in foreign science & medicine news in Germany was lower than in all the other countries; interest in news on foreign disasters & accidents was higher in the UK than in Germany and Israel; interest in foreign human interest news was higher in the US, the UK and Israel than in France, and was also higher in the US than in Germany; and finally, interest in news of foreign ceremonies was higher in the UK and Israel than in France and Germany.

8. In the UK the difference in interest between domestic and foreign news on conflict items was not significant; in France the differences for science & medicine as well as for ceremonies were not significant; in Germany the differences between ceremonies and disasters & accidents were not significant; and in Israel the differences in interest between domestic and foreign news for science & medicine and sports were not significant.

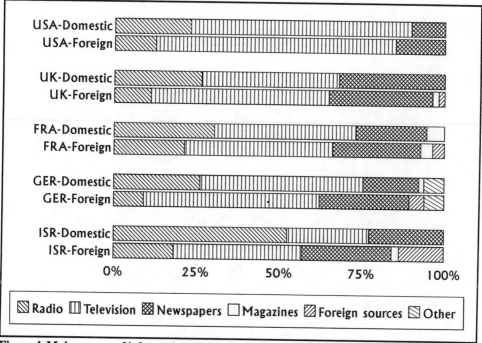

Figure 4. Major source of information about domestic and foreign events by country (in %).

important with regard to foreign news as compared with domestic news.[9] Newspapers – while in overall third place and notwithstanding much variability among the countries – were considered more important regarding foreign news as compared with domestic news, especially in Germany and Israel.

In another set of questions we asked how much attention the respondents give to foreign news when reading, listening and watching news (in newspapers, radio and television, respectively). As Figure 5 indicates, here, too, television appears as a front runner in all countries, except Israel where it is tied with radio. An analysis of variance was done among the five countries for each of the media. It was found that they were all highly significant.[10]

Perceptions of foreign news

We also asked the respondents to indicate how much of their country's main television

---

9. Research has shown that there are some limitations to the ability of the general public to give valid responses to questions about their source of routine news (Robinson and Davis, 1990; Robinson & Levy, 1995). However, there is little doubt that television plays a major, albeit not exclusive, role in the transmission of news, especially of a non-routine sort.

10. Scheffé tests indicated the following: for television, the Americans paid significantly less attention to foreign news than did the Israelis, the French, and the Germans; for radio, the Americans and Germans paid less attention than did the Israelis; and for newspapers, the Americans paid less attention than did the Israelis and the Germans.

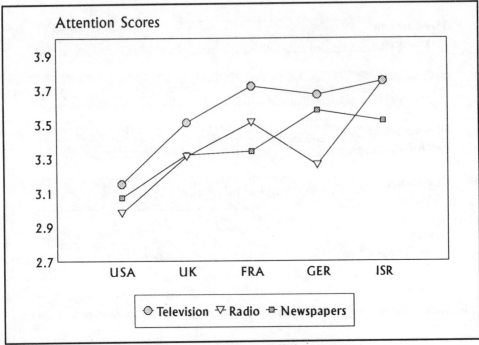

Figure 5. Attention paid to foreign news in different media by country.

news bulletin *is* devoted to foreign news and how much *should* be devoted to foreign news. Figure 6 shows that the respondents in the three European countries indicated a higher level of interest in foreign news, both as they perceive it to be and as they want it to be. The Israeli respondents were somewhat lower on both measures and the American participants were the lowest of the five countries on both measures.

The figure also shows that there was a clear shift in all the countries indicating an interest in increasing the foreign news portion of the newscasts. In all the countries there was a decrease in the 'less than 25 per cent' category from the perceived actual portion of foreign news in the newscasts to the desired portion of the newscast. In the European countries there was a similar decrease in the '25 per cent' category while in Israel and the United States there was an increase in that category. The most dramatic finding, however, is the increase of the '50 per cent' category in all the countries except the United States.

Reinforcing evidence for this trend can be found in the number of people who indicated a preference for more or less foreign news in their country's newscast. Across the five countries, 10.4 per cent wanted less foreign news; 60.8 per cent preferred no change from the existing portion of foreign news; while 28.8 per cent said they would like to see more foreign news in the newscasts.

Understanding foreign news

Using 4-point scales, the respondents were asked how easy or difficult it is for them to

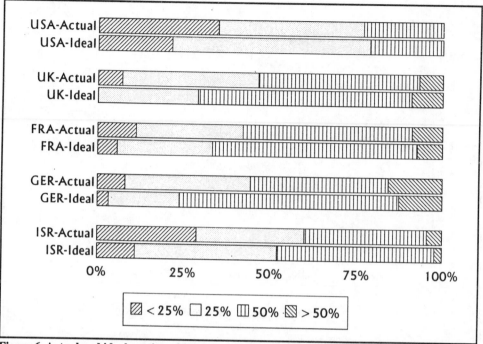

Figure 6. Actual and ideal portion of foreign news in newscast by country.

understand domestic and foreign news stories. Not unexpectedly, as the data in Figure 7 indicate, people find domestic news items less difficult to understand than foreign news stories. This was found to be the case in all the five countries. The overall perceived level of difficulty both for domestic and foreign items was significantly different among the five countries.[11]

Judging journalists

While the previous data dealt with various aspects of the respondents' self-reflexive attitudes, namely, what they think about the news, what they find interesting in it, how much foreign news should be broadcast, etc, the next two sets of questions probe the audience's perceptions of things that could be attributed to journalists and producers of foreign news. Two specific aspects of the news were dealt with in two respective series of questions: the reasons for or the functions of broadcasting foreign news; and the criteria used by journalists in selecting foreign news items to be presented in the newscast.

Based on earlier work by Cohen (1993), the first set of questions related to four possible functions of the news: to tell the audience what is happening; to help the audience form

11. The Scheffé test, however, indicated that only the Israeli respondents were significantly different from the United States, the United Kingdom and France for domestic news and that the Israelis were significantly different from all the other countries regarding foreign news. In other words, the Israeli respondents perceived both categories of news to be easier to understand than in the other countries.

115

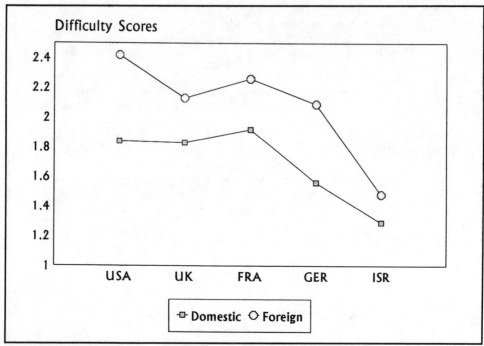

Figure 7. Difficulty of understanding news by country.

its opinion on its country's foreign policy; to show that other countries also have problems; and to enable people in one country to identify with other peoples' problems. The questions were formulated as statements to which the respondents were asked to indicate how strongly they agree or disagree with them. Four alternative responses were given to each statement ranging from 'strongly agree' to 'strongly disagree'.

The data in Figure 8 reveal two main points. First, in all the countries studied, 'knowing what is happening' was consistently considered the most important function of the news. In fact, using paired t-tests, this function was significantly higher than all the others in the five countries. Moreover, there was no significant difference across the countries using a one-way analysis of variance.

Second, identifying with other peoples' problems was considered to be the least important function of broadcasting foreign news. This finding was significant in three of the five countries (the USA, Germany and Israel) using the appropriate paired t-test vis-à-vis the next highest (and intermediate) functions – showing that other have problems and helping to form public policy. Moreover, the significant one-way analysis of variance across the countries was attributed to the large difference between the UK (high) and Israel (low). These two countries also show the most extreme differences between the highest and lowest functions.

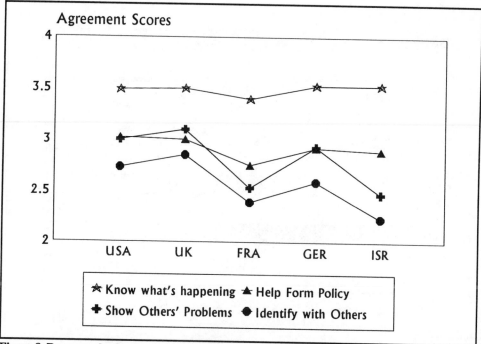

Figure 8. Reasons why foreign news is broadcast by country.

Foreign and domestic news compared

In a final series of questions we asked respondents to compare foreign and domestic news on the prevalence of three specific attributes: bad news, good news, and credible news. The questions were formulated as follows: 'Comparing news about your country and about foreign countries, where is there more ..'. The possible responses were 'Local News', 'Foreign News', 'About the same', and 'Don't know'.

Overall, Figures 9a–c indicate that a non-trivial number of respondents claimed not to be able to determine if a given attribute was more prevalent in domestic or foreign news, or even if it was equally prevalent in both realms. While in Israel the 'don't know' category was utilised by 2–11 per cent (depending upon the attribute), in Germany the range was 10–30 per cent of 'don't know' responses. These respondents were not removed from the analyses, however, since we believe that making such an assertion is a meaningful one.

Moreover, across all four attributes it is clear that there is no unequivocal distinction in how respondents perceive domestic and foreign news. On the contrary, in each of the countries and for all the attributes there were many respondents who said that there was no difference between domestic and foreign news. Thus a range from 26 per cent (in the USA) to 46 per cent in Israel said that the prevalence of good news is about the same in the domestic and foreign realms. For bad news the range was from 22 per cent (in France) to 41 per cent (in the UK); and for credible news the range was 42 per cent (in Israel) to 61 per cent (in the USA).

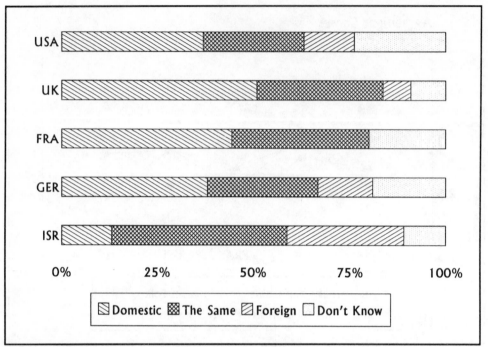

Figure 9a. Where is there more good news by country? (in %).

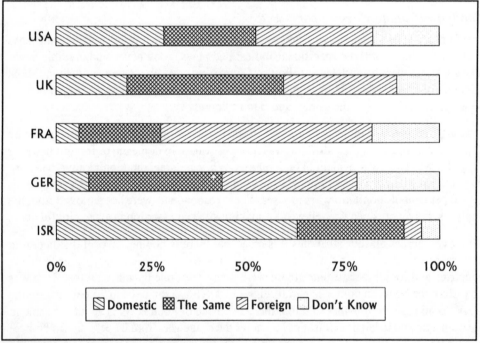

Figure 9b. Where is there more bad news by country? (in %).

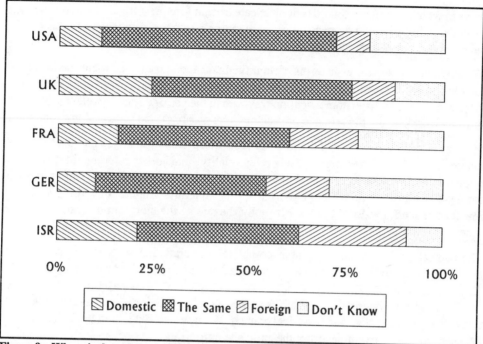

Figure 9c. Where is there more credible news by country? (in %).

And yet, simultaneously looking at Figures 9a and 9b, we see that in all the countries but Israel good news is perceived to be predominant in the domestic realm whereas bad news is perceived to be predominant in the foreign realm. It should be pointed out that in France none of the respondents thought that there was more good news in the foreign realm. In Israel the opposite is the case, and in very dramatic proportions. Finally, Figure 9c shows that there was very little difference in the perceived credibility of domestic and foreign news in the US, France and Germany. In the UK, domestic news was perceived to be somewhat more credible than foreign news whereas the opposite was the case in Israel, namely, foreign news was perceived to be slightly more credible than domestic news.

How different audiences understand foreign news[12]

In addition to filling out a questionnaire and engaging in the editorial role-playing exercise just described, each focus groups was shown tapes of local news broadcasts of three stories – one on political unrest in South Korea; a second portraying the plight of refugees from Kuwait in the period leading up to the Gulf War, and a third reporting a massacre on a train in South Africa. Our purpose here is first to present some additional analysis of the

12. The first draft of this section was written by Professor Anandam P. Kavoori and is based on his unpublished doctoral dissertation, *Globalization, Television News, and Media Audiences: A Comparative Study of American, British, Israeli, German, and French Audiences*. College of Journalism, University of Maryland, 1994.

ways in which national journalists domesticate certain foreign stories. Moreover, we will extend our discussion of domestication from journalists to their audiences, for, as will be seen shortly, viewers too engage in a kind of domestication of foreign news.

We examined news stories in terms of their thematic and narrative elements and we tried to arrive at some conclusions regarding the degree to which they were domesticated in different countries. High domestication was seen in the use of culturally relevant markers or frameworks, while the absence of such markers was regarded as 'low domestication'.

In examining the transcripts of the focus groups' discussions we ranged audience domestication around the categories of 'self referentiality' and 'other referentiality'. By self referentiality, we mean themes and issues in story interpretation that draw from self/local contexts (national, ethnic, religious). Other referentiality implies that the discussion revolved around non-local contexts (usually the site of the story but extendable to any other contexts).

The two categories are not, of course, completely separate and unrelated, as sometimes the focus on the 'other' was an extension (or an opposition) of the 'self' and vice versa. Degrees of domestication across these five countries were thus based on the range of interplay between features of the 'self' and the 'other' and their contextualization in each country's socio-political and historical context. We now present a thumbnail description of these with some examples from the audience transcripts.

Encoding and decoding the news: United Kingdom-style

The British stories all showed high levels of domestication with extensive use of cultural markers (British or 'western'). The Korean unrest story focused on themes of democracy and the Olympics. The refugee story weaved a number of motifs – including those common in representations of the third world: political incompetence, political brutality, suffering. Equally crucial was the regenerative role played by British agents – missionaries, aid agencies and the reporter himself. The British South African story (much like the American story discussed below) focused on Black on Black violence – a frame that drew on historical frames of imperialism and contemporary frames of immigration in the United Kingdom.

South Korean unrest

The Korean story constructed by the BBC story had two dominant themes. One was the possibility of a democratic change, with the students portrayed as its active agents. The second, linked to such change, was the possibility that the site of the 1988 Olympic games (Seoul) might have to be shifted due to the demonstrations.

The anchor introduced that possibility by raising the specter of Korea being on the 'verge of martial law tonight, after the government warned that it would take extraordinary steps to curb the growing student violence'. The two dominant themes came into play as the news reader provided context to the violence. He referred pointedly to the fact that the 'students whose support is growing are demanding democratic election'. The justification for those elections was then set in conflictual terms: 'President Chun says that they will have to wait until after South Korea stages next year's Olympic games. But the protestors say democracy first and Olympics later'.

Having positioned the roles to be played by the two actors in this drama, the anchor points out that 'the United States today joined the Soviet Union in insisting that their athletes won't go (to Seoul) if they might be at risk. And already Los Angles and Berlin have offered to take over the games.' By reiterating the role of the Olympics, the British story framed the theme of democratic change as a possibility – as something to be determined conditionally rather than as a natural process, as the American story discussed below seems to imply. Lexical and syntactic choices used in the British story strongly suggested a sense of active engagement by both sides. The government's position was described using words such as 'warned' 'extraordinary steps' 'insists' 'take all powers, meaning martial law', while the students and the 'revolution' were described with terms such as 'struggle' (twice) and 'demands', and their aims as 'bringing down dictatorship'.

Participants in the British focus groups dealt cursorily with the actual site of the action (Korea, the students, democracy and the Olympics) but offered a strong critique of media practices. They dealt with the issue of democracy by looking at media practices – both Korean and British – and discussed how processes of democratic action were impinged upon by media frames. Here are two examples:

> They (the South Korean media) would have concentrated on the government troops. Their efforts to suppress the disorder, rather than concentrate on the students. You wouldn't have shots of the students ... and all their banners so much. You would have had more detail on the government efforts to suppress or to put down, to put into context, to keep everything firmly shut down rather than to try to heighten their attention.

> (On British media coverage) There was a shot of, um, I don't know whether it was a water cannon or whatever was on there and the actual voice-over said: 'This could threaten the Olympic Games'. So, there hasn't been any attempt to put it in any context, other than it threatens the Olympic Games because that's the news point. I would prefer to know more about the background.

Thus in terms of self referentiality, the audience focused on how the British media function. Discussion revolved around whether the British media collaborated (i.e. like the Korean media) intentionally or unintentionally with the British government, as seen in these comments:

> Oh, they can show things. They can show things in a very pleasant way. They can just show certain aspects of demonstrations and make it appear a lot more violent than it really is.

> During the miner's strike ... it was totally fabricated. The actual charges of the police were reversed and things like that ... So, there are interventions. You can't say the government has no hand at all in that.

Does this imply that the audience had less to say about democracy itself and more about the media? That may be the case in part, but one could argue that a critique of media practices is part of the articulation of democratic concerns, both as an act of reiteration of those ideals and as an act of participation by the audience.

Gulf refugees

The Gulf refugees story framed the refugees as actors in a tragedy of epic proportions – the victims of political conflict; of the brutality of nature; of Third World incompetence and of their own ineptitude. The possibilities of regeneration were offered explicitly through the actions of Western agencies, medical officials, British missionaries and implicitly through the reporter.

The reporter developed one theme of the story – trapped prisoners of fate/politics – by focusing on victims of dehydration and other illnesses. The camera lingered inside the hot tents of the victims and then followed them to medical tents where they were treated. The camera repeatedly focused on doctors pouring water over patients and applying injections. An unusually long closeup of an injection was presented and juxtaposed with a patient moving his head in pain. The reporter punctuated this with descriptions of the victims conditions using terms such as 'collapsed', 'exhaustion' 'suffering', 'racked with fever'. He summed up their chances by focusing on one refugee and saying with a sense of exactitude: 'In these conditions it is touch and go whether he will live'. The doctors, too, the reporter said 'are exhausted, and so are their supplies'.

The story provided context to the situation with the use of a specific British cultural marker – the British chaplain in Jordan. In addition to being British, the reporter added to his status by pointing out that the chaplain was 'once an aide to the Archbishop of Canterbury'. The camera followed him as he walked around the camp.

Given the high degree of domestication in the British story and its dramatic/empathic portrayal of the refugees it was not surprising to find some of those themes reflected in the audience comments, who reiterated textual features in the story and expressed sympathy and compassion:

> I think it's a real human interest story. Bringing in children, women and infants to generate interest and sympathy for the victims of a war situation. Highlighting the desperate plight of these people, the efforts of the relief agencies and the relative difficulty of getting these people back to their own homelands.

> I thought it was very disturbing. That picture of the man suffering from dysentery, having convulsions. I found it very disturbing.

As part of other referentiality, the audience focused on Saddam Hussein. For example:

> I think it's monstrous that one man in this world can have gained so much power that he can literally destroy the lives of all these people and others.

In addition to dealing with Jordan and Saddam Hussein, the discussants paid greater attention to the refugees' countries of origin (India, Pakistan) to which the refugees were trying to return. they were harshly critical of those countries painting a picture of political ineptitude, disinterest and lack of will on the part of those countries. For example:

> They (the refugees) have just been basically disowned by their own countries, you know. Well, disowned is the wrong word. But they've been forgotten by India, Pakistan, Bangladesh because they've got their own problems. They don't want another 70,000 there.

South African violence

The verbal framing of the BBC story on South Africa emphasised the race/violence dimension of the event and the political consequences of the violence. The violence was introduced in dramatic terms. It was described as a 'rampage' caused by 'gangs armed with guns and machetes'. The reporter reinforced this image of uncontrolled violence by describing the event as a 'massacre', the station as a 'battlefield' and the killers as having 'butchered indiscriminately'.

Following comments by onlookers as to what happened, the reporter developed the primary frame – political uncertainly due to racial violence – and said that 'the carnage represented a frightening escalation in a month long war'. The imagery of uncontrolled violence was further developed through the use of the metaphor of flood: 'the conflict is now threatening to engulf the disenfranchised Black community and undermine attempts to negotiate a new democratic society'.

After an interview with Mandela, the reporter returned to this frame (and the metaphor) in his closing statement: 'The most ominous aspect of this indiscriminate slaughter is that after several weeks of bloodshed, South Africa's township war seems to be spilling over into the cities'.

The British audiences negotiated the story by focusing again on issues of media practice. They showed high levels of both self and other referentiality. In fact, much as it was with American audiences, it was difficult to analytically separate the concern with the other from a simultaneous consideration of the self. Given the history of imperialism and contemporary race related conflicts in Britain, the audience's concern with issues of race and racial conflict showed high levels of involvement. It was articulated by presenting a strong critique of apartheid and race relations in South Africa, but doing so through a critique of media presentations:

> They picked on the racial point. I would have taken away the racial conflict. The real point of the whole event was the political conflict which was undermining the attempts by Nelson Mandela to try and establish an end to apartheid. That's the real force.

> What strikes me in watching is that it was totally unnecessary to show all these dead native people. And also, that although Nelson Mandela and the point of view at the end was given an airing, the first few lines of the news story which clearly

said this was a Black on Black conflict, which is what people would think. But I mean, I think this, I mean in the light of things that happened I think there may be another angle to what's happening in these countries. But, you know, all I would say is, that it is sensational to make a news story out of it. They must have showed, must have showed maybe a minute of dead people. I don't see any need to show them.

I think it must build on White paranoia in a country like South Africa. Where they're living in a state of luxury, but that luxury is in a state of siege, perpetual siege. And that is presenting the worst fears to the White mind.

German perspectives on news and viewers

Unlike the British stories discussed above, the German stories we examined showed comparatively low levels of domestication, in that they displayed few culturally relevant markers. In their overall presentation, however, there were marked differences from stories broadcast by the other services. The stories were the least dynamic, slower in pace and showed little of the dramatic-mythological elements of the other stories. The German audiences' discussions of these stories were also not easy to pigeonhole in terms of involvement. There was a marked emphasis on analyzing media presentations. It differed, however, from the British audiences' approach which looked at media practices generally and less to the text. The German audience, on the other hand, focused narrowly, and with a lot of analytical sophistication, on how the news text was constructed.

South Korean unrest

The German story on South Korea shared some features of the British stories (and of the American and Israeli accounts which we will examine shortly), but the German item differed in its near complete emphasis on the Olympics. One domestic marker was evident – that Berlin might hold the Olympic games if the political conditions in Seoul worsened. The visual footage and the students' unrest that dominated the stories in other countries were markedly absent from the German story. The story consisted mostly of a long anchor introduction and commentary. Its framework was evident in the first line of the story, which said baldly, 'the ongoing riots in South Korea may endanger the Olympic games next fall in South Korea's capital, Seoul'.

It then outlined the crises facing the Olympics in great detail. Soviet and American offers of hosting the games were discussed and Senator Kennedy was quoted as saying that the situation is 'a threat to the games, as long as democracy has not been established on a broader basis'. The possibility of Berlin was discussed but only briefly and in somewhat legalistic language ('Hansen, President of Germany's National Athletic Association suggested Berlin as an alternative location in an interview with *Bild*, if the International Olympic Committee would cancel its contract with Seoul').

This report used none of the dramatic, poetic elements that one might expect in a story using cultural markers (one could easily have expected such a story, given the possibility of Berlin as an alternate Olympic site and given the symbolic significance of the last Berlin Olympics – Hitler, Owens, etc).

Overall, the anchor introduction was neutral, standardised and showed a low level of story involvement. When the narrative cut to the reporter the pace of the story changed due to the visual footage of students rioting and the police firing tear gas. However, what stood out was the absence of the application of a democratic frame, so abundant in the American and the British stories. It was presented much like a routine political conflict/violence story. The reporter's frame relied heavily on numbers and official sources ('according to police, 140 people took to the streets in Seoul'; 'As the police headquarters stated, on Thursday 137 protestors were put under arrest').

The visual footage, too, was of a staple variety. These included in chronological order: a crowd of students throwing stones and running; an overhead pan of students pushing against a police picket line; police pushing against the students with their shields while the students push and fight their way against the policemen; a ground level pan of students running pell-mell, covering their faces as the smoke from the tear gas scatters about; students fighting with policemen and with each other; shots of bystanders as they cover their noses with handkerchiefs; students protesting, pumping fists and marching in a demonstration.

These images, while located in Korea, were characteristic of riots and political demonstrations across the world. The preponderance of such staple images could imply a relatively low level of story involvement, despite the dramatic quality of some of the visuals.

German audiences showed an acute awareness of story form and genre. They discussed in great detail the theme of the Olympics and how it played into a story on democracy and political conflict. Awareness of the Korean 'other' was focused on but not to the same extent as the British, or as we shall see, the American audiences did. Rather, it was replaced by a discussion of democratic struggles generally, with reference to a variety of countries – China, Japan, South Africa and Israel.

Further, the discourse of democracy evident in the Anglo-American accounts received little elaboration here. Instead, the focus was on the violence in South Korea which was seen as typifying violence in the Third World. One example:

> Well, I wanted to say the following: what I noticed especially was the incredible number of people who clashed there. We do not have this in Europe: this density of policemen and demonstrators, and this brutality with which they hit each other is really something... for us Europeans. I have a close neighbour who was in Japan who says that the demonstrations there are pretty tough. In comparison to this, our demonstrations on the Kurfuerstendamm are child's play.

Examples of self referentiality were present in the German audiences' recall of similar incidents in Germany, especially the riots at the nuclear power plant at Brockdorf; riots in the German cities of Kreuzberg and Wackersdorf; demonstrations in the former East Germany and demonstrations by Palestinians in Israel.

Gulf refugees

The story of the Gulf refugees on ZDF was similar in many ways to the Korean story in its low level of involvement. It differed from the other refugee stories in its visuals. The differences were so large that it seemed as if they were shot at two entirely different camps. We detail the visual progression of the story as illustrative of its general orientation. After the anchor introduction, the visuals began with an overhead pan of refugees walking about quietly and talking amiably to each other in the desert camp. The camp in turn looked clean; no wind was blowing or dust clogging up the air. Next came a quick close up of garbage and waste of the desert camp, followed by pictures of two men taking a bath from a bucket of water.

What followed next were elaborate images on the theme of order and quiet. Men stood in line, chatting and looking at the camera as they waited for water to be distributed. A man was then seen as he carried a box full of water bottles. He stopped to say a few words and smiled at the camera and then walked off to his tent. The reporter chatted with another man who held a bottle of water and discussed its quality. The camera then switched to a scene inside the medical tent where doctors were treating patients.

Unlike the other stories, no patients were stretched on the ground. One was having his eyes and throat examined. Another lay on a bed while a doctor attended to him. The camera again switched to the outside where men stood around a truck, talking and sipping water. The next cut was a still shot of a can of corned beef with 'Not for sale, Gift of the European Economic Community' stamped on it. The reporter talked with a refugee holding the can. The story ended with a long shot of Bangladeshis sitting in their tent eating and talking.

As the visuals clearly demonstrate, the thematic structure of this story was very different from that of the American, Israeli and British stories. It lacked drama, action and conflict. The verbal commentary complemented the pictures in its reliance on numbers, official sources and a relative absence of stylistic features. This was evident both in the story's lead and close. The lead began with the anchor pointing out that:

> In Jordan more than 100 thousand people are still waiting for their return trip home. This was announced by the UN emergency aid agency. Most of the refugees come from Asian countries and are without any means of support.

The reporter's closing line was similarly bland and reiterated that, 'supposedly there are still up to 2 million foreign workers waiting for their return trip to Jordan'. The bulk of the narrative developed the story of the refugees not as a tragedy or a disaster but rather as one of suffering caused by shortages. It said that the 'living conditions are getting unbearable ... they have to endure this situation for three weeks or longer, until they can continue their trips home'. The situation in the camp, said the reporter, had become tense because of the heat, shortage of water, lack of medical facilities and lack of food.

While the other nations' stories often had shown near anarchy, the German story's verbal framing painted a picture of struggle. The visual narrative displayed a sense of order (perhaps evoking stereotypical expectations of German culture). The only explicit cultural marker that surfaced in the story was the image of the food can donated by the European community, which the reporter said was being sold by 'a clever tradesman trying to make a profit from this predicament'.

The German audience's concerns with issues of the self were manifested in their discussion of how the plight of the refugees recalled similar experiences faced by East Germans in the waning days of that country. But a comparison was also drawn between the refugee camps and the concentration camps of Nazi Germany, followed by a reference to Palestinian camps in Israel.

Each of these themes was discussed and compared with the situation facing the refugees in the Gulf. In this sense references of the 'other' were mediated through a consideration of the self. The shortages of food, water and other necessities were compared with those faced by East German refugees. The most striking comparison, however, was that with concentration camps in Nazi Germany. One participant argued that the presence of the Gulf refugees in the camp was, in a sense, 'voluntary' while the Jews in Nazi Germany had no choice. Other participants went into a detailed discussion comparing refugee camps with work camps and concentration camps. For example:

> Concentration camps and refugee camps have something in common. Somehow the effect is somewhat similar. In both cases people have to live under the worst conditions and maybe they'll even die from it because they cannot survive under such conditions. But the concentration camps were the final station for the people and these refugee camps are supposed to be a kind of stepping stone. There should be hope.

Underlying the focus on concentration camps were crucial themes of German post-war discourse, such as Germany's Nazi past and the conflict between those who lived in Nazi Germany and their children. One participant put this very explicitly:

> In fact I see here something very personal. There was this film, *Holocaust,* and after they saw it, my children – I have four teenage boys – reproached me terribly. They said: well you lived around then, why didn't you do anything. I think it is important that the young see things like this and that simply nobody can do anything about it. I think that's right because the young see these reports and have a slightly different opinion about it. They say – well, a personal involvement won't change anything around here. That's why I think it's so important.

South African violence

The level of involvement in the South African story, broadcast by ZDF, was difficult to judge because the words and pictures were at odds with each other. While there were no culturally specific markers, the use of dramatic verbal framing may have oriented the story

127

in ideologically relevant ways (much like the British and American stories). The story's visuals, however, were neutral, dramatically featureless and emotionally flat.

The paradox lay in contrasts such as a long pan of a metro train as it pulled into an empty station in broad daylight. A big board displays the station's name – 'Denver'. It is a very uneventful and commonplace shot (very different from the American and British stories). In contrast, the reporter's lexical and syntactical choices are about 'a bloody attack', 'bloodiest massacres' '(the station) seemed like a morgue ... fear spreads throughout South Africa'. The visuals in the rest of the story were staple images of people being taken to hospital; medical personnel helping wounded people; ambulances driving into hospitals and wounded people taken on stretchers. The verbal frame meanwhile characterised the events as a 'senseless blood bath':

> Unidentified men attacked travellers... with rifles, knives and axes, the attackers butchered whoever came near them without saying a word, without regard for women and children.

The visual narrative then switched from the hospital to the a press conference with reporters bustling around waiting for ANC leader Mandela. The camera followed Mandela as he came in, sat down and made a long statement. It was a generic press conference sequence with little drama or stylistic features. The visual narrative ended with the camera focusing on a poster over Mandela's head, with the words 'there shall be peace and friendship' over the painting of a Black women surrounded by flowers and a white dove.

The reporter then recounted Mandela's statement, and footage was shown of Mandela comparing the violence to the Renamo movement's activities in Mozambique (a South African supported insurgency aimed at toppling the Marxist government). Mandela's indictment of a hidden hand offered an explicit framing of the violence, and it further complicated the overall orientation of this story, by shifting it away from themes of Black violence or even of political violence to themes critical of apartheid.

The German audiences' discussion of the South African story showed very low levels of self and other referentiality. The discussants directed their comments to the story and its dominant features. There was considerable comment about the story's verbal and visual structure and the audience quickly critiqued the lack of fit between the visual and verbal framings of the story. The audiences' capacity to key into those differences did not hide what was otherwise a fairly straightforward reading of the event – the state of race relations, criticisms of apartheid and an affirmation of Mandela's status. They also critiqued media representations of the conflict in South Africa that left viewers at a loss as to the parties involved. For example:

> I'd say I feel a kind of confusion because the news we had earlier from South Africa always talked about Whites against Blacks, and now we hear all of a sudden about Blacks against Blacks. So you lose your idea of who is the enemy, who actually is the bad guy. They are not even real Black groups that are making these attacks, but rather something like terrorists.

A more common refrain was a critique of apartheid. The example below illustrates that theme and Mandela's claim about those behind the violence:

> Until now the word was spread that these are tribal conflicts between ancient tribes of Blacks in South Africa. Mandela supposes now that there is a wire puller around who is fomenting these conflicts independently and with no regard to any tribal frontiers, in order to create unrest, rebellion, and the impossibility of ruling the country ... this is just an excuse in order to be able to reinstate the old repressive conditions as they were common in South Africa since the Whites had the power.

Telling stories in France

The three French stories examined were similar to the German stories in their low level of involvement. The French audience, however, showed generally high levels of self referentiality. In addition, what marked the French audience's response was a critical engagement with the story, that combined media analysis with issues that related directly to French society and experience.

South Korean unrest

The Korean story from French television story focused neither on democracy or the Olympics, but rather on the student violence – a frame of reference easily accessible to French audiences, given the collective memory of students demonstrations in the sixties as well as more recent strikes. However, the violence was framed largely as emanating *from* the students, rather than on them. The story used dramatic visuals that conveyed a sense of immediacy and progression. This was especially evident in the long shot/close shot sequence which was used repeatedly. The story began with a long shot of students rioting and throwing stones, followed by a close up of students protesting and throwing clothes and police equipment into a pile of burning rubble. The reporter framed the event with a powerful lead: 'A policeman was crushed by a bus driven by a protestor'. He then pointed out to the viewers a detail that they may have missed out: 'look closely at this policeman shown in blue, retreating in front of the demonstrators'.

The visuals in the rest of the story showed a confrontation between an armed car spewing tear gas shells and students who attacked it. The students were seen running around the vehicle hitting it with rods but eventually having to retreat. The verbal framing too was dramatic and spoke of the 'sea of tears' and 'the strip of gas fumes' caused by tear gas shells, and the attempts by people to protect themselves by wearing 'diving masks and plastic bags'.

While focusing a good deal on media presentations, the French audience remained essentially within the parameters of the narrative elements of the story. They debated the issue of student riots in some detail and in almost every case the discussion was revealed concerns that showed high self referentiality. The audience initially identified two themes that dominated the conversation – one was the student riots in France in May 1968 and the second defined the events in Korea as evidence of 'anti-riot repression' (with students being repressed).

The student riots in Paris in 1968 were discussed, with different audience members debating their significance; where they were when it happened; media coverage of the event; how the Korea story reminded them of the past ('There are some nostalgias', said one participant. Another said: 'We immediately think about May 1968. It's eye-catching news... It recalls feelings').

The theme of student riots and repression straddled both other and self referentiality. One issue in the debate arose from the story's framing of the students as agents of violence rather than just victims of repression. Some participants compared the riots in Korea with those of Paris and felt that the magnitude of the violence implied that a good deal was at stake (e.g. 'such serious riots with such young people – the picture says something'). Others felt that because of their historical experience the French were predisposed towards supporting students and their efforts to bring about change:

> As to the report here, what struck me, well, usually when a riot and a repression are broadcast, we always tend spontaneously to feel sympathy with the rioters... that is to say, the police force which will beat up those poor youngsters is a nasty one.

Other participants pointed out that the student rioters were agents of violence. Their comments were based on references in the story that the rioters had bought arms in the black market. The audience singled out this point in discussing issues of riot repression. Two examples:

> The commentary said precisely that all sorts of arms were bartered on the black market. We had the feeling that the commentary was trying to achieve balance in order to show that after all, these rioters were not angels.

> It's about showing riots in which nobody wins, since at the start we saw a squad of a hundred policemen being beaten by students, then there are gas masks on the black market, there are people who take advantage, it seems that they are bad. They are all bad, they are really unworthy people, we don't even know why they are fighting. On the whole we, in France, are really protected; they are savage people there.

The last part of this respondent's comment is indicative of another theme of other referentiality. Participants located violence in a cultural context pertaining to the 'other' that seemed to indicate a certain imperative to be violent. This was evident in general statements (such as 'they are bad on all sides, they fight one another') as well as comparisons with similar conflicts in Japan, ('there are frequently very violent demonstrations in Japan. The demonstrations in Tokyo are very similar. From the commentary we can assume it's identical; it could also be violent manifestations in Tokyo'), China and the Far East generally ('I would say it's a kind of Asiatic violence, it's usually more violent than when they show us a demonstration in Europe. We see very often very violent demonstrations in Korea, in Japan, in Philippines, we cannot say it's something typical of Korea').

Gulf refugees

Thematically, the French story on the refugees from the Gulf presented a combination of elements that emphasised both political ineptitude and human suffering. The focus on human suffering was not presented either in terms of total anarchy (as in the British or American stories) or in terms of order (as in the German story) but rather a combination of the two. The visuals offered telling evidence of the balance of these two motifs. Emphasis on disorder appeared at the beginning of the story.

The correspondent's report began with a pan of a jeep travelling a dusty road with crowds of refugees lined up on both sides. The refugees sat on their belongings, others moved or ran around in confusion. The anchor introduced the story as one where the refugee 'situation is serious and getting more and more serious'. The reporter then described the refugees as 'packed in and abandoned .... they have fled Kuwait ... all need food, shelter and clothing'.

Having thus established a frame of human suffering and disorder, the story did not develop it further, as in the British and American stories, but rather proceeded to use general footage that was featureless and not overly dramatic. This included visuals showing children playing; men walking around with jerry cans; doctors attending to a patient; general camp shots with trucks and water tankers; people walking about and talking.

The second theme was that of political ineptitude. Those accused of political ineptitude were the countries immediately responsible (e.g. Jordan), but the thrust of the criticism was aimed at the refugees' countries of origin – Pakistan, India and Sri Lanka. The report developed this theme in both explicit and implicit ways. It was present explicitly in the reporter's syntactical choices, when he described their situation as 'without shelter, without support. Their respective countries will not volunteer political and economic support.' Late in the story the political ineptitude of these countries is contrasted with the continued arrival of goods from international (Western) agencies. A picture of boxes stacked up with the 'UNICEF' insignia emphasises the reporter's comment.

The French audience negotiation of the story showed high levels of self referentiality. The dominant themes in their discussion were strikingly similar to those of the British audience groups, which focused on the efforts by the Western countries to alleviate the chronic problems of the Third World. The discussants focussed on both the issue of human suffering and that of the Western response. In addition the French audience also inter-twined issues of immigration from the Third World into their response to the story, as seen in the examples below:

> It reaches the general topic of discarded people, like the boat people, and all the starving people in Africa, who wish to go to France or to any other wealthy country and the question here is, what are we going to do with all those starving people, can we all welcome them at home? Then what comes out, either those people will

die on the spot, or they will be welcome somewhere. Their country, too, is starving. Shall we then welcome some or will France and all the other countries close their doors?

I am more concerned by what happens in France. We can't ignore what happens abroad, but we've got our own problems to resolve. We've spent so much money, in vain. It's right, we made so much effort for foreign countries' sake that in the end we've injured ourselves. We must add that France is financially unable to provide help to our new poor people as well as the poor people here. We must make a choice.

South African violence

The low level of involvement by French viewers in the South African story was reflected in both the absence of cultural markers and the lack of dramatic footage. The footage fitted the thematic frame of the story as a violent act (but *not* Black on Black violence) to which was attached a political explanation, provided by Nelson Mandela. The first theme of the story (a violent act) was developed in a fairly straightforward manner. It used footage from the incident, supplemented by file footage of an ordinary train journey to and from Johannesburg, showing people hanging onto the train, men standing in the door, people playing an imaginary drum on the side of the coach. The theme of violence was portrayed with relatively staple pictures of the wounded being attended to or carried off on stretchers into helicopters, and being wheeled into emergency rooms and operating tables.

The political frame was provided by Nelson Mandela who said that the government must, in some sense, bear responsibility for the violence. The anchor began the story with a shot of Mandela smiling; a map of South Africa followed, showing the location of Johannesburg. Mandela's press conference on the event formed a major part of the story's interpretation. In addition to footage of the conference, the reporter described Mandela's statement as having 'caused a stir' and further elaborated by locating Mandela as the primary agent of change in South Africa.

The audience's discussion was keyed to the political frame provided by the story. The discussants talked extensively about Mandela's past, his release, his claims about who was responsible for the violence, and the prospects he held for South Africa:

> In the case of South Africa, the whole world thought during the release of Nelson Mandela that once he was released, then the whole world would be nice and good, and everything would work out. And then we found that after he was released he met the representatives of all the world countries and nothing worked out, and the tribal fights continued.

Further discussion of the theme of race relations in South Africa triggered comments similar to those made by audience members in other countries – that by portraying Black on Black conflict, the story 'demonstrated that once a country in Black Africa achieved its independence, it was unable to govern itself'. But criticism was also directed at the media for the use of violence as a frame without providing enough context. As one participant said:

> If a Martian were on earth watching this report, he wouldn't understand.... Why did the Zulus or the Black people in Soweto or anywhere else kill one another with axes? This question is not answered.

Stories and audiences from the United States

The American stories all used extensive cultural markers. The South Korean story was framed on American television as a story of political change and movement towards democracy; the Gulf refugees story included staples of foreign news coverage (chaos, disasters) in addition to demonstrating continuities with other dominant American cultural themes (freedom, democracy); the South African story was similarly framed in terms of Black on Black violence, echoing a persistent contemporary concern of American society and politics.

The American audience zeroed in on these concerns. Members of the focus groups showed high levels of self referentiality for all the stories and discussed them in terms that related to the dominant themes of the story. A high level of self referentiality may be regarded as an American cultural orientation, inasmuch as it reflects an (almost stereotypical) tendency in American culture toward concern and preoccupation with the self.

South Korea unrest

In the story about the political unrest in Korea the themes that were repeatedly echoed were those of democracy and freedom, and thus showed some similarity to the British coverage considered above. Images of students clashing with armed police could be seen as evocative of similar incidents in American society during the height of the Vietnam war. Unlike the British story which mentioned 'student violence', the US coverage portrayed the Korean students as positive agents of much-needed political change, their actions contextualised as democratic revolution; the Korean government, on the other hand, was seen as an inert defender of dictatorship.

Themes of the cold war and democracy were also present throughout the stories. The issues were also contextualised in terms of political change in Eastern Europe and the violence against student protestors at Tienamen square.

Jim Laurie's report for ABC News emphasised the positive nature of the students protest with the assertion that '*even* the state-controlled Korean news agency *admitted* that 80,000 students took part in anti-government rallies nationwide'. The implication was clear: the political strife was of such a magnitude that even the official news agency – presumably given to distorting the truth – had to concede the sheer scope of the protest. The story also focused on two scene setting events – the student hold-out at a church and then a candle-light demonstration. The 'impressive candlelight rally attracting some 10,000 people', Laurie said, constituted a 'growing movement for greater democracy in Korea'. The story's visual elements emphasised its dominant themes. The police in their riot gear, wearing masks reminiscent of assorted characters in *Star Wars*, were easily identifiable as villains. These masks, which rendered the policemen faceless, were contrasted to the surge of students as they tried to break through police lines, pushing their bodies against the armor of the police. Visual contrast also played a role in the candlelight demonstration where the obvious peace and serenity of the demonstrators holding candles in the dark was contrasted with the armour and power of the police. These images clearly presented the students as an individualised and personalised force facing a dehumanised, impersonal police force.

The participants in our focus group saw the story as political drama and related it to the theme of a 'struggle for democracy', attributing positive motives to the students and negative ones to the government. 'Democracy', said a participant, 'the poor Koreans have been trying to get it. They've been thwarted.' 'The democratic process', said another participant 'is having difficulty getting established in South Korea'. The students' struggle was also contextualised in terms of the political changes in Eastern Europe and as part of a historical movement towards democracy. 'All through the ages', said one discussant, 'people have been willing to put themselves at risk for what they believe in and for what they want. History has always shown that when we get tired of something you have some type of revolution, that in itself is history.' A second participant said, 'it was the same in Tienamen square. We can go back all the way to the Boston tea party. People are constantly looking for a change.'

What about the agents involved in this revolution? The students were characterised in heroic terms, battling a heartless state. 'Students were the catalyst', said one participant. 'Everybody else was tired but the younger people had the guts to rise up', said another. 'They are the ones who get fed up the quickest and they start movements which are then picked up by other people.' Moreover, in spite of the violent action by students, the movement was characterised as peaceful. 'It was a peaceful march, it was pretty, it was like they were not going to give up', said a participant. There was a great deal of emphasis on the visual quality of the candlelight procession and the 'peace' it exuded. It was repeatedly pointed out as an example of the intentions of the revolution and as an attribute of those involved in it. The presence of nuns among the protesters was pointed out by the discussants as added evidence of the peaceful nature of the protest.

By contrast, the government was framed negatively. This was especially evident in the differential evaluation of violence in the story. 'The government over there seems to be against the democratic society', said one participant. Another said, 'the government came down and they were willing to do anything to stop those people from getting across what they wanted to get across. They were ready to use violence right in there rather than talk. An armed force means that they're ready to do that rather than listen or negotiate.' A third participant compared the Korean situation to that in Kent State University. In both, she said, there 'seemed like an excessive amount of force was used'. At the same time there was either no mention of the violence by the students or there was implicit approval of it, by virtue of it being part of a 'revolution'. One participant clarified this further. Referring to a student attacking the riot police kung-fu style he said: 'I guess he really believed in what he was protesting... they had him blocked off, so you know he had to use force on them, just like they were using force on him.' A second participant said, 'I was impressed by the youngsters who were doing the kicking and all that. Really fighting, literally fighting for their rights'.

Gulf refugees

In the Gulf story, domestication took place through a focus on Mr. Yakoob, an Indian refugee endowed by the reporter with American virtues. The story of Mr. Yakoob is not one of an average man. He is described as a man of good means (he owned 'cosmetic stores, a construction company') and of hard work. He is also portrayed as a successful self-made man, a quintessentially American entrepreneur. His self made-ness is implicitly contrasted with the grasping and rapacious nature of Saddam Hussein's acts, who bears the responsibility for Mr. Yakoob's plight. At the conclusion, as the reporter Ed Rabel, hands the story back to anchor Tom Brokaw, the latter thanks him for 'that tragic story'.

Members of our audience readily identified the story as an example of the general chaos that exists in the outside world. The story was most commonly seen as an example of a 'violent world ... just sad, just pitiful – what it has come to'. The condition of the refugees was seen as another example of generalised suffering in the world ('it is happening everywhere. People suffering') and specific to some parts of the world ('in Africa, in South Africa, the starving over there, Ethiopia – all those countries ... the refugees are suffering in all those ways – shelter, food, water'; 'the situation in Uganda with Idi Amin'; 'starvation in Africa, certain parts of South America, Mexico City and Mexico').

The story's images of chaos and imminent disaster, so emblematic of the portrayal of the Third World on American television, were contrasted by our viewers with the stability and order in their own country. There was a mix of empathy with the victims and gratitude that it did not happen in America. One comment typified responses elsewhere:

> I was thinking about oppression. I was just thinking how depressing it was and how lucky the Americans are to have everything like they have got. We can't take what we have for granted. I mean we have never been in the situation where we had to go to a different country and live in a desert under a tent or anything. So, I feel for them but I really cannot say that I understand what they are going through.

In addition to identifying the story as symptomatic of the chaos in other parts of the world, the audience also discussed what had not been done to help the refugees. They criticised the failure of other countries to rescue their citizens ('Why can't they just get some planes to take them. It's irresponsible that they are still there') and praised their own government's efforts to rescue its own citizens ('we did the best we could to get our people on airplanes and back to the United States').

Finally, the audience saw Saddam Hussein as responsible for the plight of the refugees. He was described as 'greedy', a 'second Hitler', who 'invaded a small territory because he was after black gold'. His actions were compared to 'World War II when Hitler invaded some of the countries with Jews and it was the same situation with Stalin and Lenin'.

South African violence

Broadcast by ABC News, this story was one in a series of similar stories reporting violent incidents in South Africa. Like other stories in this vein it was short, heavily dependent on the visual material and verbally framed in oppositional terms. The story's power lay in its visuals. In all but one of the frames it displayed pictures of the dead and dying. Scattered in stark poses of death, the victims, all Black men and women, lay in pools of blood. Harsh police lights and the hard grey floor emphasised the horror of the event: the inside of a blood spattered subway car; the heart wrenching sight of a woman's shoe and handbag lying in a corner, with the woman herself, huddled in death. On the platform, the rush and noise of ambulances and the revolving lights of police cars punctuated the darkness of the night beyond the station. The camera focused and lingered on each body, zooming in to show details of bloody faces, shot up bodies and agonised survivors. The natural sound – an eerie silence punctuated with the whine of police sirens – was only interrupted by the comments of one bystander and one relief official. Both spoke with the platform scene framed behind them. Visually, the narrative did not move outside the violence on the platform and the pictures of the dead. Nelson Mandela made a brief appearance for a few seconds and then was replaced with the picture of the platform.

Perhaps not surprisingly, the audience's focus on the violence in South Africa and its critique of apartheid was inspired by an evaluation and discussion of race relations in America. Links to the theme of Black-on-Black violence provided the anchors for domesticating the story. In this case, domestication took place almost simultaneously at the level of the self and the other. Black on black violence was linked through a critique of media practice to issues of African- American consciousness and those of South African resistance.

The participants commented that 'the major thing was death ... they showed almost every body they could show', with the result that almost 'every piece of film had a body in it'. This was followed by of the story's implications. 'We all know that what is going on over there is purely political', said one respondent. 'What comes out of there definitely is controlled by the [South African] government. When the government kills students, you don't see that kind of bloodshed. They like the kind of story we just saw'.

In addition to criticizing the media for presenting images that were regarded as favouring the South African government's view, the participants tried to provide a historical and empirical context for the killings. They criticised the report for not detailing the 'differences between the ANC and the Zulus. They did not show why they are different, why they are opposing each other or why it had come to this point of violence'. The story, they said, just presented a 'group of crazy Black guys with guns', without 'showing any reason for the violence'. There was 'little background about why this is, why it had to happen'. To the participants, the reasons 'why it had to happen' lay in the history of race relations and in the South African government's actions. The killings emanated from 'oppression and the search for freedom', the response of a 'people in bondage ... it's so bad they don't know if there is anybody to fight. So they just fight anybody, anything. They are at their wits end. The solution is not in sight, so take it out on the next door neighbour.' The government, it was felt, was 'not doing a big deal to help out', and in fact was 'taking a stand by letting these people fight it out [and] just kill each other off'.

While themes common to dominant American cultural discourse (freedom, democracy) were explicit in the Korean and the Gulf refugee stories, they were subordinated in the South African story. However, issues of media portrayals, race relations and the struggle for civil rights are closely linked in the American mind with those of freedom and democracy. Taken in its entirety, the audiences domestication had a recursive quality, indicating a discourse bound by a set of narrowly defined public values (e.g. democracy) that are continually displayed.

Israeli domestication of the news

The Israeli stories on South Korea and South Africa had relatively few cultural markers while the story on the Gulf refugees showed high levels of domestication. Overall, the Israeli audience showed high levels of self referentiality and relatively low levels of other referentiality. What stood out was the limited set of referents that were continually re-deployed within the dimension of self referentiality. These dealt with issues of internal conflicts and historical referents – especially the Holocaust – and a critique of foreign media coverage of Israel.

South Korean unrest

The Israeli story on South Korea began with an anchor identifying its foreign origin ('in world news') and said that it was about '200 students who had barricaded themselves in the Catholic Church in Seoul'. There was a straightforward and bald treatment of the subject matter and its protagonists. According to the story the students had 'acceded to the request of the authorities and stopped their protest strike'. The authorities in turn had 'promised that nothing would happen to them'. The anchor introduction then changed to a voice over as footage from the student protests was shown.

The first cut was of the crowd running through a street and towards the camera, which then followed the crowd, panning across the field of vision until their backs were to the camera. The second cut repeated the process with the policemen running after the protestors. This time the camera pan ended with the policemen stopping at the head of the street where the protestors had gone. In the third cut, the camera zoomed in on the protestors, who were shown running helter-skelter, pushing each other, skirting around cars that had been abandoned on the road and trying to escape from the tear gas fired by the police. The policemen, meanwhile, were shown in the foreground, dressed in black with gas masks and wielding large riot shields and batons. The fourth cut moved the narrative to a different locale – a sit-in demonstration with students waving two large flags and a church silhouetted in the background.

The voice-over contextualised the visuals by pointing out that 'thousands of students supporting the strikers cheered the protestors when they walked out of the building to the buses in the nearby street'. Further context was provided by the commentary that the 'students have demanded that President Chun Du Hwan call for free elections and resign'. Altogether, this was a relatively short generic, tell story, with no specific Israeli markers. It was fairly characteristic of the presentation of much 'foreign' news on Israeli television, judged to be on the very margins of public interest. Perhaps paradoxically, the domestication of the story lay precisely in the absence of any genuine domestication.

The Israeli audience related to the Korean story in the same remote, uninterested fashion. The participants were initially asked to retell the event in their own words. Their accounts were more descriptive than evaluative, although they revealed a note of support for the students struggling for democracy and free elections:

> The riots happened because they want South Korea and North Korea to unite. The students demand that they unite. The students want more democratic rule – the rule there is not democratic – they want free elections and to change the president.

> The students wanted more rights, more freedom of speech, so that they can do things. The government opposed this and as a result the riots started and the violence began. The students had no choice, they had to resist and enter a cathedral.

> The students were protesting against the South Korean president. The students started a sit down strike in the great church of Seoul, I suppose. Here they are showing pictures of how they are being evacuated, and what accompanies it, all this for demanding free elections.

Other audience members did not even show descriptive interest in the story and were forthright about their lack of involvement in the event. One said that 'it doesn't really interest us what is happening in Korea', while another said that 'this isn't a news story of great importance here in Israel'. Others showed some irritation with the site of the event:

> The Israelis don't care about what is happening in South Korea, what exactly are the problems there and what the population does not have and is demanding through the students. The viewers don't know what is the form of government there and what the problems are.

Despite the lack of interest on the part of some discussants there were elements of self referentiality, relating different elements in the story to issues of Jewish identity and conflicts within Israel. For example, unrest in Korea was likened, implicitly and explicitly, to Arab-Israeli conflicts and the Intifada. Student unrest in Korea was implicitly seen as something akin to civil unrest (by Palestinians) in Israel. As one participant put it, 'it's not our students, it's Arabs. They (our students) don't want to revolt against the government, it's the Arabs.' Civil unrest was seen as something that should not happen in Israel for both political and historical reasons:

> It (civil unrest) is something that repeats all over the world. And we as Israelis that were once a beaten people should make sure that such pictures will not come

out of here. Not that it won't get out of here. If it happens it has to get out, but it shouldn't happen here.

And, in the natural progression of the conversation, coverage of violence in Israel by foreign media was critiqued, as the following dialogue between several focus group participants shows:

Here, when even one person is killed or hurt or whatever, it gets covered by reports at least as large as this one and more.

The whole world is against you.

Right.

There were demonstrations against the war in Lebanon. The army wasn't involved and no one was killed, but there too pictures were shown abroad.

It's frightening. When I see such a report I immediately translate it to our situation.

Gulf refugees

The story aired by Israeli television's Hebrew-language evening newscast on the Gulf refugees in Jordan was in stark contrast to the Korean student story. It used compelling footage in tandem with commentary that was heavy in drama, metaphors and vivid imagery. Stylistic markers such as anaphora and hyperbole were also evident. The story showed high involvement with the event. It was presented as a voice-over (with a brief anchor introduction) and was dominated by themes of strife and despair.

The visuals were the most dramatic evidence of this. The opening shot of the story was a slow pan of a truck driving into the refugee camp, seen murkily through clouds of dust and shimmering heat. The camp was in pandemonium, energised, it seems, by the arrival of the truck, bearing water and food supplies. Men ran around it, and as they clambered up the sides of the truck they were pushed/beaten down, but clawed their way back up to get bottles of water and pass them down to relatives milling around the halted truck.

The second cut shows a Jordanian policeman addressing a crowd of refugees who stand at a distance of 100 yards or more. They look as if they have been rounded up and made to stand quietly. The policeman explains in a loud voice that they need to come to the truck 'one by one'. He speaks slowly and loudly and his attitude is that of someone addressing people that are slow and witless. The refugees add to that perception. They stand mute, framed against the yellow sand and the clear blue sky. The third cut reveals that the refugees did not get the message. It follows a policeman as he walks arrogantly towards the refugees, twirling his baton.

The fourth cut shows refugees running around crazily, raising clouds of dust. The camera switches to a policeman running amongst the refugees, swishing his baton in all directions. The refugees scatter in his wake. A change in locale takes place with the next shot: the refugees are walking with their bags and bundles of belongings, the camera pans them as they struggle with their awkward bundles. A close up is offered of some refugees, their faces hot with sweat, their clothes dirty as they struggle to give their passports to Jordanian border officials, who stamp and return them.

The verbal component of the story complemented the dramatic visuals and contributed to the story's high level of relationality. The story was emphatic in tone, identified with the refugees and portrayed them as victims who have turned desperate. It said that the thousands of refugees are losing patience and violent clashes are taking place. The refugees are 'fighting for every drop of water and every piece of bread'. The commentary used anaphora (exact repetition of a word or phrase) to convey confirmation of their status: the refugees were getting 'one cucumber, one tomato and one pita a day'. Metaphorically, the story painted their situation as one primed for disaster. The disaster metaphor came literally from identifying it as an explosion – it described their current status as a 'barrel of explosives inside Jordan' and as a natural disaster ('Jordan is stemming the flood that threatens it'). The story did not hold out much hope for the refugees. Their status was seen as one of 'hardship (that) increases from day to day because of a mix of neglect and apathy towards those who used to be the menial workers of Kuwait.' In addition to focusing on Jordan's predicament it also points out that Turkey faced a similar problem, that of 'the challenge of this horrible movement of populations'.

The Israeli audience also critiqued the motives of Jordan and Iraq, especially the former. As the quotes below show, Jordan was seen as using the refugees to generate support – financial, political and in the media:

> I think they showed it only to create international sympathy to help Jordan's tough situation, and they are in a tough situation. Considering the fact that Jordan is facing tough economic times, and we know that is the case, then Jordan has to face a very hard problem and Jordan needs broad international assistance to solve the refugees problem.

> It is propaganda for Jordan, so that it can ask for money for all kinds of things to show that it has refugees and doesn't have money to give them. It did all this propaganda to ask for money.

> The Jordanian government wants to show that this is hard for them. They are fighting against bringing these refugees. Maybe they want to get aid and contributions from other countries, then they will show how much more pressure this puts on them.

One participant speculated on the possibility of the refugees coming to Israel and said:

> They [the refugees] would come here, see a little, stay in a rest house; get some food, some water, recuperate and then gain their strength and pick a fight with us.

Another participant discussed the possibility of taking refugees into Israel by combining it with a criticism of the government:

> Knowing our government we would expect them to show the refugees how nice we are, how good we are. We are always worried that we need to look good.

A third participant linked the treatment of the refugees to concerns about how Israel is viewed abroad – a concern expressed in the aftermath of the incident on the Temple Mount, in which Israeli police clashed with Arab worshippers, causing a large number of casualties – and reiterated here:

> No one cares [about refugees getting beaten up]. What do they care? As long as it isn't the Israelis that are hitting. Who cares about a few Arabs or whatever?

After contextualizing the refugee story in these terms, the discussion shifted almost completely toward concerns with the self, turning to a more focused discussion of the Israeli/Jewish experience in relation to migration and refugees. Images lodged in the Jewish collective memory were invoked. One example:

> Unfortunately, the pictures we saw on TV reminded me of the Jews in the time of the Germans, how they were with suitcases, women and children. And this is a heavy burden. We as Jews are reminded a bit of what happened once. We have to understand that this is a great fear.

It is worth pondering whether the television news editors had these concerns in mind when putting together this story.

South African violence

The Israeli story on South African violence was similar to other 'foreign' news stories in that it used few, if any, culturally relevant markers. It framed the event as one incident in a chain of similar incidents ('Another bloody night took place in South Africa, 53 were killed in clashes between Blacks in townships around Johannesburg'). The story was marked by the absence of drama and poetic elements. It was a 'tell story' that conformed to the norms of that genre: reliance of official sources ('police said that at least 400 houses and ten huts were burnt down') and political figures ('The wife of the Black leader, Nelson Mandela, today visited the hospitals, police stations and impoverished refugee camps and heard the Blacks complaints') and the use of numbers as evidence ('thousands of Blacks are leaving .... 53 people killed .... 400 houses burnt .... 800 casualties').

The audience displayed a low level of other referentiality and discussed the conflict as an example of inter-tribal conflict. One participant pointed to the historic intractability of this problem and said that:

> This is a case of history repeating itself. Who remembers that in 1800 or something, the beginning of 1900, the Zulu was also against other tribes and the British. The Zulu was always like this.

Some discussants focused on the future of Israel's relationship with South Africa:

> We had a very good relationship with White South Africa, the apartheid one. I don't know how it will be tomorrow when the Blacks are the majority and they will be in power.

Self-referentiality surfaced again through the perceived parallels with the Israeli-Palestinian conflict and the occupied territories. The issues (as indicated in the quotes below) ranged from a critical evaluation of Palestinian motives, to the factional fighting amongst the Palestinians and possible conflicts between Israel and a future Palestinian state:

> I see this business of South Africa as it applies to Israel. Those that are in the occupied territories, those that are in Israel, for them Israel is like America, and they should understand how good they have it here. Why make problems for Israel?

> We can conclude many things regarding our situation. It has many consequences. In our case, for instance, on the Palestinian side they want their own country. We can see what happens amongst themselves. If in the future we would offer them something, there might be a war between the different factions.

> I am talking about the ambitions of a certain nationality to get independence. This situation as it was there is very similar to the situation here. They have an ambition to get independence, to be the ones that run their own country. That's what's happening there. The Palestinians want to get a part of the country that we want. And they present themselves as a united Palestinian people that want their own state. I don't think that it is exactly true, because we see what happens amongst themselves.

To summarise then our qualitative review of stories and audiences from Great Britain, Germany, France, the United States and Israel, we found that stories were domesticated differently country-by-country, not in some absolute fashion but rather by a set of predilections towards issues of self and other referentiality. Differential domestication of television news should thus be seen as an important process that allows for the reiteration of a given country's specific orientations, as well as its connections to more inclusive categories such as Europe or the West. This process, it needs to be emphasised, is usually structured oppositionally, i.e. by contrasting the self with generalised others (the East, Third World, the Orient) and specific others (Iraq, Korea, South Africa).

5 Eurovision and the Globalization of Television News

This final chapter has three main purposes. First, as a way to shed additional light on the process and consequences of globalised television news, we will make a limited comparison of the news values of EVN journalists and of viewers in five countries. To the extent that there is agreement, we will take that as one piece of evidence supporting the notion of globalization. Second, as is expected in all scholarly writings, we will self-critically examine the strengths and weaknesses of the overall study presented here. And third, we will return to the three broad sets of research questions which have structured our efforts at a start-to-finish study of the Eurovision News Exchange and the creation, contents, and consequences of television news on a global scale (See Chapter 1). In particular, we will focus on what we believe are the two core theoretical foci of this study – the metaphor of the 'global newsroom', which appears (in the plural form) as early as the title of this monograph and which guided much of our work on the institutional aspects of the news exchange process; and our explication of the notion of news domestication, a concept which ties together the work of journalists, the content of the news, and the audience as decoder of mass media messages. Finally, we will speculate briefly about the future of the Eurovision News Exchange.

News values: professional and public

Has the globalization of television news produced a journalistic culture in which global newsworkers and their audiences have come to share a more or less common notion of what is newsworthy and important? Recall that Chapter 2 (Table 4) presents findings from our survey of Eurovision Contacts which asked these professionals to rank how interested they thought news viewers in their respective countries would be in six types of news. In addition, in the first part of Chapter 4 we presented survey data on the degree of interest in the same news categories as expressed by viewers in five countries.

Since the audience members were asked to indicate how much interest they had in an array of ten news categories, including the six specifically asked of the Eurovision Contacts, we were able to create Table 1 which compares two sets of rankings: the direct responses of the Contacts and the inferred rankings of the audiences for the relevant six relevant news categories. The six news categories are presented in the table in the order obtained from the Contacts.

Table 1. Rankings of Eurovision Contacts and audiences on preference for foreign news items and categories

Categories	Audiences	Contacts
Science & medicine	1	4
Accidents & disasters	2	2
International relations & conflicts	3	1
Culture & art	4	6
Internal politics	5	3
Ceremonies and festivals	6	5

The Kendall Tau correlation coefficient between the two rankings was $r = 0.37$. While the two data sets are clearly based on different populations (i.e. news contacts from 33 countries and samples of audience members from only five countries) and while the data was collected at different times (1990 for the audience members and 1994 for the News Contacts), the rather moderate correlation can still be taken as an indication of a significant discrepancy between what the EVN journalists think the audience members are interested in and the actual (or at least expressed) interests of the audience members.[1]

In short, we believe that even if the two data sets were collected simultaneously the current data would still support the notion of an existing culture whereby professionals – in our case study, broadcast journalists – are at best ignorant of their clients' preferences – here news viewers – and are largely guided by their self-proclaimed expertise, criteria and norms. This phenomenon, well known within most newsroom seems to be manifest also within the more global context.

There are a number of ways this modest disparity might be explained. First, it should be noted that, unlike doctors or lawyers, journalists do not personally know their 'clients' nor do journalists interact directly with readers and viewers on a one-to-one basis. Indeed, what most journalists know about the audience, if they know anything, is likely to be 'the numbers', i.e. how many people read the newspaper or watch the newscast. Thus, journalists are not likely to have the first-hand knowledge which would lead them to share news values with their audiences.

Another explanation might lie in the notion of variability. Individual differences exist both at the personal and at the national levels. It seems fair to say that in recent years there has been a significant transformation of television news in many countries, based at least in part on the perceived differences among peoples' interests and tastes. Testimony to this growing phenomenon are the mushrooming of news stations exhibiting new genres of news, and the fact that these different formats do seem to attract audiences, albeit small

1. For a similar finding about newspaper journalists and their readers, see Bogart (1989).

ones at times. These include such diametrically opposed prototypes as 'headline' news vs. in-depth analysis; local all-news stations vs. international all-news services; single language vs. multi-language news; sanitised-for-violence news vs. sensational programmes, such as the American tabloid television shows, 'Inside Edition' and 'Hard Copy'. Add to this the specialised news services such as those dedicated to business, sports, entertainment, etc., it seems that there is little limit to the variety of news products that can be produced.

While the majority of Eurovision member services are public broadcasting organizations, whose main product is the more traditional middle-of-the-road news format, it is clear that these services, in most if not all countries, are facing growing competition with the newer formats described above. In order to provide material for such a variety of audiences' interests and tastes the items made available by Eurovision must conform to these more trendy innovations.

Other studies have concluded that the reference groups for many journalists are either other journalists or the people they write about, not their readers or viewers (Gans, 1979). It seems that the Eurovision News co-ordinators and News Contacts who set the agenda for their organization and influence in varying degrees the news content of the member services are no exception to this rule. They seem to perceive their audiences – to the extent that they both do think about such matters in the first place – within the more traditional framework. The Eurovision Contacts believe that the most interesting topics to viewers are traditional hard news categories such as international relations and conflicts (perhaps because they deal mainly with international news), accidents and disasters, and internal politics. While the data clearly show that the audience members find interest in these news stories, they also have interest in other topics, such as health, science, technology, culture and art, which the Eurovision News Exchange perhaps provides too little of. Indeed the findings in Chapter 3 (Table 8) clearly attest to this deficit with stories on health and culture appearing halfway in the list of topic categories, while science and technology stories appear last.

This problem is exacerbated by the fact that Eurovision does indeed deal with a very heterogeneous group of nations, from Western to Eastern Europe, from North Africa to the Middle East, from Scandinavia to the Mediterranean Rim. At the cross-national level the interest in news, as well as the interpretation given to it, probably vary even more than they do within single countries and societies. While surely some major events are of interest to virtually all nations and audiences and will not go unreported, even such stories are read and interpreted differently in different cultures, as our focus groups reported in Chapter 4 clearly indicate. Should we be surprised, then, that journalists in the Global Newsroom do not and cannot fully enunciate the sentiments expressed by viewers in a variety of countries?

It's difficult studying global news

We do not believe that it is immodest to say that this study, or more accurately this entire

145

project, was a very ambitious undertaking. We were aware from the outset that the broader our scope, the more likely we were to get into some kind of 'trouble'. Before dealing with the shortcomings, however, we want to point to what we think is the major methodological achievement of the project. As the findings presented above illustrate, we were able to bring together a variety of data sets from journalists and audiences, using different methodologies of data collection, into what we believe is a comprehensive and coherent picture of a very complex media system.

We believe this study also represents a good example of how quantitative and qualitative methods can be combined to produce different meaningful interpretations of mass media messages. At a time when scholars still debate, often vehemently, the relative merits of each of these approaches, we have tried hard to score points in both fields thereby producing deeper appreciation for the topic under investigation.

Finally, on the plus side of the ledger, our study confirms again that television was considered by audiences in all the countries we investigated (and possibly in those that we did not study as well) to be the most important medium for foreign news and that there is substantial interest in international news among TV viewers. One might ask, of course, how much does Eurovision contribute to the world's news discourse. We will discuss this question more in the next section which deals with the competitive news environment. It is sufficient to say here that, based on our study, if the Eurovision News Exchange did not exist then someone would have to invent it. Despite its weaknesses, the overall benefits of the exchange clearly make it a valuable contributor to the flow of globalised news. In its 34-year history, not a single service has deserted it, while the number of member services, transmissions, and news items has steadily grown.

As for some limitations of this study, first of all, it took much longer than we had hoped it would. Timeliness is important when one is studying a dynamic phenomenon. In any event, to rectify this situation we added, as noted earlier, the final round of research in 1994; and as late as Spring, 1995, we were still in contact with key EVN personnel. We believe we have succeeded in this and that we have provided not only a partial historical picture but also a current view of the Eurovision News Exchange and its complex relationships, both among its members and with the agencies and organizations with which it must deal (and compete) on a daily basis.

Time-to-completion aside, one of the main difficulties with our study, or with any study of news for that matter, has to do with the sampling process. Whereas in many areas of research a merely random selection of 'stimuli' is sufficient in order to obtain a valid representative sample, when sampling news we are faced with the problem of item specificity. By this we mean that each news item has both common and unique charac- teristics, thus no two items can even be considered as precisely identical even using the notion of probability. An earthquake in one place is both similar and dissimilar to an earthquake in another place; an election campaign in one country is like and unlike an election in another. Therefore, when sampling a certain number of news items, even a fairly large number, at best what we can say is that we sampled what was presented by the media in a certain time and at a certain place. But given the variability in world (and local) events and hence in the news, this week's sample will not necessarily be representative of last week's or that of next week. A partial remedy for this is to take large samples and to spread them across time. Our samples spanned two weeks, separated by about four months, but obviously with more resources it could have been larger.

As indicated above, in our sample there were very few stories on science and technology, for example, or animal stories. From our discussion with the Contacts and News Co-or-dinators we know that they indeed like to provide soft news such as animal stories. Does this mean that our sample was flawed? Probably not, but still we know that it is lacking in certain respects. In this connection we must add that even the selection of the countries and the services implies non-random decisions which surely might have limited the external validity of the findings in (unknown) possible directions.

The global newsroom: one or many?

The Eurovision News Exchange has been our research site for collecting empirical evidence to support our concept of the global newsroom. Although our attention was focused primarily on the EVN, it was always clear that there was never one unified and global newsroom. Rather, what we were observing was a system of interlocking news-rooms and news organizations: some large, some small; some profit-seeking, others non-commercial; some with great sweep and influence; others far more marginal to the commerce of international news flow.

One way to situate the Eurovision News Exchange in the global newsroom metaphor is to ask how it relates to the competitive environment of television news.

One set of challenges to the EVN comes from what we will call 'the wholesalers of TV news footage', World Television News (WTN) and Reuters Television (formerly Vis-news). Both of these video news agencies have been in the business of distributing television footage longer and in far larger quantities than the Eurovision News Exchange. WTN, housed in a renovated gin-warehouse in north London, was founded in 1952, when the print wire service United Press teamed up with 20th Century Fox Movietone News (Waite, 1992). Eighty per cent of WTN is owned by the US-based ABC News, with Britain's Independent Television News and Australia's Channel Nine, controlling the remainder. Reuters Television, then called Visnews, was started five years after WTN, when the BBC, the Rank Organization, the Australian Broadcasting Company and the Canadian Broadcasting companies banded together to form the British Commonwealth International Newsfilm Agency. Within a few years, NBC News from the US became a major partner and the name of the agency was changed to Visnews. In 1992, the BBC and NBC sold their shares to Reuters, resulting in a change to the organization's current name.

Of the two agencies, WTN is the smaller and is said to be the less profitable ('WTN Puts Half...', 1994). However, recently it has gained some important new clients ('WTN Signs ...', 1994). Thus the struggle between these arch-rival agencies may continue on. Together, WTN and Reuters have customers in almost 90 countries, stringer camera crews in 70, and a total of forty bureaus, some, of course, quite obviously one-person operations. Depending on the size of the country and the amount of footage made available, clients of the agencies pay anywhere from US$10-15,000 a year on up to several million.

When we first began our field work in 1987, one characteristic which distinguished the agencies from the EVN was what we saw as the almost constant transmission of news materials by the agencies. Compared to two or three EVN's in a normal day, it was somewhat startling for us to discover that WTN and Visnews were 'on the air' almost all the time. Here for example, is how Visnews' Andrew Ailes described part of his agency's scheduled satellite transmissions:

> One-thirty in the morning we come out of New York and we go into Japan. 03.30 in the morning we come out of New York and we go into Thailand and Malaysia. 03.50 we come out of New York and go into Australia. 04.10 we come out of America ... into Europe. 04.30 we come out of Tokyo into Europe ... 07.45 we are going into Europe, the Middle East, and Africa. At 17.00 we are going into Europe [and] Africa. 20.10 we're going from Europe into Japan. At 21.30 we're going from Europe into Asia. At 21.40 we go from Europe into North America and, lo and behold, two hours later, we are coming back out of New York.

What this frenetic schedule demonstrated is first, that the global newsroom never sleeps (it's always time for a newscast somewhere) and second, that the strength of the video news agencies is their ability to target their transmissions to geographically specialised clients, while using much of the same television footage, with limited or no re-editing.

On the face of it, then, the existing video news agencies seem like formidable competitors for the Eurovision News Exchange. Indeed, in 1993 there was some speculation that the Tokyo-based Kyodo News International and Agence France Presse were about to get into the video agency business (McClellan, 1993). Moreover, Associated Press has started a video news agency, providing customers with pre-packaged news stories to which subscribers must only add a local voice-over narration.

Thus, at first glance, it is difficult to see how the EVN continues to survive, let alone, as we have seen, grow and prosper. One seeming impediment, particularly when compared to the resources of WTN and Reuters, is that the EVN is nominally a 'regional' exchange, whose policies give priority to footage from EBU members services. What if, as so often is the case, the big news of the day is not happening within the national boundaries of the EBU members. How then does a regional broadcaster obtain those all-important video images? Moreover, since many EBU-affiliated services are either official government agencies or have some more or less formal tie to their national governments, this necessarily raises doubts particularly in the minds of Western journalists about the journalistic objectivity of items supplied to Eurovision.

This quasi-official relationship of some member services may even preclude that service from covering 'sensitive' events altogether. (During the height of the Intifada, for example, the Israeli Broadcasting Authority was unable to provide footage of the violence, because its reporters, fearing for their safety, were often reluctant to roam the alleys of the refugee camps and the main streets of Gaza.)

A second potential handicap for the Eurovision News Exchange is this: the major European and US television networks rarely need its news footage, since they are well-heeled enough to generate their own international coverage, without depending on what one US network executive once called the 'headless journalism' of the news exchanges. Finally, the Eurovision News Exchange is a creature of the EBU and that ties it, for better or worse, to the public service broadcasting tradition. If, as some suggest (Blumler, 1992), public service broadcasting is vulnerable to the changing media marketplace, then one might wonder whether the Eurovision exchange too is at risk.

While the Eurovision News Exchange is no doubt challenged by these factors and forces, it has, we believe, managed to accommodate itself to the emerging media environment, in part by skillful adaptation and innovation, and in part because the significance of some of these so-called challenges are in truth over-stated.

First, the Eurovision News Exchange has developed a number of mechanisms which allow it to transcend its 'regional' and often 'official' base. Part of Eurovision's regional handicap has been overcome by the growth of other regional news exchanges, most especially Asiavision. Links with other regional exchanges have created a system of region-to-region cooperation, making it possible for the Eurovision News Exchange to 'cover' the world far beyond Europe and the Mediterranean rim.

Even more important, however, than its ties to other exchanges has been EVN's complicated but beneficial relationship with the two dominant international video agencies (Reuters Television and WTN). What complicates the situation is that the video agencies offer their footage both unilaterally to individual national news services and to national broadcasters through the Eurovision News Exchange. This EVN-agency relationship is at least partially symbiotic: EVN needs the agencies to extend its reach into areas where there are no EBU members or where, for various political or technical reasons, the EBU member service can not adequately provide what is needed. For the agencies, the Eurovision exchange is another outlet for its product and, through the technical facilities of Eurovision and its member nations, a cost-free means to transmit agency materials from the field to London for further distribution.

Moreover, it does not appear that CNN is often a serious competitor for the Eurovision News Exchange, since CNN's strengths are not what EVN members services need on a day to day basis. First, many EVN services claim that CNN is simply too US-oriented, that it provides pictures of too much coverage of made-for-the-media events in Washington or sensational, but essential American stories, (e.g. the O.J. Simpson trial). Second, EVN journalists say that CNN does not do an especially good job providing stories with natural sound and clean video, the sort of materials that an EVN national service can use in its normal newscasts and for which it has come to rely on the Eurovision Exchange.

The second challenge to EVN – its general irrelevance for the wealthiest national newscasters – is not completely true in the first instance and seems in the second to be more than a little narrow-minded and elitist in its assumptions, even if it is. EVN usage data presented in Chapter 2 addressed this first point and showed that even the most illustrious and well-off broadcasters of Europe and elsewhere do air news footage from EVN feeds.[2] As to the elitist assumptions of those who would readily dismiss the significance of EVN to the work of 'important' news organizations, we would remind them that from a global perspective, there is more to broadcast news than what's offered by the broadcasters of the US, UK, and other industrialised nations. The BBC's *News at Nine* or ABC's *World News Tonight* are not seen by many people of the planet.[3] Other nations have newscasts too, and news organizations in those countries, perhaps less well financed but certainly no less dedicated, have come to depend on the efforts of the Eurovision News Exchange to inform their citizens.

News challengers, retail

Meanwhile, broadcasting, both public and commercial, is moving rapidly in new and not completely understood directions. Indeed, it is no exaggeration to say that never before in the history of the world have there been so many television channels available to the home viewer, nor has there ever been more opportunity to see news on television. This abundance of new providers of television news may well have a potential impact on the future of the Eurovision News Exchange. When the first EVN was fed down the line, the broadcast terrain of Europe and much of the world certainly was substantially different from today. Most countries had only one or sometime two national broadcasters, and most European television stations were firmly rooted in the quasi-governmental model known as public service broadcasting. Even today, in a worldwide growth of multi-channel broadcasting, the core, some might say the soul of EBU and its Eurovision News Exchange, remains public service oriented. But while commercial stations and satellite-delivered channels may have sprung up like mushrooms after a spring shower, it is important to remember, as Parker (1994) observes: 'Globally, the majority of people still live in countries where public broadcasting monopolies have no domestic private competitors' (p. 5). Indeed, the largest public broadcasters, i.e. the BBC, Italy's RAI, and Japan's NHK, have annual revenues at least equal to the income produced by the giant US

---

2. Of course, the 'big boys' do not need the video news agencies all that often either. However, there have been some notable exceptions (e.g. footage of an Israeli ambush of Hezbollah leader Sheik Abbas Musawi in Lebanon; the failure of a coupe in Venezuela; and even CNN's much-vaunted reporting from Baghdad during the early days of the Gulf War) in which the only pictures available to the US networks came from the news agencies (Waite, 1992). Moreover, given the continuing squeeze on US network news budgets, network executives are quick to admit that relying on the agencies is enormously less expensive than maintaining their own correspondents and crews (Kimball, 1994).

3. In fact, some of the regular US network news programmes *are* now being transmitted outside the United States via satellite and then rebroadcast by 'foreign' cable systems. Thus, for example, SKY News carries the CBS Evening News. Needless to say, the principle audience for such programmes is likely to be expatriates and travelling business people, and thus US news is unlikely to draw many viewers away from locally-created newscasts.

networks, even though the non-profit broadcasters operate in significantly smaller markets.

More specifically, newscasts produced by national public service broadcasters seem to be doing very well in the ratings. Challengers to public service newscasts come in two types: so-called global broadcasters, such as Ted Turner's Cable News Network International and the BBC World Television News; and domestic news programmes, produced by for-profit networks. With regard to the global broadcasters, we would argue that their mass appeal is much exaggerated. At the moment, for example, Cable News Network International (CNNI) can be seen in only one per cent of all households worldwide. While one per cent of the globe's total population is most certainly a very large audience, there is little evidence to suggest that many of these potential CNNI viewers tune in. Rather, CNNI and similar worldwide broadcasters have become, in the words of one knowledgeable observer, 'the office intercom of the global elites' (Rich Zharadnik, quoted in Parker, 1994, p. 16). Of course, providing the globe's politicians and technocrats with news is potentially of major importance. But, except in rare moments of international crisis, it seems unlikely that the influence of broadcasts like CNNI even on elites would exceed the impact of locally produced news programmes.

Indeed, even in national broadcast systems where there are sometimes a half dozen or more potential newscasts available, there apparently is a general pattern of viewer preferences for the more established, public-service news programmes. As Parker notes:

> [W]hat's striking is how many viewers continue to choose public broadcast news as their first choice over any of the private alternatives. In Britain, the number one news programme is on BBC1, in France on TF1, in Germany on ARD 1, in Italy on RAI, in Spain on TVE 1 – all supposedly 'withering' public broadcasters threatened by the private-sector upstarts' (p. 22).

To sum up, then, we would conclude that the Eurovision News Exchange has found, for the time-being at least, a niche for its activities. Even in an age of fierce institutional competition, the EVN continues to grow in its capacities to provide news to its members. Several questions arise, however, about EVN's future. We can not possibly offer certain answers to any of them, but we think they are worth posing, because they point to possible future research based on the concept of the global newsroom.

The first question is this: Given the current state of cooperation and symbiosis between the Eurovision News Exchange and the handful of other regional exchanges and video news agencies, could a single institution arise which combined all these elements into an unequivocally global newsroom? The expansion, for example, of the Eurovision News Exchange to include the Eastern European broadcasters who used to be part of Intervision suggests that historic changes in the political scene might produce a more centralised, read globalised, news exchange system.

On the other hand, given the current economic health of many Pacific basin nations and their broadcast systems, the Asian Broadcasting Union news exchange scarcely seems like a target for take-over by EVN, even if, as is completely unlikely, the governors of EBU wanted to undertake such a move.

And then there is question of what economic model a single, centralised global video service might follow? Would it be more likely based on the governmental or quasi-governmental example of, say, the EBU? Would it be more likely grounded in a profit-making model, such as that established by Reuters Television or would it emerge as a spin-off of, say, CNN International?.

There is simply no way to know. But there is one precedent worth considering. As curious as it may seem, historically among the strongest supporters of public television in the United States are the commercial television networks. Why? For many reasons, including the poorly-kept secret that commercial broadcasters see public television as providing some, if not most, of the 'quality' programming that appeals to a relative small audience. If public television meets this need, the for-profit broadcasters say, they can concentrate on more popular fare, aimed at larger and hence more commercially lucrative audiences.

Perhaps, then, a similar logic might be at work in the case of news around the world. The wealthier national broadcasters, especially those in the US, Western Europe and Japan, might continue to largely ignore the not-for-profit Eurovision exchange and its peers. Perhaps, if news budgets were particularly pinched, the better-off broadcasters would forge somewhat closer, more active ties to the public news exchanges. Far more likely, however, the 'big boys' of broadcast journalism would go about their business, throwing an occasional bouquet to the fine work of the news exchanges, but secretly pleased that they are independent of the exchange system, its ties to public service broadcasting, and its news values which do not give preeminent importance to events in the Industrial Seven.

News domestication

The notion of domestication has emerged as one of the core characteristics of the process explored in this monograph. Its theoretical import in this study is twofold. First, it serves as a counterpoint to the notion of 'globalization' that underlay the conceptual origins of this project. Second, it serves to conceptually link media professionals and their audiences. Theoretically, the notion of domestication can be seen to be an aspect of, perhaps a 'sub-process' of the processes of encoding and decoding. Inasmuch as the concept refers to the ways in which news stories are being shaped and tailored to fit in with (assumed) audience interests, expectations and cognitive framework, it refers not only to the encoding process itself but indeed specifies its *direction*. It suggests that reporters and correspondents, working either in far-away lands or at home, view the events they witness as if through the eyes of the local audiences and attempt to tell the story accordingly.

Thus, our use of the concept, domestication, may be thought of as a necessary corrective to discussions of media globalization. Assumptions and arguments concerning the globalization of television news are often so imbued with the spirit and the vision of the 'Global village' that they typically ignore the counter-pull generated everywhere by audiences situated within their own cultures (Ferguson, 1992). Our focus group data clearly illustrate the manner in which television news viewers anchor the meanings of news stories – or any other cultural products for that matter – in their own extant cognitive frameworks. In other words, they 'domesticate' the meaning of the stories they watch. This finding might not be a novelty to many readers, and yet it is important to highlight it as the opposite pole of the process of globalization.

Clearly, then, the notion of domestication thus applies both at the encoding and the decoding levels. Before they engage in 'domesticating' a story for their audiences, reporters first *decode* the event they report about in a similarly domesticated fashion. They bring their own cultural perspective to bear on, and define the meaning of the event which is then encoded into the story. Thus, instead of viewing the 'production' and 'reproduction' of meaning as semi-independent and separate processes these processes apply to both journalists and audience members, resulting in 'understandings' that dovetail each other.

There are echoes here to Bakhtin's insistence on 'the dialogic model' of communication. In Bakhtin's words, 'Dialogic relationships are a much broader phenomenon than mere rejoinders in a dialogue laid out compositionally in the text ... Neither individuals nor any social entities are locked within their boundaries. They are partially 'located outside' themselves ... To be means to be for another, and through the other for oneself' (Morson & Emerson, 1990, pp. 49–51). Applying this model to our concerns the 'dialogic model' of communication – be it interpersonal, public or mass – suggests that every utterance is jointly produced by speaker and listener. The speaker, Bakhtin suggests, is responsible 'for not more than 50 per cent of his words (signals/message), for the other 50 per cent responsibility lies with the receiver'. Thus, the listener/ viewer's understanding is a 'responsive' one and the knowledge generated is 'dialogic'. The journalist who tells a story does so successfully only if and when he or she couches the story in the language, mythologies, norms, conventions, ideologies of the culture within which he or she and their listeners are situated.

It follows, then, that 'global communicators' must retain their domestic cultural identity. As foreign reporters they must not assimilate into the culture – the foreign soil – within which they happen to work or about which they happen to report. To be able to conduct the 'dialogue' with their audiences at home they must be able to impose their own, and their society's perspective on the perspective of the 'other' society. And indeed, most of them do so almost instinctively, not because they are adapting to their audiences' point of view, but because they *are their audience*. Also, this might be a reason why news organizations tend to prefer limiting the period of time for their reporters to stay abroad as foreign correspondents.

The small band of truly 'global communicators' – not the foreign correspondents and their ilk, but Eurovision's News Co-ordinators and those who serve the global news agencies – must therefore find themselves in no-man's land. Deliberately detaching themselves from their own cultural identity, and slipping into a 'regional' or a global one, they are probably incapable of 'domesticating' their news products in any meaningful way. In fact, this is precisely what they aim to be. It is the supra-national, and supra-cultural ground on which they prefer to stand. The only 'dialogue' they can therefore enter into is the 'professional', artificial one they conduct with their distant colleagues. It is on the shoulders of these distant 'local' colleagues that the true burden of domestication rests.

In sum, then, the Eurovision News Exchange can be thought of as an interperspectival dialogue. The daily conferences, presided over by the News Co-ordinators, have a manifest function of exchanging the information necessary to run the exchange. But the daily conference and the news exchange system itself also may be thought of in larger, symbolic terms.

Throughout history, there has been a tension between the human desire to belong to larger groups (clans, tribes, faith communities, nation-states or whatever) and the equally compelling urge to be an individual, free to pursue one's own goals and visions with limited or little constraint from others. However mundane its purposes, the Eurovision News Exchange can still be seen as a site of intercultural negotiation (as we discussed mainly in Chapter 2) where understandings and their limits are continuously expressed. At times this negotiation process can even become a harsh struggle. Tugging in one direction is the McLuhanite vision of a global culture – a worldwide village based on shared values and experiences, created by the technology of communication, a utopian vision of equality and equity, an almost primitive communism where the class struggle has been replaced by consensual communication.

Pulling in the opposite direction is that sort of human experience often summarised by the metaphor of the Tower of Babel. As the Hebrew Bible teaches us, the human race 'was of one language and one speech ... And they said 'Come let us build us a city and a tower with its top in heaven and let us make us a name' (*Genesis*, 11). And as the Bible records, God confounded man's audacious effort by destroying the tower and the common language (and hence shared culture). Ever since, with or without the Deity as causal variable, and like it or not, the world has been culturally and politically divided.

What strikes us, in conclusion, is how the Eurovision News Exchange is characterised by a tension between the particularistic and the common; the shared world and the divided one; the effort to defend cultural borders and, at the same time, the effort to blur them. Our study is in the final analysis a call to reflect and meditate about borders – boundaries that are both existing and non-existing, easy and impossible to cross.

References

Blumler, Jay (1992) 'Vulnerable values at stake' in Jay Blumler (ed.), *Television and the Public Interest*. London: Sage Publications.

Bogart, Leo (1989) *Press and public: who reads what, when, where, and why in American newspapers*. 2nd edition. Hillsdale, NJ: Lawrence Erlbaum Associates.

Boyd-Barrett, Oliver & Thussu, Daya Kishan (1992) *Contra-Flow in global news: International and regional news exchange mechanisms*. London: John Libbey & Company, Ltd.

Cohen, Akiba (1993) 'Israelis and foreign news: perceptions of interest, functions, and newsworthiness' *Journal of Broadcasting and Electronic Media* 37, 337-347.

Cohen, Akiba & Bantz, Charles (1989) 'Where did we come from and where are we going?: Some future directions in television news research' *American Behavioral Scientist* 33, 135-143.

Ferguson, Marjorie (1992) 'The mythology about globalization' *European Journal of Communication* 7, 69-93.

Fisher, Harold (1980) 'The EBU: Model for regional cooperation in broadcasting' *Journalism Monographs*, 68.

Flournoy, Don (1990) 'Emergence of the international news exchange: The new global journalism' Paper presented at the meeting of the International Association of Mass Communication Research, Bled, Yugoslavia.

Gans, Herbert (1979) *Deciding What's News*. New York: Pantheon.

Hjrvard, Stig (1991) 'Pan-European television news: Towards a European political public sphere?' Paper presented to the Fourth International Television Conference, London.

Kimball, Penn (1994) *Downsizing the News: Network Cutbacks in the Nation's Capital*. Washington, DC: The Woodrow Wilson Center Press.

Kressley, Konrad (1978a) 'East-west communication in Europe: The television nexus' *Communication Research* 5, 71-86.

Kressley, Konrad (1978b) 'Eurovision: Distributing Costs and Benefits in an International Broadcasting Union' *Journal of Broadcasting* 22, 179-193.

Lanispuro, Yrjo (1987) 'Asiavision News Exchange' *Intermedia* 15(1), 22-27.

McClellan, Steve (1993) 'The growing focus on global news' *Broadcasting & Cable*, pp. 40–41.

Melnik, Stefan (1981) *Eurovision News and the International Flow of Information: History, Problems and Perspectives, 1960-1980.* (Studies in International Communication, Vol. 1). Bochum: Studienverlag Dr. N. Brockmeyer.

Morson, Gary Saul & Emerson, Caryl (1990) *Mikhail Bakhtin – Creation of a Prosaics.* Stanford, CA: Stanford University Press.

Parker, Richard (1994) *The future of global television news.* (Research Paper R-13). Cambridge, MA: Harvard University, The Joan Shorenstein Center, John F. Kennedy School of Government.

Pollock, Donald & Woods, David (1959) 'A study in international communication: Eurovision' *Journal of Broadcasting* 3, 101–117.

Robinson, John & Davis, Dennis (1990) 'Television news and the informed public: An information-processing approach' *Journal of Communication* 40(3), 106–119.

Robinson, John & Levy, Mark (1995) 'News media use and the informed public: A view from the 1990s' Paper presented at the annual meeting of the American Association for Public Opinion Research, Ft. Lauderdale, FL.

Roeh, Itzhak & Dahlgren, Peter (1991) 'Stories nations tell themselves' *NORDICOM Review* 1, 48–52.

Sherman, Charles & Ruby, John. (1974) 'Television news in Eurovision and Intervision' *Journalism Quarterly* 51, 478–485.

Varis, Tapio (1989) 'The influence of international television: A case study' *Journal of Moral Education* 13, 23-32.

Waite, Teresa (1992) 'As networks stay home, two agencies roam the world *The New York Times*, p. 5.

Wallis, Roger & Baran, Stanley (1990) *The Known World of Broadcast News.* London: Routledge.

WTN puts half profits into equipment and coverage. (1994, 27 July) *Broadcasting & Cable*, p. 42.

WTN signs with CBS. (1994, 19 September) *Broadcasting & Cable*, p. 42.

Appendix A
Members of European
Broadcasting Union

'Active' Members

Algeria
  Enterprise Nationale de Télévision (ENTV)
Austria
  Osterreichischer Rundfunk (ORF)
Belarus
  Belaruskaja Tele-Radio Campanija (BTRC)
Belgium
  Belgische Radio i Televidenie (BRTN)
  Radio-Television Belge de la Communaute francaise (RTBF)
Bosnia-Herzegovina
  Radio Televizija Bosne i Hercegovine (RTVBH)
Bulgaria
  Bâlgarsko Nationaino Radio (BR)
  Bâlgarska Nationaino Televizija (BT)
Croatia
  Hrvatska Radiotelevizija (HRT)
Cyprus
  Cyprus Broadcasting Corporation (CYBC)
Czech Republic
  Cesky Rozhlas (CR)
  Ceská Televize (CST/CT)
Denmark
  Danmarks Radio (DR)
  TV2/Danmark (TV2/DK)
Egypt
  Egyptian Radio and Television Union (ERTU)

Estonia
    Eesti Raadio (ER)
    Eesti Televisioon (ETV)
Finland
    MTV Oy (MTV3)
    Oy Yleisradio Ab (YLE)
France
    Europe 1
    Télévision Française 1 (TF1)
    France 2 (FT2, formerly A2F)
    France 3 (FT3)
    Canal Plus (CPF)
    Radio France
    Radio France Internationale
    TéléDiffusion de France (TDF)
Germany
    Arbeitsgemeinschaft der offentlichrechtlichen Rundfunkanstalten der
        Bundesrepublik Deutschland (ARD)
    Zweites Deutsches Fernsehen (ZDF)
Greece
    Elliniki Radiophonia-Tileorassi SA (ERT)
Hungary
    Magyar Rádió (MR)
    Magyar Televízió (MTV)
Iceland
    Rikisútvarpid (RUV)
Ireland
    Radio Telefís Éireann (RTE)
Israel
    Israel Broadcasting Authority (IBA)
Italy
    Radiotelevisione Italiana (RAI)
Jordan
    Jordan Radio and Television Corporation (JRTV)
Latvia
    Latvijas Valsta Televizija (LTV)
    Latvijas Valsta Radio (LR)
Lebanon
    Radio Liban/Télé-Liban
Libya
    Libyan Jamahiriya Broadcasting (LJB)
Lithuania
    Lietuvos Radijas ir Televizija (LRT)

Luxembourg
CLT Multi Media (includes RTL, Radio-Television Luxembourg)
Macedonia (Former Yugoslav Republic of)
MKRTV (MRT)
Malta
Broadcasting Authority-Malta
Moldova
Teleradio-Moldova (NRTM)
Monaco
Groupement de Radiodiffuseurs monégasques (RMC/TMC)
Morocco
Radiodiffusion-Télévision Marocaine (RTM)
Netherlands
Nederlandse Omroep Stichting (NOS)
Norway
Norsk Rikskringkasting (NRK)
TV2 AS (TV2 Norway)
Poland
Polskie Radio i Telewizja (TVP)
Portugal
Radiodifusaõ Portuguesa EP
Radiotelevisaõ Portuguesa SA (RTP)
Romania
Societatea Româna de Radiodifuziune
Societatea Româna de Televiziune (TVR)
Russian Federation
Radiotelevidenie Ostankino (RTO)
Rossijakoe Teleradio (RTR)
San Marino
San Marino RTV
Slovakia
Slovensky Rozhlas
Slovenská Televizia (CSTA)
Slovenia
Radiotelevizija Slovenija (RTVSL)
Spain
Radiotelevisión Espãnola (TVE)
Sociedad Espanola de Radiodifusion
Sweden
Sveriges Television och Radio Grupp (SVT)
Switzerland
Société Suisse de Radiodiffusion et Télévision (includes Schweizrische Radio und Fernsehengesellschaft, SRG and Societe Suisee de Radiodiffusion et

Television, SSR)

Tunisia
    Établissement de la Radiodiffusion-Télévision Tunisienne (ERTT)

Turkey
    Türkiye Radyo-Televizyon Kurumu (TRT)

Ukraine
    Natsionaina Radiokompanya Ukrainy and Natsionaina Telekompanya Ukrainy (DTRU)

United Kingdom
    British Broadcasting Corporation (BBC)
    Independent Television News (ITN)

Vatican State
    Radio Vaticana

'Associate' Members

Albania
    Radiotelevisione Shqiptar

Australia
    Australian Broadcasting Corporation (ABC)
    Federation of Australian Commercial Television Stations
    Special Broadcasting Service

Bangladesh
    National Broadcasting Corporation (BTV)

Barbados
    Caribbean Broadcasting Corporation (CABC)

Brazil
    TV Globo Ltda. (TVG)

Canada
    Canadian Broadcasting Corporation (CBC)
    CTV Television Network Ltd.

Chile
    Corporación de Televisión de la Universidad Católica de Chile (Canal 13)

Cuba
    Instituto Cubano de Radio y Televisión (ICRT)

Gabon
    Radiodiffusion Télévision Gabonaise

Greenland
    Kalaalit Nunaata Radioa

Hong Kong
    Asia Television Ltd.
    Metro Broadcasting Corporation Ltd.
    Radio Television Hong Kong
    Television Broacasts Ltd

India
   All India Radio
Iran
   Islamic Republic of Iran Broadcasting (IRIB)
Japan
   Asahi National Broadcasting Company Ltd. (TV Asahi)
   Fuji Television Network Inc.
   National Association of Commercial Broadcasters in Japan
   Nippon Hoso Kyokai (NHK)
   Nippon Television Network Corporation
   Tokyo Broadcasting System Inc.
   Tokyo FM Broadcasting Co. Ltd.
 Republic of Korea
   Korean Broadcasting System (KBS)
   Munhwa Broadcasting Corporation
Malawi
   Malawi Broadcasting Corporation
Malaysia
   Radio Television Malaysia (RTVM)
Mauritius
   Mauritius Broadcasting Corporation
Mexico
   Televisa SA de CV
   TV Azteca
Nepal
   Nepal Television Corporation
New Zealand
   Radio New Zealand Ltd
   Television New Zealand Ltd
Oman
   Oman Directorate General of Radio and Television (ODGRT)
Pakistan
   Pakistan Television Corporation
South Africa
   South African Broadcasting Corporation (SABC)
Sri Lanka
   Sri Lanka Broadcasting Corporation (SLRC)
Syria
   Organisme de la Radio-Télévision Arabe Syrienne (ORTAS)
United Arab Emirates
   United Arab Emirates Radio and Television (UAERTV)
   United Arab Emirates Radio and Television - Dubai
United States

Capital Cities/American Broadcasting Companies Inc. (ABC)
CBS Inc.
Corporation for Public Broadcasting (CPB)
Public Broadcasting Service (PBS)
National Public Radio (NPR)
Public Radio International (PRI)
National Broadcasting Company Inc. (NBC)
Turner Broadcasting System Inc. (TBS)
United States Information Agency (USIA)

Venezuela
Corporacion Venezolana de Televisión CA
Radio Caracas Television/Radio Caracas Radio

Zimbabwe
Zimbabwe Broadcasting Corporation

Appendix B

Questionnaire for News Co-ordinators and Contacts

European Broadcasting Union Union Européenne de Radio-Télévision

Geneva, 23 March 1994

Dear colleague,

This questionnaire is being sent to all Eurovision contacts. It is part of a comprehensive study of the Eurovision News Exchange that is being done by the College of Journalism at the University of Maryland, USA. This is not an official EBU project, but we are pleased to cooperate in every way with it.

Please answer all the questions and return the questionnaire in the accompanying envelope as soon as possible.

For each question indicate the most appropriate response or fill in your response, in most cases in a word or two.

Please note this study is about news items only, not sports.

All answers will be pooled for purposes of statistical analysis. No one will be individually identified in the final report.

Thank you very much for your cooperation.

Sincerely yours,

Tony Naets
Director, News

Adresse postale/Postal address
Case postale 67
CH-1218 Grand-Saconnex (GE)
Suisse/Switzerland

Bureau/Office
Ancienne Route 17A
Grand-Saconnex
Genève/Geneva

Tél. (+4122) 717 21 11
Téléfax (+4122) 717 24 81
Tx. 41 57 00 ebu ch
Télégr. Uniradio Genève/Geneva

1. Which service (e.g., NRK, NOS, BBC) do you work for? _____

2. How long have you been working in the field of TV news?
    1. Less than one year
    2. 1 to 2 years
    3. 3 to 4 years
    4. 5 to 10 years
    5. 11 or more years

In which of the following have you taken formal courses in journalism?
(Please place an X in the appropriate place for each kind of programme)

Programme	None	1–2 courses	3–4 courses	6+ courses
3. College or University				
4. Professional or technical school				
5. Trade union				
6. Society of professional journalists				
7. On the job				
8. Other (specify) _____				

9. How long have you been working for your service?
    1. Less than one year
    2. 1 to 2 years
    3. 3 to 4 years
    4. 5 to 10 years
    5. 11 or more years

10. How long have you been the Eurovision Contact of your service?
    1. Less than one year
    2. 1 to 2 years
    3. 3 to 4 years
    4. 5 to 10 years
    5. 11 or more years

Have you ever been ...
(Please place an X in the appropriate column for each job)

	Never	1–2 years	3–4 years	5–10 years	11+ years
11. a reporter or correspondent for TV					
12. a reporter or correspondent for radio					
13. a newspaper reporter or correspondent					
14. an editor or sub-editor for TV news					
15. an editor or sub-editor for radio news					
16. a newspaper editor or sub-editor					
17. an administrator in TV news					
18. an administrator in radio news					
19. an administrator for a newspaper					

20.   In addition to being the Eurovision Contact, what other job, if any, do you currently have with your service?
Please specify

_____

21.   What job, either at your service or elsewhere, did you have immediately preceding your appointment as Eurovision Contact for your service?
Please specify

_____

22.   And what job did you have before that one?
Please specify

_____

23.   In your opinion, which of the following is the best description of what it means to be a Eurovision Contact?
1. A reporter or correspondent
2. An editor or sub-editor
3. An administrator
4. Other (please specify) _____

24.   In your service, how long does a person usually serve as the Eurovision contact?
1. There is no fixed rule on this
2. 1-2 years
3. 3-4 years
4. 5 years or more

25. Overall, how satisfied are you with being a Eurovision Contact?
   1. Very satisfied
   2. Somewhat satisfied
   3. Not very satisfied
   4. Not at all satisfied

As a Eurovision contact, how rewarding are each of the following to you?
(Please place an X in the appropriate column for each function)

	Very rewarding	Somewhat rewarding	Not so rewarding	Not at all rewarding
26. Interacting with colleagues from other countries				
27. Helping to shape the news agenda of many countries				
28. The intellectual challenge of the job				

29. In your service, who usually initiates requests to Eurovision for news materials?
   1. I do, as Eurovision Contact
   2. The foreign news editor (or someone comparable)
   3. The foreign editor and I decide together

30. In general, how often does *your* service request news items from the News Exchange?
   1. Hardly ever
   2. About once a month
   3. About once a week
   4. Several times a week
   5. Almost daily
   6. Several times each day

31. In general, how often do Eurovision members request materials from *your* service through the Exchange?
   1. Hardly ever
   2. About once a month
   3. About once a week
   4. Several times a week
   5. Almost daily
   6. Several times each day

32. In general, how often do the newscasts of your service *use* Eurovision news items?
    1. Hardly ever
    2. About once a month
    3. About once a week
    4. Several times a week
    5. Almost daily
    6. Several times each day

33. In general, do you think there are certain topics about which too *many* items are offered through the Exchange?
    1. No
    2. Yes (please specify which topics) _____

34. In general, do you think there are certain topics about which too *few* items are made available through the Exchange?
    1. No
    2. Yes (please specify which topics) _____

35. When you make an offer to the Exchange and it is not accepted, how do you generally feel?
    1. I get quite annoyed
    2. I get a little upset
    3. It really doesn't bother me

When news items in the following 6 categories take place *abroad* which category do you think is of most interest to viewers in your country, which is the next most interesting, and so on. Please rank all six categories from 1 to 6 (1 being the most interesting and 6 being the least interesting).

Category	Rank
36. Accidents and disasters	
37. Advances in science and medicine	
38. Artistic events	
39. Ceremonial events	
40. Conflicts between nations	
41. Internal politics of foreign nations	

42. In your view, how much agreement is there among broadcast journalists around the world regarding what makes events newsworthy?
    1. There is almost complete agreement
    2. There is substantial agreement
    3. There is some agreement
    4. There is very little agreement

43. What percentage of your service's <u>main</u> evening newscast is foreign news?
    _____ per cent

44. About how much of that foreign news comes from Eurovision?
    _____ per cent

45. Beyond Eurovision, does your service have any arrangements with other services or agencies to get news material?
    1. No
    2. Yes, with (please specify)

    _____

46. In approximately how many countries does your service have permanently stationed foreign correspondents?
    _____ countries

47. Have you ever attended the annual meeting of the Eurovision Contacts?
    1. No
    2. Yes, about _____ times

48. Generally, how useful do you think are the annual Eurovision Contact meetings in helping <u>you</u> do a better job as a Eurovision Contact?
    1. Very useful
    2. Quite useful
    3. Not very useful
    4. Not useful at all

49. Generally, how useful do you think are the annual Eurovision Contact meetings in improving the way the News Exchange operates?
    1. Very useful
    2. Quite useful
    3. Not very useful
    4. Not useful at all

50. Have you ever attended a meeting of the Eurovision News Working Party?
    1. No
    2. Yes, about _____ times

51. Generally, how useful do you think are the News Working Party meetings in helping *you* do a better job as a Eurovision contact?
    1. Very useful
    2. Quite useful
    3. Not very useful
    4. Not useful at all

52. Generally, how useful do you think are the News Working Party meetings in improving the way the News Exchange operates?
    1. Very useful
    2. Quite useful
    3. Not very useful
    4. Not useful at all

53. Do you currently also serve as a News Co-ordinator?
    1. No
    2. Yes
    3. I did in the past but I no longer do

54. When you are serving as the Co-ordinator, do you ever decide to accept or reject an item based on the needs of your own service?
    1. Almost never
    2. Sometimes
    3. Frequently
    4. Always
    5. Not relevant, I am not a Co-ordinator

55. Please imagine a situation in which you are the News Co-ordinator and no service is interested in a particular item being offered. Would you nonetheless decide to accept the item?
    1. No, because I follow the rules of the Exchange
    2. Yes, because I would hope that some service would ultimately use it
    3. Yes, because I know that my own service would be interested in the item

56. Do you generally read the weekly reports submitted by the News Co-ordinators in which they sum up their week's work?
    1. I read every report
    2. I read some of them
    3. I read very few of them
    4. I don't read any of the reports

169

57. If you read the Co-ordinator weekly reports, please use the space below to describe what you find interesting and/or important in them. On the other hand, if you do <u>not</u> read the reports, please indicate what you might wish to see in them and which may increase the chances that you would read them. Please use the reverse side of this page if you need more space.

58. Did you graduate from college or university?
    1. Yes (please specify your major field/s of study)_____
    2. No

59. How old are you?
    1. 21-25
    2. 26-30
    3. 31-35
    4. 36-40
    5. 41-45
    6. 46-50
    7. 51-55
    8. 56-60
    9. 61+

60. Are you a:
    1. Female
    2. Male

Thank you very much!
Please return this questionnaire in the envelope provided and send it via Air Mail.
If you have any questions or comments, please feel free to contact:
Professor Mark Levy, College of Journalism, University of Maryland, College Park, Maryland 20742, USA.
Telephone (301)405-2389 Fax (301) 314-9166

Appendix C

Questionnaire for Focus Group Participants

Generally, how interested are you in events that occur in ___?[1]
1. very interested
2. quite interested
3. a little interested
4. not so interested
5. not at all interested

Usually, how interested are you in the following news topics when they take place in _?

	Very interested	Quite interested	Not very interested	Not at all interested
Problems of Law and order in ___	1	2	3	4
Conflicts between ___ and foreign countries	1	2	3	4
Meetings of ___ leaders with leaders of foreign countries	1	2	3	4
Sports events in ___	1	2	3	4
Artistic and cultural events in ___	1	2	3	4
Disasters or accidents in ___	1	2	3	4
Ceremonies and festivals in ___	1	2	3	4
Internal ___ political events	1	2	3	4
Human interest stories in ___	1	2	3	4
Scientific or medical developments in ___	1	2	3	4

Generally, how interested are you in events that occur in other countries?
1. very interested
2. quite interested
3. a little interested
4. not so interested
5. not at all interested

---

1. In this and other questions, the name of the country in which the questionnaire is administered is substituted for the blank space (e.g. '... events that occur in France'?).

Usually, how interested are you in the following topics when they take place in foreign countries?

	Very interested	Quite interested	Not very interested	Not at all interested
Problems of law and order in foreign countries	1	2	3	4
Conflicts between foreign countries	1	2	3	4
Meetings of leaders of foreign countries	1	2	3	4
Foreign sports events	1	2	3	4
Foreign artistic and cultural events	1	2	3	4
Disasters or accidents in foreign countries	1	2	3	4
Ceremonies and festivals in foreign countries	1	2	3	4
Internal political of foreign countries	1	2	3	4
Human interest stories in foreign countries	1	2	3	4
Scientific or medical developments in foreign countries	1	2	3	4

Which, would you say, is your major source of information for news about what is happening in_____?
1. _____ radio stations
2. _____ TV stations
3. _____ daily newspapers
4. a news magazine published in ___
5. radio from another country
6. TV from another country
7. a news magazine from another country
8. other _____

Which, would you say, is your major source of information for news about what is happening in foreign countries?
1. ____ radio stations
2. ____ TV stations
3. ____ daily newspapers
4. a news magazine published in ___
5. radio from another country
6. TV from another country
7. a news magazine from another country
8. other _____

How often do you read a newspaper?
1. every day
2. almost every day
3. a few times a week
4. seldom (once a week or less)
5. never

When you read the newspaper, do you read items about foreign countries?
    1. always
    2. sometimes
    3. seldom
    4. never

Which newspaper do you usually read? _____

How frequently do you listen to news on the radio?
    1. at least once each day
    2. at least once, almost every day
    3. a few times a week
    4. seldom (once a week or less)
    5. never

When you listen to the news on the radio, do you pay attention to items about foreign
    countries?
    1. always
    2. sometimes
    3. seldom
    4. never

How often do you watch the news on ___ TV?
    1. every evening
    2. almost every evening
    3. a few times a week
    4. seldom (once a week or less)
    5. never

When you watch the news on TV, do you pay attention to items about foreign
    countries?
    1. always
    2. sometimes
    3. seldom
    4. never

Do you discuss new events with family members or friends?
    1. yes, but only news events in ___
    2. yes, but only news events in foreign countries
    3. yes, both news events in ___ and in foreign countries
    4. I don't discuss the news at all

Do you ever use non-___ sources (like foreign radio, TV, or newspapers) for foreign news?
  1. never
  2. seldom
  3. sometimes
  4. often
  5. always

To the best of your knowledge, how much of ___ TV news is devoted to events taking place in foreign countries?
  1. the entire newscast
  2. about 3/4 of the newscast
  3. about 1/2 of the newscast
  4. about 1/4 of the newscast
  5. less than 1/4 if the newscast
  6. there is no foreign news on ___TV
  7. I really have no idea

In your opinion, how much of ___ TV news should be devoted to events taking place in foreign countries?
  1. the entire newscast
  2. about 3/4 of the newscast
  3. about 1/2 of the newscast
  4. about 1/4 of the newscast
  5. less than 1/4 if the newscast
  6. there is no foreign news on ___TV
  7. I really have no idea

How strongly do you agree or disagree with the following statements?

	Strongly agree	Somewhat agree	Somewhat disagree	Strongly disagree
TV news reports on stories from foreign countries in order for us to know what is happening abroad				
TV news reports on stories from foreign countries in order to show that other countries also have problems?				
TV news reports on stories from foreign countries in order to help us identify with other peoples' problems				
TV news reports on stories from foreign countries in order to help us form an opinion on ___ foreign policy				

Usually, how easy or difficult is it for you to understand TV news stories about
events in ___?
1. all stories are easy
2. most are easy and some are difficult
3. some are easy and some are difficult
4. most are difficult and some are easy
5. all stories are difficult
6. I don't know because I don't watch the news

Usually, how easy or difficult is it for you to understand TV news stories about events
foreign countries?
1. all stories are easy
2. most are easy and some are difficult
3. some are easy and some are difficult
4. most are difficult and some are easy
5. all stories are difficult
6. I don't know because I don't watch the news

Comparing news events about ___ and about foreign countries, where is there more...

	Local news	Foreign news	About the same	Don't know
Good news	1	2	3	4
Bad news	1	2	3	4
Credible news	1	2	3	4

Thank you very much for your cooperation!

Index